Between Birth and Death

Between Birth and Death

FEMALE INFANTICIDE IN
NINETEENTH-CENTURY CHINA

Michelle T. King

STANFORD UNIVERSITY PRESS
STANFORD, CALIFORNIA

Stanford University Press
Stanford, California

This book is published with the support of a Publication Grant from the University Research Council of The University of North Carolina at Chapel Hill.

Library of Congress Cataloging-in-Publication Data

King, Michelle Tien, author.
  Between birth and death : female infanticide in nineteenth-century China / Michelle T. King.
      pages   cm
  Includes bibliographical references and index.
  ISBN 978-0-8047-8598-3 (cloth : alk. paper)
  1. Female infanticide—China—History—19th century.   I. Title.
  HV6541.C6K56 2013
  304.6'680820951—dc23

                                                            2013017259

  ISBN 978-0-8047-8893-9 (electronic)

Typeset by Westchester Publishing Services in 11/14 Adobe Garamond

To my parents, Stanley Shih-Tung King
and Ellen Huang King

Contents

Figures and Tables

Tables

Acknowledgments

Writing a book is often compared to giving birth. But the metaphor is not quite apt. Writing a book is actually a lot more like raising a child: you pour all your attention, love and energy into it, trying to prepare it to step into the world on its own, and fret all the while that you should be doing more. This, I think, is why books take so much longer than nine months to emerge—authors, like parents, have a hard time letting go. This book project has been many long years in the making. Along the way, I have incurred the debts of many people. I am grateful now to offer my deepest thanks for their generous and gracious material, intellectual and emotional support.

The research and writing of this project were made possible with the financial support of several organizations through the following fellowships or grants: Council on Library and Information Resources Mellon Fellowship for Humanities Research, Peking University/Harvard-Yenching Institute Fellowship, Mabelle MacLeod Lewis Memorial Fellowship, University of North Carolina at Chapel Hill Grier-Woods Presbyterian Initiative Fellowship for China Studies, University of North Carolina at Chapel Hill Junior Faculty Development Grant, University of North Carolina at Chapel Hill University Research Council Small Grant and University of North Carolina at Chapel Hill Publications Grant. I also received a semester of leave from the History Department at the University of North Carolina at Chapel Hill, which provided a crucial window of time to work on the manuscript. I thank these organizations and their staffs for providing this material aid; scholars cannot live, travel or work on ideas alone.

Source materials used in this project were collected at the following libraries and archives, whose staffs I thank for their time and assistance: the British Library, the School of Oriental and African Studies Library, the Wellcome Library, the Cambridge University Library, the Bibliothèque nationale de France, Robert Bonfils at the Archives de la Province de

France de la Compagnie de Jésus, the Peking University Library, the National Library of China, the Shanghai Library, Boston University Libraries, the Harvard-Yenching Library, the Widener Library at Harvard University, Bruce Williams and Tomoko Kobayashi at the C. V. Starr East Asian Library at the University of California, Berkeley, and Hsi-chu Bolick at the Davis Library at the University of North Carolina at Chapel Hill. My very special thanks go to Wang Renfang, head librarian at the Shanghai Library Bibliotheca Zikawei, who went above and beyond the call of duty in providing critical assistance to locate rare source materials, and to Leonello Malvezzi, archivist at the Pontificium Opus a Sancta Infantia, whose warmth and generous hospitality ensured that my stay in Rome was memorable as well as productive. I am also grateful for the help and friendship of Shen Xiaohong, Yang Ke and Shen Penghua, who were steady anchors during my time in Beijing.

Many scholars gave generously of their time to provide critical feedback at different stages of my work; any remaining infelicities in the text remain my own. The insights and continued encouragement of Wen-Hsin Yeh and James Vernon have indelibly shaped my intellectual journey, for which I will be forever grateful. Andrew Jones offered sensitive readings that opened new avenues for thinking about my work. Sadly, Frederic Wakeman and Allan Pred both passed away before seeing this book, but their examples continue to inspire me as I make my way through the world as a teacher and a scholar. Joanna Handlin Smith, Larissa Heinrich and Janet Theiss provided keen insights on different portions of my work in the form of conference papers, and audiences at the Association for Asian Studies meetings, the University of Michigan, the University of North Carolina at Chapel Hill, and Stanford University helped to sharpen the presentation of my ideas through their questions and comments. Ye Bin, Liu Wennan and Leslie Wang provided me with source materials and references on contemporary PRC practices. I would like to give special thanks to Henrietta Harrison, Kathryn Edgerton-Tarpley, Jonathan Ocko, James Vernon, Wen-hsin Yeh, Kathleen DuVal, Michael Tsin, Kwangmin Kim, Charlotte Cowden and two anonymous readers at Stanford University Press, who read versions of the manuscript in its entirety and offered detailed critical commentary, which was invaluable in guiding me through the revision process.

While at Berkeley, I had the great fortune to meet a group of strong, fabulous women whose friendship and support have sustained me through many years: Charlotte Cowden, Berta Rodriguez, Edna Tow, Maika Watanabe, Sandy Yu and Angie Yuan. I have continued to rely on the calming influence and advice of Dorothy Duff Brown, whose own book I look forward to someday reading. I thank Stephanie Heit for sharing with me the joys and sorrows of the writing life, over the course of many conversations and many years.

Finally, I wish to thank the members of my family, whose love and support have lightened the load for me during these years in countless ways. Ellen King, Margaret King and Brenda Frans provided loving childcare during critical junctures of producing this book, allowing me to focus on the task at hand. Michael and Margaret King offered their steady love and encouragement; Todd and Laura King cheered for me and buoyed my spirits every step of the way. Penelope King has been a boundless source of joy and laughter throughout the final stages of this whole enterprise. Ian King deserves special thanks: he commented on more drafts of this book than any person should be expected to do in a lifetime, while enriching our shared life every day, in both words and deeds. Finally, I give my deepest thanks to my mother and father, Ellen and Stanley King, whose unconditional love and essential support have sustained me my entire life, including at every stage of writing this book. For all they have done, this book is dedicated to them.

Introduction

In a letter to a friend, the eleventh-century Song dynasty Chinese states-man and poet Su Shi (1037–1101) tells of a story he has heard on the subject of infanticide. Su Shi's acquaintance has described to him the birth cus-toms in one rural part of what is now Hubei Province: "As a rule, common folk there raise only two sons and one daughter. Anything beyond this, they kill. In particular, they don't want daughters. Because of this, there are few women and many old men without wives among the people." Su Shi continues his acquaintance's description of how infanticide is usually car-ried out: "The newborn child is drowned in cold water. Its own parents cannot bear it, so they usually close their eyes and turn their faces away. With their hands they press it down into the water bucket. After mewling for a while, it dies." The physical immediacy of this terse description leaps across the centuries and hits us hard. The water is cold, not merely tepid. Most of us have held or at least seen a newborn—such a tiny, delicate thing— and could never imagine what it would take to drown an infant with our own two hands. The helplessness of the newborn child in Su Shi's letter is amplified by the tiny, indistinct sounds it makes before dying. The descrip-tion in Su Shi's letter—that the parents cannot bear it and must close their eyes, turning their faces away—resonates with our most basic human instincts. When Su Shi heard this story, he writes, "I felt miserable. I could not eat." His dejection is ours, melancholy shared.[1]

When I tell people my book is about the history of female infanticide in China, they usually widen their eyes and commiserate with me on what must be a depressing topic of study. By its very nature, infanticide is serious and compelling, but the challenge it poses for the historian stems less from its bleakness than from the taken-for-granted contours of its practice, persistence and meaning. Without yet having read this book, many readers will already associate the practice of female infanticide with China, or Asia more generally, based upon a steady stream of media reports about the severe sex ratio imbalances found in societies there.[2] Researchers have calculated an average sex ratio at birth in China of 118.06 males to 100 females, based on national census data from 2010, in comparison to ratios in industrialized countries from 103 to 107 males for every 100 females.[3] The magnitude of this imbalance has been attributed to a number of compounding factors, both new and old. Perhaps the most significant is the widespread use of modern technology in the form of ultrasound equipment for fetal sex identification and sex-selective abortion.[4] Another complicating factor is China's One-Child policy, first announced in 1979, which, with a number of changing exceptions, has allowed urban couples of Han ethnicity to have only one child.[5] However, these recent technological and political innovations have merely amplified the effects of a long-standing societal preference for sons, derived from a traditional Confucian value system that still lingers in protean form.

Whether in its present or past, China seems to have maintained an exceptional relationship with the practice of female infanticide, one that has been continually reinforced through contemporary media reports and historical studies. Forty years ago, historian William Langer remarked that infanticide was "often held up to school-children as an abomination practiced by the Chinese or other Asians," and mostly neglected in Western history.[6] Things have not changed much today. When I ask undergraduates in my Chinese history courses to list everything they know about China on the first day of class, rarely has a group failed to mention the practice of female infanticide. This result would be difficult to imagine in any other kind of history course, even though we can easily find examples of infanticide throughout Western history, from ancient Greece and Rome to medieval and early modern Europe to modern Britain, France, Germany and the United States.[7] Anthropologists who have researched infanticide among primates have gone so far as to suggest that it has evolved as a *human* coping mechanism of maternal stress, not tied to any one culture.[8] Yet few ever learn, for example, that Great Britain suffered from its own infanticide panic in the mid-nineteenth century, fueled largely by concerns about moral disorder on the part of serving women in the lower classes, who were driven by shame or straitened circumstances to kill their illegitimate children.[9] Infanticide remains for most people a historical curiosity when it occurs in Western societies, not one of its historical fixtures, as it has been imagined for Chinese society. What accounts for this selective forgetting and collective remembering?

This book attempts to answer that question by breaking down the naturalized and eternal relationship between female infanticide and Chinese culture and reconstructing that association instead as a product of historical processes of the nineteenth century. It takes as its explicit focus the changing *perception* of female infanticide in Chinese history, rather than its *practice*. Why make such a distinction in the first place, and why focus on the former, not the latter? There are two reasons for this choice, one pragmatic and one philosophical. The pragmatic reason for framing this book as a study of the perception of female infanticide in Chinese history is that this is the story that available historical sources are most prepared to tell. In spite of his sadness, Su Shi, like so many other Chinese male elites, had never himself witnessed an act of infanticide and had nothing in the way of firsthand experience of the social phenomenon he was so driven to write about. This was because female infanticide in late imperial China most often took place in the initial moments after the sex of the child was determined at birth, within the closed confines of the family and the even more narrowly constrained female sphere of childbirth. As a hidden social practice, it is almost never addressed in written sources by those who were most directly involved in its practice: mothers, midwives, mothers-in-law or other female relations. It is quite rare to find detailed records of actual cases of female infanticide in China involving real, historical persons; instead, we have a plethora of secondhand evidence that reveals much more about general attitudes and perceptions of infanticide on the part of the men (and it was almost always men, whether Chinese or foreign) who were doing the writing.

But there is an even more compelling philosophical reason to study the shifting perceptions of infanticide in Chinese history, rather than conceiving of it as a coherent practice. This is the only way to disrupt familiar, shop-worn narratives about the continuity of female victimhood in China from the premodern era to the present, and to introduce the possibility of historical change. Without diminishing the seriousness of the problem of excess female mortality in either the Chinese present or past, I want to reframe our understanding of this issue and widen the space between an infant girl's birth and death, so that this moment encompasses more than mere expressions of condemnation and regret. Existing historical studies of female infanticide, shaped in no small part by our contemporary understanding of the problem as a matter of victim gender and enumeration, tend to pose two questions: Why have girls been the primary victims of infanticide in China? And what has been the prevalence of female infanticide there? Although answers to both questions are essential for a basic understanding of female infanticide in Chinese history and require more elaboration in the following text, they also tend to underscore the identification of the problem as an unchanging cultural phenomenon, arising out of gender bias or profound parental indifference.

Historical studies that explain why girls were the primary victims of infanticide reinforce the idea of an unbroken lineage of antifemale attitudes in China, from the earliest dynasties to the present day.[10] Typically, such surveys open with lines from early canonical texts such as the *Shijing* (ca. 1000–600 BCE), a book of odes that contains a stanza celebrating the birth of a son while denigrating the birth of a daughter, or *Han Feizi* (ca. 280–233 BCE), a classic of political philosophy that includes the first Chinese historical reference to the practice of killing a daughter.[11] These lines demonstrate the long-standing undesirability of a daughter as opposed to a son in the early records of Chinese history, prompting treatment ranging from general neglect to intentional death. A brisk march through other textual references from subsequent dynasties often follows, with few distinctions made along the way between past and present practices. At times, the span of more than two millennia may occupy no more space than a single footnote, invoking references to female infanticide from both the third-century BCE *Han Feizi* and a 1983 news story taken straight from the headlines of the *People's Daily*.[12]

Broadly speaking, the prevalence of female infanticide in these studies is ascribed to the Confucian stress on the importance of having a son, which has manifested itself in a variety of ways. The well-worn Chinese phrase "to place emphasis on men and to slight women" (*zhongnan qingnü*) serves as shorthand for this pervasive system of patriarchal and hierarchical gender notions. One of the central concepts of Confucian filial behavior was the continuance of the family line through male progeny. Sons would remain in the natal home, supporting parents in their old age and observing the proper mourning rituals after their death. A daughter, on the other hand, was in this schema nothing but a financial and emotional burden. Even raising her to maturity required using a family's scarce resources, to say nothing of the bridal dowry she would need upon marriage, when she would leave her natal home for good to join her new husband's family.[13] Within this nexus of gender hierarchy and economic pressures, late imperial Chinese families faced with the birth of an unwanted daughter often opted for the nearest and most efficacious of solutions—a bucket of cold water, as Su Shi describes.

Yet if we look to the past without privileging infant sex as the primary reason for infanticide in China, we can see that in earlier dynasties, such as the Han (206 BCE–220 CE), there was a wide range of reasons for infanticide, including inauspicious births or deformities, family circumstances, general poverty and, indeed, infant sex.[14] During the Song dynasty (960–1279), economic reasons, such as general poverty and excessive head taxes, were still most commonly cited for not raising both girls and boys.[15] An infant's sex seems to have become the definitive motive for infanticide in China only by the late imperial period, or the Ming (1368–1644) and Qing (1644–1911) dynasties, when female infanticide seems to have predominated and male infanticide was discussed only as a rare exception to the rule.[16] This transformation over the millennia is borne out by changes in Chinese terminology for infanticide. In the Han dynasty, the most common Chinese terms referred to the non-gender-specific abandonment of children, including "to cast out/abandon an infant" (qi ying), "to not raise a child" (bu ju zi) or "to not care for a child" (bu yang zi).[17] These broad terms encompassed behaviors that might lead to infant death but did not necessarily indicate the act of killing itself, which was referred to explicitly by the less common term, "to kill a child" (sha zi). Up through the Song dynasty, the term "to not raise a child" (bu ju zi) was still most commonly used.[18] By the Qing dynasty, however, the most commonly used term for infanticide was "to drown girls" (ni nü), which specified not only the sex of the victim but also the method of disposal.

Demographic studies, which attempt to determine the incidence of female infanticide within specific Chinese populations, comprise a second common historical approach to the problem. We need to recognize first of all that calculating the rate of infanticide for any population, let alone a historical one, is neither easy nor precise. As a hidden demographic event, which most societies do not openly record, the incidence of infanticide can be approached only through indirect methods. In one of the most extensive studies of the prevalence of infanticide in late imperial China, James Lee and Cameron Campbell draw upon the vital statistics from some 80,000 individuals found in the household registries of one village in Liaoning Province, all descendants of the Qing military-administrative banner system and estimate that "between one-fifth and one-quarter of all girls born" there from 1774 to 1873 were victims of infanticide.[19] In a separate study, Lee and his colleagues estimate that "as many as one-tenth of daughters" were killed in the Qing imperial lineage in Beijing from 1700 to 1840.[20] As Lee and his coauthors elsewhere note, these are "indirect estimates from incomplete data," relying on extrapolations using models developed for European populations.[21] Nonetheless, they conclude that infanticide in late imperial China was a rational form of postnatal family planning, which, alongside a variety of other active strategies for fertility control, serves to debunk Malthusian notions of unchecked Chinese population growth.[22]

In the absence of other historical contexts, however, their estimates inadvertently reinforce the notion of late imperial Chinese parents as barbarically indifferent toward their own offspring, an attitude another scholar has described as "rational to the point of being ruthless."[23] To lend some perspective to these estimated rates of infanticide in China, it is helpful to compare them with estimated historic rates in other world regions. Although contemporaneous European and American rates of infanticide were almost certainly lower than the estimated rates for these Chinese populations, neither was the practice unknown.[24] Indeed, Thomas Coram established London's first foundling hospital in the mid-eighteenth century "to prevent the frequent murders of poor miserable infants at their birth" and "to suppress the inhuman custom of exposing new-born infants to perish in the streets."[25]

Although rates of infanticide were probably lower in Europe, rates of newborn abandonment there were still shockingly high. John Boswell's groundbreaking study of the history of child abandonment in Western Europe makes clear just how widely this related practice occurred. In eighteenth-century France, the average rate of known abandonments in the city of Toulouse ranged from 10 percent to 25 percent, and in Paris, it ranged from 20 percent to 30 percent. In Lyons, approximately one-third of all registered births resulted in abandonment. The fate of children in Italy was no less alarming: in eighteenth-century Milan, the rate of abandonment ranged from 16 percent to 25 percent, and in early nineteenth-century Florence, the rate of abandonment rose to a high of 43 percent of all registered births.[26] Although abandoning a child to a foundling home may seem to us now less outwardly cruel than infanticide, it by no means guaranteed a child's life. In the absence of adequate nutrition and medical care in these institutions, child mortality rates were extremely high. Thirty to forty percent of the children in the St. Petersburg foundling hospital, one of the best of its kind, died within six weeks of arrival there, with fewer than a third reaching the age of six. Of the 4,779 infants admitted to the Paris foundling hospital in 1818, a total of 2,370, or more than half, died in the first three months.[27] Certainly abandonment and infanticide are not the same practice, and one could well argue that their rates should not be compared. But this is more of a moral or philosophical issue regarding parental intent, and less of a distinction with regard to ultimate outcomes for unwanted children.

What should strike the modern reader, then, is less the particular cruelty or indifference of late imperial Chinese with regard to their children than the immensity of the social problem of unwanted children all over the world, both in Europe and in China. The practices of infanticide and abandonment can be understood, as Sarah Blaffer Hrdy suggests, as part of a spectrum of responses to deal with unwanted children, in eras without reliable forms of contraception or abortion.[28] It is safe to assume that the death of a young child, under any circumstances, was a far more common event in late imperial China and eighteenth- and nineteenth-century Europe than it is to us. As William Langer has remarked, "Modern humanitarian sentiment makes it difficult to recapture the relatively detached attitude of the parents towards their offspring. Babies were looked upon as the unavoidable result of normal sex relations, often as an undesirable burden rather than as a blessing."[29] Demographic explanations of infanticide alone, in other words, can do little to illuminate its most critical human dimensions.

If we wish to move beyond an undifferentiated past of Chinese gender discrimination and barbarity, then we need to frame our central question in a radical, new way. Instead of taking the historical relationship between female infanticide and Chinese culture as a given, in this book I place it at the very center of my investigation, asking, "Just when and how did female infanticide become so Chinese?" What exactly do I mean by this? In the pages that follow, I argue that female infanticide *became Chinese* in the imperialist context of the late nineteenth century, when it was immutably transformed from a local, moral, philanthropic issue into a cross-cultural, political, scientific issue of international concern. Female infanticide had been practiced in China well before the nineteenth century, of course, with Chinese historical records to prove it. But never would those early observers have considered it to be a uniquely *Chinese* problem, somehow reflecting deficiencies peculiar to Chinese culture. Throughout much of the Ming and Qing dynasties, female infanticide was perceived by Chinese male elites as a regrettable but localized "vulgar custom" (*lousu*), occurring in different parts of the empire and particularly widespread in the provinces south of the Yangtze River. Chinese sources were written for Chinese audiences, and by and large their major purpose was one of persuasion, to urge others to refrain from killing their newborn children. This mode of understanding was oriented toward local communities and local practices.

It was only in the mid-nineteenth century, after China emerged battered and bruised from its defeat at the hands of Great Britain in the Opium War (1839–42), that female infanticide was reframed as a totemic cultural marker of China writ large, in Western sources written primarily for Western audiences. Western traders, diplomats and missionaries, eager to come to China for the gain of both profits and souls, generated all manner of information about the country and its inhabitants for foreign consumption, and often referred in their writings to the Chinese practice of infanticide. Imperial relationships of power in the nineteenth century meant that this mode of understanding was inherently comparative, giving China its proper (inferior) place in the world civilizational pecking order. Moreover, it was these Western representations of the problem of female infanticide, rather than Chinese interpretations, that would go global, shaping impressions of China in the outside world. By the early twentieth century, the notion of infanticide as a particular Chinese problem had also spread within Chinese society, embedded within a reformist discourse aiming to mitigate its negative impact on the composition and size of the nation's population.

Within this framework of shifting perceptions, one point bears repeating: nineteenth-century Chinese did not require the tutelage of Westerners, or what one contemporary author has called a "moral revolution," to bring about an understanding of the abhorrent nature of the practice of female infanticide or to implement institutional solutions to the problem.[30] Chinese texts condemning the practice and philanthropic agencies attempting to ameliorate it predated the arrival of Westerners in China by many centuries. More significantly, almost every single extant late imperial Chinese source on the subject of infanticide was written to urge others to refrain from the practice.[31] This is not to say that all late imperial Chinese uniformly felt the practice was wrong; many Chinese obviously did commit infanticide, regardless of what was written publicly about it. Still, it is important not to leap to the conclusion, as did many nineteenth-century Western writers, that the abundance of Chinese sources *against* infanticide should be taken as evidence of its prevalence. The abundance of nineteenth-century Chinese sources against infanticide indicates, first and foremost, precisely just that: the publicly acceptable attitude toward infanticide, at least for literate male elites, was one of condemnation, not approbation. However widespread the incidence of female infanticide in China may have been in practice, in other words, historical voices almost always spoke out against it. Su Shi's melancholy is an important part of the story.

Yet it is also undeniable that cross-cultural interactions with Western texts and people in the nineteenth century played a pivotal role in changing the nature of Chinese discourse on female infanticide, shifting it from a concern with karmic rewards and retributions for individuals to a concern with its effect on the national population. In other words, the lives and bodies of newborn Chinese infant girls would come to mean something new and distinct in the early twentieth century when compared to the nineteenth, and this shift did not occur in a cultural vacuum. Dipesh Chakrabarty has described European thought as both "indispensable and inadequate" to explain the trajectories of varied modern histories in India, and these adjectives apply equally well to the nineteenth-century transformation of ideas about female infanticide in China.[32] The effects of these cross-cultural interactions, too, were varied—some were explosive and immediate, and others were gradual and piecemeal. At no time, however, were nineteenth-century Chinese cultural interpreters only passive recipients of Western influence; they engaged in acts of meaning-making in contradictory and unpredictable ways, selecting, adapting, adopting and vehemently rejecting different Western notions related to the practice of female infanticide.

Although the actual space between the birth and death of an unwanted Chinese daughter in the nineteenth century may seem to us all too brief, the meaning of that same short life could encompass yawning gaps in perception when refracted through the lenses of gender, culture, geography and religious beliefs. This book traces the shift in the perception of female infanticide in China during the nineteenth century, as it moved from Chinese historical contexts to Western ones, in what can be imagined as a series of ever-wider concentric circles of concerned adults surrounding a Chinese infant girl. When we expand our vision of female infanticide in Chinese history to encompass more than just the sex and number of its infant victims, we see that a newborn daughter was always surrounded by a wide array of historical actors interested in her fate: the mother, midwife, mother-in-law and other female neighbors or relations; male Chinese scholars and officials; foreign missionaries, diplomats and traders living in China and even European schoolchildren half a world away.

In Chapter 1 we begin with the example of the woman Ye (1567–1659), who drowned her first daughter immediately after birth, and consider the various factors that influenced such a decision. Here, gender is used not simply as a pretext for selecting female over male infant victims, but as a category of analysis to examine the complex and conflicting roles of many different women, including the mother, midwife, mother-in-law, other female relations and even the ghost of the unwanted daughter herself, in determining the outcome to this moral quandary.

Chapter 2 moves outward, to the circle of concerned Chinese men who were not privy to the intimacies of the birth chamber but still advocated the prevention of female infanticide in the wider public, through philanthropic endeavors within their communities. Female infanticide was most frequently described in male-authored Chinese texts as a deplorable local custom, and managed on a local or regional scale. Our guide in this chapter is Yu Zhi (1804–74), a little-known country schoolteacher, who devoted himself to the practice of good works and the improvement of moral behavior at all levels of society. Exhorting one's fellow man not to commit female infanticide was but one small part of a typical portfolio of mid-nineteenth-century philanthropy, especially in the aftermath of the Taiping Rebellion (1850–64).

The next two chapters of the book detail how Western writings shaped the perception among worldwide audiences that female infanticide was a totemic marker of Chinese society. Chapter 3 examines the writings of Western travelers, amateur scientists, diplomats and missionaries, such as the French Jesuit priest Gabriel Palatre (1830–78), who had no access to the inner lives of Chinese families yet were intent on gathering different types of evidence regarding the prevalence of infanticide in China. The exact meaning of such evidence, which notably included visceral encounters with dead infant corpses, was hotly debated, since the precise cause of death could never be discerned. Even when original Chinese texts and images generated by native male scholars were copied and translated for Western audiences as authentic proof of infanticide, the resulting message had more to say about the visual exoticism of Chinese culture and language than about the social practice of infanticide per se.

Chapter 4 takes the concern with Chinese infanticide to its widest global audience, that of nineteenth-century Euro-American Catholic school-children, who were galvanized into humanitarian action by the pontifical charity the Oeuvre de la Sainte-Enfance (Holy Childhood Association). The charity, which was originally established in 1843 to support overseas missionaries in their rescue and redemption of heathen Chinese children through the sacrament of baptism, enjoined Catholic children around the world to make regular contributions to aid this cause, deploying images and texts that promoted the idea of widespread infanticide in China. The Sainte-Enfance's annual tally of infant souls saved was an important marker of the growing worldwide success of the organization.

In the final chapter, Chapter 5, we consider the various consequences of these different perceptions of female infanticide back on the ground in China, tracing their effects into the early twentieth century. On the one hand, most nineteenth-century Chinese audiences staunchly opposed the claims of Catholic missionaries who vied for the right to gather and baptize unwanted Chinese children, accusing them instead of kidnapping and killing children for occult purposes. The most notorious episode involving such rumors was the Tianjin Massacre of 1870, where twenty foreigners, including ten nuns, were killed by a rampaging Chinese mob convinced of their mistreatment of children. The outright violence of the outcome, though, has obscured the political stakes of the conflict: the Tianjin Massacre revealed an early proto-nationalist stance on the issue of female infanticide and unwanted children in China, articulating a keen desire to find Chinese, not foreign, solutions to these problems. On the other hand, even as many ordinary Chinese overtly rejected the presence of Western missionaries and their religious notions regarding the practice of infanticide in China, other Chinese active in treaty ports gradually absorbed Western secular ideas about science and women's rights, adapting them to suit the expectations and needs of Chinese audiences. These gradual adaptations, found in the pages of new nineteenth-century treaty port newspapers, eventually paved the way for the widespread acceptance of population as the scientific measure of the nation's health and strength in the early twentieth century, when the life of each girl child was seen as essential for China's survival as a nation on the international stage.

The overall trajectory of this nineteenth-century history of female infanticide has much in common with that of other totemic markers of Chinese culture, such as judicial torture, disease or footbinding, which were fetishized within Western texts and images as repulsive markers of Chinese barbarity, grotesqueness or exoticism. Scholars have begun to historicize Western impressions of these other social phenomena, interrogating their meaning, representation and reproduction, thereby reconfiguring their rhetorical power. Timothy Brook, Jérôme Bourgon and Gregory Blue, for example, have argued that the Qing judicial punishment of "lingering," whereby a condemned criminal was put to death, then dismembered and sliced into pieces, should be understood as another kind of capital punishment within a fixed range of judicial procedures, rather than some extraordinary and diabolical torture concocted by Oriental despots.[33] Likewise, Larissa Heinrich has examined the trope of China as the "sick man of Asia," detailing how Chinese images of smallpox inoculation, among other examples, acquired their own "afterlife" in their migration to a Western context, transformed into etiological proof and enduring as images of diseased Chinese bodies.[34] Dorothy Ko has argued that images of Chinese women's unbound feet, which circulated as photographic curiosities of treaty port China in the nineteenth century, were always already inflected as grotesque for new Western audiences, laden with meanings they never had for Chinese.[35]

All of these hyperbolic nineteenth-century Western impressions of Chinese cultural practices shared the same corporeal space of the body, which, as Brook and his coauthors suggest, has always been "the most emotionally compelling site of cultural difference."[36] Western impressions of the "Chinese body"—as feminized, eroticized, weakened, diseased, impoverished, tortured, insensible or long-suffering—literally took shape in photographs and postcards marketed to foreign tourists in the nineteenth century, featuring, for example, a woman's tiny, unbound foot, an opium smoker's wasted countenance or a torture victim's mutilated corpse.[37] Nineteenth-century foreign missionaries and travelers to China tried to depict the infanticide in a similar, corporeal way, invoking the innocent, diminutive bodies of unwanted Chinese children, deserving of pity and in need of rescue.

Compared to other phenomena, however, the problem of female infanticide could never be so easily represented: at its heart it involves not bodies but their unyielding absence. A newborn infant girl was one of the most invisible members of late imperial Chinese society, by dint of both her gender and her biological immaturity. Her existence could all too easily disappear from both real life and the historical record. In the end, this is the fundamental reason why writing a history of female infanticide in China is at once such a delicate and difficult enterprise: how does one render the outlines of a body that is barely seen or articulate the sound of a voice that is barely heard? Nineteenth-century Chinese and Western advocates alike tried their hardest to fill in this profound gap by giving both voice and form to unwanted female infants in numerous elaborate and imaginative ways, hoping to make their intended audiences sit up and take notice, to see what was otherwise an invisible problem. In this book, I suggest a rather different approach, following the example of Orpheus in chasing his elusive Eurydice, the elemental shade. If we always fixate on the blank space at the center, where we would most expect to find the missing daughters of Chinese history, we will never do more than mourn their absence. Only by turning our attention away from the center can we ever hope to catch a glimpse of their brief existence, reflected in the pale light of those who always surrounded them.

A note on the text: All references to a Chinese individual's age in the following pages are given in *sui*, numerically one year older than the Western equivalent in years. All translations are my own, unless otherwise indicated.

ONE

Deciding a Child's Fate

Women and Birth

That we can say anything about the life of the woman Ye (1567–1659) is only the result of the writings of her youngest son, Chen Que (1604–77), a prominent philosopher during the transition between the Ming (1368–1644) and Qing (1644–1911) dynasties. Although it is little known, Ye's story is precious: in the course of my research it is the only example I have found of a late imperial Chinese woman describing her own experience of infanticide, in her own language.[1] Ye's recounting of the act of infanticide appears in the context of a memorial written by her son to commemorate the twenty-fifth anniversary of his father's death, when Ye herself was eighty-nine and near the end of her own life. Much of the memorial involves Ye's narration to her son of the struggles she and his father endured during their early years of marriage. This brief account is written in straightforward language; the events it describes are not unusual. Yet all the same it is a remarkable testament. In one short passage, Ye humanizes and complicates our everyday notions about female infanticide in late imperial China:

> Most of my life, I have never had any secrets to weigh down my heart. The
> only thing is when I was twenty-four, I gave birth to a girl, and drowned

her. Even now I regret it. At the time, we were so poor that we had not a thing in our house. There was just a chicken, which I was saving for after I gave birth. Right before the moment of birth came, though, someone ate my chicken.

At the same time, my father was in Hangzhou, and he sent someone home to my stepmother, urging her, "The Chens' daughter [referring to Ye's husband's family name] has given birth. Send someone immediately to look after her," supposing that something would be brought for me. Eventually my stepmother sent a servant boy, Chang Shou, to come and serve me—empty-handed. [Instead of helping me,] he found some food and made it for himself.

I was at my wits' end. My mother and father had given birth to me, but after growing up, I still had to suffer in this way. As for this mere fleck of foam [referring to her own daughter]—what would be the point of raising her? It would only be in vain: no good for me, and no good for her. So I made up my mind to drown her.

After losing so much blood during birth, I couldn't get up, so I ordered the servant girl from your grandparents' house, Si Xiu, to drown it. She put it into shallow water, but it didn't die the whole night long. I was so furious, I forced myself to get up, and shut the door in order to drown her. I turned my head, closed my eyes and then did it. I couldn't look. Alas! How could I have done such a cruel thing?[2]

What do we make of Ye's decision? Do we condemn her for committing infanticide, knowing that she still regrets this one dark deed in her life? Or do we sympathize with her—impoverished, emotionally bereft, and having just undergone the most physically draining task a woman's body ever undertakes—in all the moments leading up to that point? Ye's dilemma illuminates the very human drama of infanticide in late imperial China, and hints at the many elements influencing a woman's decision: the family's economic status, her lack of physical support, her emotional vulnerability immediately after birth and the long perspective of her experience as a woman up to that moment. Each segment of the story addresses larger themes that we will explore in this chapter, pushing an analysis of gender in infanticide beyond female victimhood to consider how it factored more broadly into family, birth experience and morality.

Clearly, Ye's tale is set within a society that, if depicted in broad strokes, valued men over women. It is easy, from our present day vantage point, to condemn the system that perpetuated this behavior. But what if, instead of judging from the here and now, we attempt instead to imagine the view from then and there: what actions would have made sense to those who were part of such a cultural system? Working within the constraints of the historical sources left to us, in this chapter I want to bring to life that crucial moment immediately after the birth of a daughter, when infanticide was not yet an act to be condemned, but a decision yet to be made. This approach brings us directly into the inner chambers of the Chinese family, into an almost exclusively female world. Not only for biological reasons but also for social ones of gender segregation, the act of giving birth in late imperial China was an arena where women prevailed. Parturient mothers were generally assisted by older female relatives or neighbors, or perhaps a midwife. Husbands normally stayed outside the birth room, and male doctors would be called upon only in special cases, for elite families who could afford their services.[3]

Yet illuminating a female perspective on infanticide in late imperial China is a challenge, because men authored all extant Chinese sources on the subject. The story of the woman Ye offers keen insights, as we are able to place infanticide as one episode within the long span of a real late imperial woman's life. But to achieve a broader understanding of women's involvement in infanticide, we must also turn to other extant sources, such as late imperial medical texts and morality books. Although neither of these male-authored genres provides direct expressions of women's experiences, they do offer some insight into normative understandings and explanations of the practice and ethics of infanticide. Focusing on the expectations leading up to birth, the act of birth itself and the assignment of moral responsibility after birth allows us to reinsert women into the history of infanticide in late imperial China as more than just the simple victims of a patriarchal system. Mothers like the woman Ye were often complicit in the decision to commit female infanticide, yet moral responsibility never fell on their shoulders alone. The most striking feature of late imperial Chinese writings about female infanticide is that they addressed a large circle of adult participants, both male and female, who were all in some way held morally accountable. At the same time, women did not avoid close scrutiny for their involvement as mothers, midwives, relatives and neighbors.

WOMAN YE, INFANTICIDAL MOTHER

The woman Ye, who is known only by her family name, was the oldest of nine siblings, all children of Ye Zhan, a successful candidate of the provincial level of the three-tiered imperial civil examination system, a status that made it possible for him to hold a position as an official.[4] Her life path followed the idealized route to happiness for a late imperial Chinese woman, as described by Susan Mann, by getting married, giving birth to a son, raising him to be a success and finding him a dutiful wife to marry (and gaining for herself a filial daughter-in-law in the process).[5] At or before the age of twenty-one, Ye was married into a family less prosperous than her own, the Chen family of Haining, Zhejiang Province, to the second of four sons, Chen Yingbo (1564–1630). Unlike her father, Ye's husband passed only the county level of the examination system, which meant status as a local elite and permission to try for the next examination level but which did not lead to a government post. Ye herself successfully fulfilled her own reproductive role in the family by giving birth to four sons and continuing her husband's family line. Her first son was born when she was twenty-two, the second when she was twenty-seven, a third at thirty-one and Chen Que, the fourth and youngest son, when she was thirty-eight. At an unspecified age, perhaps between her third and fourth sons, she also gave birth to another daughter who did live to adulthood.[6] At fifty-five, her youngest son finally married, and three years later he welcomed the birth of his own son, allowing Ye to complete what Charlotte Furth has called the "cycle connecting generations."[7] After the death of her husband when she was sixty-four, Ye lived another twenty-nine years as a widow and matriarch, recognizing sadly in her late years that "those born before me have all died, while I alone remain."[8] Apart from being the mother of the philosopher Chen Que, the only other noteworthy aspect of her life was its longevity: she outlived not only her husband but also her three eldest sons, flourishing until the ripe old age of ninety-three.

The traditional shorthand notation of Three Followings (*sancong*) refers to the three life stages governing a woman's behavior: a woman should follow her father before marriage, her husband after marriage and her son after widowhood. Directly or indirectly, the story told by Ye does indeed bear upon her relationships to the men in her life. She is telling her son a story about life with her husband, and her father appears in it as an important figure. In particular, Ye's relationship to her son is significant, as her very existence in the historical record is a result of her position as "Chen Que's mother." This is a crucial point: had Ye never borne a son, we would probably never have even learned of her regret for killing her first daughter. Only a small percentage of elite women in late imperial China were literate, and those who did write never addressed the topic of infanticide.[9] The very telling of this tale of infanticide, therefore, is not exclusively Ye's own narration, since it was ultimately written down by her son and may have been edited by him, although it is expressed from her point of view, in her voice. The eventual birth of Ye's four sons, moreover, may well have afforded her the luxury of past regret: had she given birth only to daughters, who knows how she might have felt about drowning her first?

Ye's narrative mixes a sense of wifely pride in her husband with a certain degree of frustration. More suited to a life of study than to household economies, her husband was always ready to help friends and relatives in need, but he was ill-equipped to manage his own family matters. In her retelling, his family did little to help them, and the couple was more often than not rescued by her father's generosity. Her husband had no official position, and made a meager, sporadic income through teaching, while she tried to supplement their income by spinning, weaving and buying up seeds and tools to plant their small, barren farm acreage.[10] Plagued by bad luck and misfortune, Chen Que's father fell seriously ill two years before the episode of infanticide and the couple had to pawn everything, including their clothes, to pay the doctor. Ye's own father, on his way to a funeral, stopped by to pay them a visit. Ye describes the scene to her son: "Because your father had no clothes to wear, he could not come out to meet your grandfather. Only after a long while, having sent out to borrow a garment of rough white cotton from a cloth shop . . . was he able to come out. As your grandfather asked after your father, tears streamed down his face. I too was hardly able to raise my head to look."[11]

It is all the more striking, then, that in a narrative that mostly highlights their life together as a married couple, the episode recounting infanticide belongs to the woman Ye alone. At the moment of birth, Ye seems to have been without much support from her natal family, and no mention is made of her husband or her husband's family. We see how she has had to do everything herself, carefully saving a chicken for a postpartum meal (broth was frequently cited as the best nourishment for a new mother), only to endure the indignity of someone else eating it. Her father was in another city and tries to arrange for help. But her words reveal her strained relationship with her stepmother, who was "unwilling to show the tiniest sympathy."[12] The servant boy her stepmother sends is worse than useless—he not only arrives empty-handed, he does nothing but take care of himself. Ye's decision to commit infanticide highlights the palpable connection between her present indignities and the fate of her newborn daughter. She recognizes everything her father and birth mother did to raise her, all of which has come to naught. Why should she and her daughter both suffer? Since the maid is incapable of doing the deed, Ye must, as with everything else, take care of this matter with her own two hands. Some sixty-five years later, the episode remains one of the strongest memories in her long life.

Within the context of the memorial, the episode of infanticide seems intended as yet another example of the family's struggles in their early years of poverty. The trope of the poor scholar was a common one in late imperial writing. Chen Que's parents undoubtedly had very little, but neither were they at the very bottom rungs of society. Ye's father was a passed provincial exam candidate, after all, and her husband did achieve county-level exam status. They had been allotted some acres of land by her husband's family, however barren, and they did have the help of the extended family's servants, however ineffective. Indeed, later in life, Chen Que's father eventually managed to build a family compound, however ramshackle, so that his four sons could marry. Moreover, another daughter was later born into the family and eventually married. At the moment of the first daughter's birth, however, the combination of circumstances—general poverty (or at any rate the perception of poverty), along with physical and emotional vulnerability after birth, and frustration at her own and her newborn daughter's lot in life—leads to infanticide. Looking back decades later, Chen Que's mother cannot believe her own past conduct. What comes across to readers, though, is not her weakness, but her strength. The narration of her entire life is marked by various episodes in which she always took it upon herself to do whatever was required. "I have never been one to beg from others," she remarks dryly to her son.[13]

DAUGHTERS AND SONS

One of the difficulties of writing about female infanticide in late imperial China is that even raising the topic gives the impression that parents never wanted daughters or were somehow incapable of loving girls. A daughter could indeed be a cherished child, particularly in elite families, when she would be described as a "pearl in the palm."[14] In the story of the woman Ye, for example, time and again she and her husband are rescued by her own father, rather than turning to her husband's family. It is her father who sends servants to help plow and water their fields, and then food to feed the servants when they are exhausted. He feels deeply for his daughter and her husband, and cannot help but cry when he realizes the depth of their poverty. Weijing Lu, Hsiung Ping-chen and Susan Mann have examined written accounts from Ming and Qing fathers, who doted on their daughters in life and mourned them deeply in death.[15] Mothers, too, left behind written expressions of care and grief over daughters, such as the poem by one eighteenth-century woman on the occasion of the birth of her second daughter, recalling the death of her first daughter from smallpox.[16]

Essays against the practice of female infanticide, written by male elites for audiences of other men, tried to emphasize these bonds that tied men to women within the traditional family structure. The author of a popular late imperial essay against infanticide, Gui Zhongfu, was a scholar from Hunan Province who passed the provincial exam in 1744 and later served as a county magistrate in Jiangsu Province.[17] In his essay *Jie ninü wen* (Essay Against the Drowning of Daughters), which was reprinted throughout the nineteenth century, Gui Zhongfu urged other men to consider their relationships with the significant women in their lives: "Where do our bodies come from? If it were not for my mother, how would I come into being? . . . Today's daughter is tomorrow's mother. Today's mother who bears a daughter is a girl who was not drowned in the past. Our sons and grandsons came from women who were not drowned. The wives of our sons and grandsons are daughters who were not drowned by others."[18] The worth of a daughter's life, in other words, could be measured by her future roles as a wife and a mother of sons, contained within a normal cycle of family reproduction. The practice of female infanticide, Gui lamented, meant that this natural cycle of birth and family would grind to a halt: "If one person drowns a daughter, everyone will do the same, and soon all will have no daughters. If everyone eventually has no daughters, then all will eventually have no wives. If everyone has no wives, then people themselves will die out."[19]

In these didactic essays against infanticide, daughters were rarely prized outside of their future reproductive roles as wives and mothers. Even when male essayists did draw attention to a daughter's inherent value, it was still reckoned within the bonds of the family, as a function of the daughter's filiality toward her parents. One song, cited in an essay discouraging female infanticide, for example, argued that daughters would treat their parents better than sons would, caring for them more deeply in old age:

> Daughters' natures are the most gentle and kind,
> They love their parents better than sons.
> Sons go out more often,
> Daughters remain by their parents.
> Sons are more disobedient,
> Daughters always listen to their parents.
> Sons go on long journeys more often,
> Daughters stay near their parents.
> Sons are less prone to sorrow,
> Daughters always cry for their parents.
> Daughters have filial hearts,
> And always help their parents.
> Daughters with a good husband,
> Will always show it to their parents.[20]

The cozy idea that daughters would stay near their parents while sons traveled long distances may have been more optimistic than realistic, given that daughters generally married out into their husband's homes.[21] Those near their natal homes might come back for occasional visits, but those married out into more distant families might find it harder to return. Distance was no barrier to feeling, however, and certainly the emotional bonds between daughters and their parents could be deep. The song concluded with a long list of the deeds of filial daughters throughout Chinese history, often no more than teenagers, who were historically renowned for their willingness to sacrifice on behalf of their parents and in-laws.[22] During the Han dynasty (206 BCE–220 CE), for example, Cao E leaped into a river to recover her drowned father's corpse for proper burial, only to surface holding it days later, having sacrificed her own life. Likewise, Ti Ying wrote a moving letter to the Han emperor, begging to be allowed to offer her life in place of her father's, who was to be subjected to bodily punishment and had no sons to come to his aid.[23] Thus the well-known historian of the Han dynasty, Ban Gu, was to have remarked, "One hundred muddle-headed males are not worth one Ti Ying alone."

Despite such efforts to remind people of the value of a filial daughter, would-be parents continued to go to great lengths to ensure the birth of a son, primarily by attempting to influence the yin and yang forces that determined the sex of the fetus. In Chinese medicine, yin and yang were understood as the two dynamic cosmological principles that formed the fundamental building blocks of the universe. Although yin represented the female, yielding force and yang represented the male, active force, yin was not exclusive to women, nor was yang limited to men. Both forces waxed and waned in male and female human bodies, at different life stages and under different conditions of health and sickness. Moreover, yin and yang permeated the environment, taking shape in everyday aspects of life: yin ruled the dark, cold and night, and yang ruled the light, hot and day. Odd numbers and the left side were considered yang, and even numbers and the right side were considered yin. It was this fluctuation of yin and yang forces that ultimately determined fetal sex. If yang forces were ascendant, then a male fetus would result. If, on the other hand, yin forces were ascendant, then a female fetus would result.[24]

Historians Charlotte Furth, Lee Jen-der and Angela Leung have described different strategies for influencing fetal sex from early and late imperial China, in which the central goal was to reproduce a son.[25] Cosmological factors at the time of intercourse, what Lee Jen-der calls the "arts of the bedchamber," were considered influences on fetal sex since the early Qin times (221–206 BCE).[26] These bedchamber methods proliferated in early China, particularly before the sixth century, and usually included some form of calendrical timing or spatial orientation. Certain auspicious days could favor conception of sons, as could the timing of intercourse after the cessation of a woman's menses. Specific recommendations varied, but usually depended on some calculation of odd and even days. The famous medical master Chen Ziming, for example, wrote in the eighth century that intercourse on the first, third and fifth days after a woman's period—all odd and yang numbers—would result in a boy, and on the second, fourth and sixth days—all even and yin numbers—would result in a girl.[27] Specific locations, the directional orientation of the bedroom or weather patterns could also influence the success of conception.

The health status of each parent also needed to be taken into consideration. A woman's menstrual blood was, not surprisingly, considered full of yin force and represented her bodily contribution to conception. A man's essence, which took form as semen, was full of yang force. Depending on which force was stronger when the two essences met, a male or female fetus would form. A sixth-century medical master, Chu Cheng, explained: "If yin blood arrives first and yang essence then dashes against it, the blood opens to wrap around the essence; essence enters making bone and a male is formed. If yang *qi* [fundamental life-force] enters first and yin blood later joins it, the essence opens to surround the blood; blood enters to make the foundation and a female is formed."[28] Beginning in the seventh and eighth centuries, herbal prescriptions proliferated, commonly used to take care of parental imbalances with regard to reproduction, such as weak yang *qi* in the man.[29]

Even after conception, a mother's behavior could continue to extend the influence of yin and yang forces into gestation. Echoing early imperial texts, a sixteenth-century medical manual suggested that a pregnant woman could influence offspring characteristics through her behavior: "After three months, the fetus beings to form and [the mother] can pay a visit to the mothers of aristocratic personages. If she wants a boy, she should touch a bow and be transported by spirited horses. If she wants a girl, it is enough to wear bracelets, earrings and other jade pendants. If she wants the child to be beautiful, she should play often with white jade and admire peacocks. If she wants it to be wise, she should read to it the Classics and listen to noble music."[30] Another Qing manual on pregnancy and childbirth, which echoed early imperial texts, suggested that one could foretell the sex of a fetus by observing the mother's behavior: "When the pregnant woman goes to the bathroom, have her husband call to her from behind. If she turns her head left, it will be a boy; if she turns her head right, it will be a girl. Males are conceived on the left, so the left side is heavier. Females [are conceived] on the right, so the right side is heavier. This is how you can tell, since the [mother's] head turns to protect her heavier side."[31]

Another approach, which increased in frequency with the spread of Buddhism in China during the Tang dynasty (618–907), was to pray to celestial beings, with special attention to the Boddhisattva Guanyin, who in one of her many aspects was named "Guanyin, the giver of sons" (*Songzi Guan-yin*).[32] Guanyin was also the protector of women in childbirth and young children. Iconography of this aspect of Guanyin depicted her as a white-robed woman, carrying a baby boy in her arms.[33] Buddhist miracle tales about Guanyin had appeared already in the fourth century, but exploded in popularity after the late Ming. These tales recounted the stories of faithful devotees without sons who prayed to Guanyin, chanted or distributed sutras or did other good deeds and were rewarded with the birth of a cherished son. So strong was the desire for sons that in one case, after the death of a husband, Guanyin was reported to have the power to change the sex of an existing daughter to a son, causing her to grow a penis.[34] In spite of the miraculous outcomes described by such tales, parents no doubt understood through practical experience that all of these methods could never guarantee results: the moment of birth was the final arbiter of "success," when parents would know for certain if they should celebrate the arrival of a son or lament the arrival of a daughter. The decision to commit female infanticide, then, would have been made as a last resort, after all other prenatal methods for sex selection—cosmological, medical or religious—had obviously failed.

ASSIGNING RESPONSIBILITY
FOR INFANTICIDE

One of the most popular childbirth manuals in late imperial China, *Dasheng bian* (On Successful Childbirth), first published in 1715 and frequently reprinted even through the early twentieth century, provides us with a glimpse of one male medical practitioner's ideal vision of a birth room.[35] At the very least, a laboring mother could use the help of "two or three experienced and calm persons," by which the *Dasheng bian* author meant older female relatives or neighbors.[36] If wealthy enough, the family might also call upon the paid services of a professional midwife.[37] At all times, an expectant mother was to keep in mind three short phrases: "First: Sleep. Second: Withstand pain. Third: Be slow in calling for the basin."[38] It was essential that a laboring woman not try to "call for the basin" too soon, which was shorthand for the penultimate moment of birth, when a mother exerted herself to the utmost, and her attendants had a basin ready to catch the newborn. The assistance of other women provided both physical and moral support to a laboring mother. Physically, she could use the external support of other women to maintain an upright sitting or squatting position for an extended period of time, positions that were believed to allow a child an easier course out of the mother's body.[39]

It was the moral support of birth assistants, however, that was most critical, since a parturient mother mostly required a quiet, restful environment. More than two or three female assistants, the author warned, were not necessary and were even potentially harmful: "As for all other female relatives, tactfully thank them but refuse politely. Do not allow them to enter the room." Birth attendants should "move gently and talk softly, and not say too much," occasionally reminding the mother to "remain calm and assured, to bear the pain and rest." By no means, the author cautioned, should anyone in the room "make a big fuss over nothing, murmur into another's ears, or heave great sighs or gasps. . . . No one should pray to gods, make vows, or cry out loudly to heaven and earth in front of the mother." All of these activities might disturb the laboring woman, adding to her anxiety or nervousness. After much patience and pain, the mother would finally be ready to push. When would a woman recognize this moment? Only "when all the bones in your body loosen, your chest cavity falls, and your abdomen is so heavy that you feel the need to defecate and urinate all at once. You will see an explosion of fireworks in your eyes. *This* is the right time." Then and only then, cautioned the author of *Dasheng bian*, should the birthing mother push, but only for "as much time as it takes to drink a cup of tea."[40]

Imagine then that moment, after a lifetime of being schooled in the essential role of providing a male heir, after a woman has done everything in her power to ensure the conception of a son, who will not only continue the family line but also support her in old age, after ten lunar months of gestation and nervous waiting, after the excruciating pain of an ordinary childbirth, to say nothing of any additional life-threatening complications—imagine what it would have meant to give birth to a daughter. At that moment, the news could have been devastating. Early imperial medical texts cautioned against allowing anyone, including the mother herself, to ask about the sex of the child immediately after birth: "When the child has completely emerged, all people, including the mother, are forbidden to ask whether it is a girl or a boy."[41] Such silence was essential in order to preserve the new mother's emotional balance, which made her weakened physical condition all the more precarious.

Who was ultimately to be held responsible for female infanticide in late imperial China? In most texts of the period, there was no shortage of possible culprits to blame besides the mother, even though she might be the one to act, as in the case of the woman Ye. For example, one essay writer objected vehemently to "the oppression of bystanders" on the mother after birth. "The most hateful thing," he complained, "is when others egg [the mother] on. When someone has just had a daughter, it's hard to avoid provocation. Bystanders should use their mouths to urge them to refrain [from infanticide]. What reason is there to egg them on?"[42] A mother deserved pity, not blame. The tactless comments of tongue-wagging bystanders served only to push her over the edge:

> There's the type of neighbor or relative who doesn't care about committing a sin, or who is a hateful enemy. Once they hear that someone's had a daughter, they say sharp and biting things, or they laugh behind her back, so that the birth mother burns up inside, and drowns the child in anger.
>
> Then there's the type of false flatterer, who devilishly says solicitous things, purposely sighing and saying it is a pity. That just heaps more de-

pression on the birth mother who is already depressed, so that she drowns the child.

Then there's the type of mother-in-law or sister-in-law, who curses and makes trouble behind her back, making the birth mother so uncomfortable that she cannot but drown the child.[43]

This apportioning of responsibility across a wide group of participants is distinctive from the typical portrayal of infanticide in Europe during the same period, where mothers alone bore the brunt of the blame, as the solitary subjects of criminal prosecution or mental health examinations, or as public figures for condemnation or sympathy in the newspapers.[44]

Our sources for understanding the moral dimensions of infanticide in late imperial China come from a genre of texts known as morality books (shanshu).[45] As didactic texts, they cannot be read as straightforward historical records of actual behavior, but they can be used to illuminate common patterns of normative thinking. These texts shared the same basic universal creed of karmic retribution: do good and you will be rewarded, do evil and you will be punished. The earliest and best-known morality books, dating from the twelfth century, included a wide range of behaviors but mentioned no more than a single line against "committing infanticide or inducing abortion."[46] One popular morality book from the late Ming, the Gong-guo ge (Ledgers of Merit and Demerit), made such moral calculations even more explicit by assigning specific positive and negative point values to different behaviors, as adherents attempted to yield a positive balance each day.[47] "Urging someone to drown a child or have an abortion," for example, was among the most serious crimes, for which the maximum 100 demerits were deducted, and its positive counterpart, "Preventing someone from drowning a child or having an abortion," gained a person 100 merits.[48]

Morality books from the nineteenth century were more specialized and often devoted to a single topic, such as female infanticide. Each book might contain a wide variety of expressive forms, including essays, stories, illustrations, songs, poems and even institutional guidelines for philanthropy. Most of these texts were written in very simple language, for easy comprehension, and were often distributed for free at examination sites where elite men gathered, as an act of religious merit. Moral tales, which make up a significant portion of morality books devoted to infanticide, never varied in purpose and were never ambiguous in message: they always featured a person receiving a reward for preventing infanticide, or a person being punished for committing, aiding or abetting it.[49]

Although different members of a family or the community at large were held accountable in morality books for their actions or inactions in preventing or abetting in infanticide, men and women did not enjoy equal chances for a happy outcome. In my survey of late imperial morality books devoted to the topic of infanticide, I categorized the ninety-three stories they contained by the main character's gender (male or female) and ultimate consequence for the main character (punishment or reward).[50] The largest group, with thirty-six examples, featured the punishment of female characters. The second largest group, with twenty-eight examples, featured the reward of male characters. A smaller number were devoted to the punishment of male characters, with sixteen examples. An even smaller number detailed rewards given to female characters, with five examples. The remaining tales were considered as either punishments or rewards assigned jointly to a married couple, with eight examples. Why would there be such a distinct division in the types of stories featured in morality books against infanticide, with the greatest number featuring karmic punishments for women and karmic rewards for men?

In the first instance, because these didactic texts were written by men for audiences made up primarily of other men, it should come as no surprise that the framework of moral authority surrounding infanticide would largely favor males. A second factor, however, may have been the special role that women played as the primary assistants during childbirth. A midwife, mother-in-law or other female assistants would have been present in the crucial moments immediately following a birth, when they could exert immediate pressure over the birth mother in ways that men could not. A father's involvement in the act of birth was often minimal: recall that the woman Ye's husband, Chen Yingbo, is not even mentioned when she delivers her first daughter. Late imperial Chinese fathers could be away from their families for years at a time, sojourning in other towns or provinces as officials, merchants, teachers or examination students. Although they might return long enough to ensure conception, they would not necessarily return for the birth of their children.[51] This is not to suggest that fathers were entirely free from blame for infanticide, but it does suggest a dynamic in which a mother was in many ways left to fend for herself when dealing with an unwanted daughter. As in the case of the woman Ye, she might have only herself to rely upon, or fall under the influence of her female birth assistants.

MIDWIVES AND MOTHERS-IN-LAW

The midwife was a common target of moral blame for her supposed willingness to drown a daughter after birth at the request of parents, since the midwife had no blood ties to the child. Midwives did not enjoy a good reputation among male medical professionals in late imperial China, who accused them of trying to hurry the birth along by telling the mother to push too soon, massaging or pressing on the mother's belly or even using their hands to feel around in the mother's womb instead of allowing birth to slowly take its natural course.[52] Midwives were also commonly accused of being greedy, since midwifery was a special service requiring payment. The following birth scenario taken from an 1871 gazetteer from Fujian Province highlights all of a midwife's most odious qualities:

> The mother is dizzy and weak, and moreover afraid to touch the water [because of a taboo against newly delivered mothers touching water]. Men do not enter the room. The sisters-in-law and mother-in-law are all of the weaker sex, and most are fearful or timid. Only the midwife is in control at that moment; for her it has become something of a habit and by degrees something natural. She also has no feeling for the newborn, as she shares with it not one drop of blood. Thus her heart is ruthless and her hands are cruel. As soon as the baby emerges, she picks it up with both hands and examines it closely to see if it is a girl. Then, with one hand, she turns it over to put it in the basin, asking, "Keep it or not?" The answer is no, so she sits and calls for water, dragging the infant into it head first. Sometimes the baby is healthy and struggles or cries, so the midwife presses it down more forcefully. The baby tosses about for a moment, and suffers terribly. The mother sobs uncontrollably. After a while, the child makes no more sounds and doesn't move. The midwife then gets up, straightens her clothes, demands payment in food, wine, and money and goes complacently on her way.[53]

In this particular scenario, the midwife is more culpable than the mother, who is too physically and emotionally exhausted to do anything more than weep, while mother-in-law and sisters-in-law meekly stand by and the husband waits outside the room. As Charlotte Furth suggests, this generalized description of midwife behavior may have exaggerated her motivations and emotions, revealing more about male anxieties than a midwife's actual character or healing skills.[54] All the same, there is little reason to doubt the description of the scene of birth as a traditionally female domain, or the immediacy of the decision to commit infanticide. James Lee estimates that mortality rates for daughters in the Qing imperial lineage were ten times higher than for sons on the day of birth, four times higher in the first week, and twice as high in the first month.[55]

Morality tales did not differ greatly from other negative accounts of midwives, except in the ultimate assignment of karmic rewards or punishments. In the following example of a morality tale, a ruthless midwife is described as ignorant, greedy, conniving and manipulative, and in the end she receives her justly deserved karmic punishment:

> In the Taiyuan prefecture of Shanxi, lived a woman named Wang who was thirty. She specialized in midwifery. She had a mean and ruthless character. When she came into a room to deliver a child, she would rock the pelvis and rub the belly of the expectant mother. If the baby did not arrive at once, she would wildly claim that it was a transverse or breech presentation. Then she would secretly use a knife to cut it, breaking its hands and feet, using force to pull it out. She would call this a success and demand payment; it made no difference if it harmed the child or endangered the life of the mother. When this evil midwife went to a rich family and saw that the wives and concubines did not get along, she would take the bribe of one woman and hurt the child of another woman. Then she would lie and say that the fetus was damaged. . . . She delivered babies for twenty some years. Her family was well-off. At the age of sixty she already had three grandchildren. Because they were planning a party for her, they were all in the kitchen when it suddenly toppled. She was smothered along with her entire family. Each of Wang's hands and feet were broken. She wailed for several days before she died.[56]

Karmic punishments in death and the afterlife were often meted out directly onto the body, corresponding to whatever had been done in life to deserve it. In the case of the midwife Wang, her hands and feet are broken before she dies, since she broke the hands and feet of babies she delivered. A midwife's tongue might be cut out by demons, for example, for urging a birth mother to drown her daughter, rather than urging her to keep the child (Figure 1.1).[57]

These excruciating bodily punishments fit within grander visions of Chinese Buddhist hell, popularly depicted as a series of ten halls of judgment, each presided over by a different judge or overlord.[58] Those committing infanticide would be sent down to the seventh hall to have their fingers burned or their tongues pulled out or would be forced to swallow their own blood.[59] Punishment for infanticide could also be extended to family members by association, particularly sons, through their death or through the

Figure 1.1. Morality book illustration of a midwife receiving a punishment for encouraging infanticide, by having her tongue cut out in an underworld court of justice. The presiding judge is seated while various demons and ghosts assist him. Source: *Guobao tu* (1872), from the collection of the National Library of China.

removal of any future sons from a family's fated lineage. One story punished both a birth mother and the female neighbor who brought the bucket to drown her daughter, by having the son of the first woman kill the son of the second woman before he himself is executed for murder.[60]

Another common villain in late imperial morality tales about infanticide was the mother-in-law. Impatient for a grandson, she might force her daughter-in-law to drown a granddaughter or might commit the evil deed herself. More broadly, mothers-in-law were blamed as part of a wider family dynamic, for abusing the child brides of their young sons. Child brides (*tongyangxi*, or "daughter-in-law raised from childhood") were given up for adoption by a girl's family at a very young age and raised by the future groom's family until reaching maturity, when she would then be married to the chosen son.[61] The arrangement could be advantageous for both families, as the bride's family no longer bore the burden of raising a daughter and the groom's family gained a bride cheaply, who could then be trained by the mother-in-law to serve as the perfect daughter-in-law. According to Guo Songyi, almost one-third of Qing gazetteers he surveyed recorded the custom of child brides, with the greatest number of references in the southern provinces of Sichuan, Jiangsu, Zhejiang, Fujian, Guangdong, Jiangxi and the northern province of Zhili.[62] In almost half of the cases, child brides had been given over for adoption sometime between birth and the age of five, and others were given up at older ages, often after the death of one or both parents.[63]

Adoptive families could be indifferent or even abusive, and most families, according to one morality book essayist, treated their young daughters-in-law no better than they treated domestic servants. "In one family, they all eat happily and nosily, while the child bride stands in a remote corner. In another family, they all wear nice, warm things, while the child bride's coarse frock is in tatters. In another family, they all sleep sweetly and soundly, while the child bride doesn't get to sleep all night. Her food is the same as that for dogs and pigs, which she swallows with cold tears."[64] The main culprit was the mercurial mother-in-law, who could make life a living hell for a girl: "If a girl doesn't come near her mother-in-law, she is cursed for keeping her distance. If she comes a bit closer to her mother-in-law, she is cursed for keeping an eye on her. If she doesn't talk to other people, she is cursed for not being as clever as other people's daughters-in-law. If she occasionally talks to someone, she is cursed for talking about her mother-in-law behind her back."[65] Convincing an evil mother-in-law not to abuse her daughter-in-law was a matter of reminding her that this young girl would someday grow up to be the mother of her grandchildren and continue the family line. The young girl would also eventually serve as her mother-in-law's caretaker when the mother-in-law turned old and gray. Sympathy in any case was deserved, if a woman stopped to consider her own experience as a daughter-in-law and as a mother of a daughter: "You are the daughter of others. What if your mother-in-law had mistreated you this way? Your own daughter will marry into another family. If her mother-in-law abused her as you abuse your daughter-in-law, will your own heart not ache?"[66] This last line of reasoning neatly paralleled Gui Zhongfu's arguments for men, to think of their own mothers and wives, and reinforced the network of familial relationships that accorded every individual a proper place in it.

Reported abuse of child brides made parents hesitate to hand their daughters over to strangers, since they might be only condemning her to a worse fate. "Since the custom of abusing child brides is so widespread," lamented the same anonymous essayist, "those who have heard about it and seen it do not dare to or want their daughters raised that way. They can only drown their daughters, since they are forced to do so by those who abuse child brides." A girl trapped in a bad family as a child bride had no recourse to appeal to her natal family, and no way to defend herself. "In such a situation, they want to cry, but don't dare. They want to run away, but have nowhere to run. They want to cry out to heaven, but there is no response. They want to bury themselves under the earth, but have no way to do it." At that moment, a girl might regret her very existence, and rue the day that her parents had let her live past birth, asking, "Why didn't you just drown me on that day?" Her parents, too, would come to regret their decision: "Why didn't we just turn her over into a bucket of placid water? It would have been so quick and clean, and saved so much misery and heartache."[67]

Occasionally, the formulaic black and white universe of morality tales yields some surprising shades of gray. In one story, a mother-in-law in a poor family is widowed at thirty. Subsequently she forbids her two daughters-in-law from raising any of their own girls, and tries to force one to drown a newborn. For this, the mother-in-law is punished by a bevy of small ghost children and dies. Although this karmic punishment would have been the obvious message for readers and listeners of the time, we have the luxury of another possible interpretation. Justifying her rationale for female infanticide, the mother-in-law says, "All daughters would have the same bitter fate as me. It would be better to put her into a bucket of water at the start."[68] Such a sentiment echoes the feelings of the woman Ye at the beginning of this chapter, who wishes to spare her daughter her own experience of suffering. In this example, the sparse Chinese text never specifies whether the woman's "bitter fate" is that of being a woman, being a widow, being poor or a combination of all three injustices.

GOOD NEIGHBORS AND SISTERS

Occasionally women were rewarded in the universe of morality tales for preventing female infanticide, most often a female neighbor or friend who used her personal influence to sway a mother in the crucial moments immediately after the birth of a daughter. In the following example, one woman's moral behavior is enough to overcome the deficiencies of her son's shoddy examination paper, creating the opportunity for his success in spite of his lackadaisical study habits:

> In Fujian, Putian County, a poor woman gave birth to a daughter. She called her aunt to fetch water to drown it. Her neighbor, Lin, heard the noise and hurried over, urging her to stop. "You mustn't! You mustn't!" She helped them with money and food, ordering them to raise it. Just at the moment when Lin was urging them to stop, the poor woman's aunt suddenly saw a god in the air above her, holding a small book and writing in it. Later, Lin's son went to take the civil exams. His writing was not exemplary. The examiner was about to set aside his paper, when he saw a hidden god cry out, "You mustn't! You mustn't!" He knew that this paper had some secret merit and gave it passing marks. After the names of successful candidates were listed, Lin's son paid his respects to his teacher, who had been told by the examiner the reason for his passing the exam. At a loss, Lin's son went home and asked his mother about it. She thought for a long time. She began to understand that "You mustn't! You mustn't!" were the very words she had uttered that day when she urged them not to drown their daughter.[69]

Because morality books involved the karmic reckoning of good and bad behaviors, they often featured otherworldly beings, particularly Buddhist and Taoist deities. Whether or not humans were aware of it, invisible gods were always watching and recording their behavior, for future rewards or retribution. For example, the god Wenchang, patron saint of scholars, had in his possession the Cinnamon Record, in which he recorded the fates of all mortals, which could be altered by the performance of good or bad deeds.

As described earlier, the Boddhisattva Guanyin, goddess of compassion and mercy, could reward good deeds by giving a son to a couple. Yama, king of the underworld, was responsible for judging the recently dead. Those who needed to atone for their earthly sins were punished, often gruesomely, and those who were innocent could often be sent back to earth as demons to torment those who had done them wrong.[70] All of these gods had powers to judge and punish unrepentant humans or reward exemplary ones, and made appearances in morality tales. They were joined by a host of otherworldly denizens, minor demons, ghosts and wronged spirits, who crowded the landscape of popular beliefs and assisted in meting out rewards and punishments for good and bad human behavior. In the woman Lin's story, the god's repetition of her exact words makes the causal connection between actions taken against infanticide and her son's later examination success explicit.

Ironically, the nature of the most common reward for women only reinforced the overwhelming importance of sons that lay at the heart of the problem. No matter the good deed, it yielded the same ultimate reward for women and men: the birth of a fine son or male success in the civil examination system. This was true even for women well past their child-bearing years: one fifty-nine-year-old woman who prevents her neighbor from drowning a daughter is rewarded, along with her sixty-five-year-old husband, by the miraculous birth of a much unexpected son (Figure 1.2).

Although a man's good deeds might directly benefit himself, a woman's good deeds almost always contributed to the success of her husband, her sons or her husband's family line. Examination success served as the de facto karmic reward not only for preventing or refraining from infanticide but also for countless other good deeds, such as liberating captive animals or refusing to sleep with another man's concubine.[71] One of the appeals of examination success as a karmic reward, a trend notable by the late Ming period, was, as Cynthia Brokaw suggests, that a person "no longer needed to wait until death for an essentially spiritual reward; he could expect examination degrees, sons, and official appointments in his own lifetime as long as he accumulated merit in the proper state of mind."[72]

One unusual example about a karmic reward given to a woman for preventing infanticide can be found in an 1872 collection of twenty-four stories of filial piety aimed specifically at girls. In this story, set during the Ming dynasty, Yang Xiuzhen of Xinjian County demonstrates both her quick thinking and her compassion when she convinces her mother and grandmother not

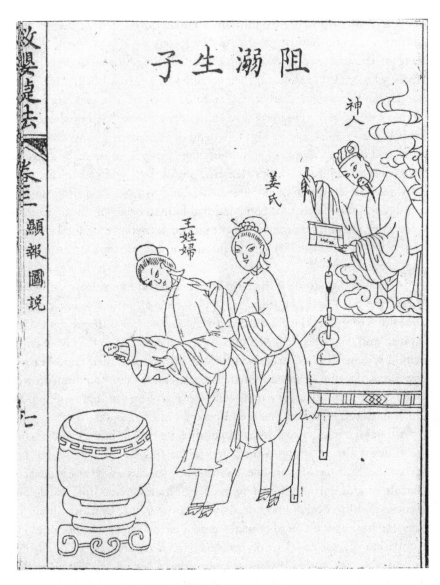

Figure 1.2. Morality book illustration of a fifty-nine-year-old woman preventing her neighbor from drowning a newborn daughter, for which she and her sixty-five-year-old husband will be rewarded by the miraculous birth of a son. The god in the cloud on the right is secretly recording her good deed. Source: *Jiuying jiefa* (1882), from the collection of the Harvard-Yenching Library.

to drown her newborn younger sister. Already at the age of ten, Xiuzhen has shown her filial qualities when she serves her father "day and night . . . without ever closing her eyes" during his illness. Three years later, her mother, having had three daughters already but no sons, gives birth once again to another girl. Xiuzhen's mother is so angry that she wants to drown it:

> She had already put it into a bucket of water when Xiuzhen, who was thirteen, rushed over to pick it up. She knelt and begged, "Mother, you wish to have a son, but if you kill this daughter, I fear there will be even less chance of having a son." The grandmother was angry and said, "You little wench, you don't know anything about the ways of the world! How could we have any extra food to feed a girl? Just hurry up and drown it!" Xiuzhen cried and knelt, begging, "Buddha's way is to show mercy. Granny, you read sutras every morning. If today you see death and don't prevent it, then why read sutras? If you say there is nothing to eat, I want to eat frugally and abstain from meat, and save a little money every day to raise this little sister." The grandmother was touched by her words, and let the child be raised. Two years later, they had a son. Her father dreamt that he saw his great-grandfather, who said, "If you had not raised your fourth daughter, then this son wouldn't have been born. Wise Xiuzhen, you are my family's lucky star." Later Xiuzhen married a scholar and had a son, who achieved the rank of assistant minister. She was awarded the honorary title of Lady of Highest Rank.[73]

On the one hand, this story reinforces the general framework of son preference, in that the ultimate consequence is the birth of a baby boy for Xiuzhen's parents, saving the family line, as well as the birth of a successful son later for Xiuzhen and her husband. Indeed, one could say that no reward for a woman, which might include good fortune or a long life, was complete without examination success for her male offspring. On the other hand, the story of Xiuzhen is unusual, since her actions teeter on the edge of propriety, given her subordinate position as a daughter and granddaughter. Ultimately, though, reasoning and begging with both her mother and grandmother is not framed as an act of defiance, but reclaimed as an act of gentle remonstrance, an extension of her filial qualities and worthy of a special titled reward.

BAD MOTHERS AND GHOSTLY DAUGHTERS

The one woman *never* rewarded as an individual for her behavior with regard to infanticide in morality tales was the birth mother herself. In all of the ninety-three moral tales on infanticide surveyed for this chapter, there was no instance of a mother being rewarded or receiving credit for actions taken to save her own daughter, though she might share the reward as part of a couple whose husband decides to refrain from committing infanticide. Why should this be? There is certainly no shortage of representations of good mothers in other genres of Chinese writing, and the mother was a powerful figure in family life. The story of Mencius's widowed mother, for example, who moved their household three times in order to find him a proper environment for his studies, is the Mother of all mother stories. The relationship between mother and son in late imperial China could be of monumental importance, and mothers were frequently and reverently remembered by their literati sons as symbols of virtue or suffering.[74]

One way to think through the problem is to consider what a good mother in an infanticide scenario might look like. It might be a moral behavior for a birth mother to refrain from drowning her child, but it would be disobedient and unfilial for her to defy her parents-in-law or husband, or, in the case of a concubine or servant, the head wife or mistress. Francesca Bray has explored the complex web of female-female "reproductive hierarchies" in late imperial China, mapping the dominance of the primary wife over the reproductive decisions of concubines and female servants.[75] If any of these people in a dominant position should force a birth mother to drown her daughter, they would be punished eventually in a karmic schema for their actions, but the birth mother herself could not defy their wishes and still be considered filial.[76]

If a woman did decide to preserve the life of her daughter, it could only be with the acquiescence of her husband, meaning that the husband would be credited with the good deed. A story of a poor scholar's wife who adopts an abandoned girl, for example, was placed under the heading of "Good Rewards Given to Poor Scholars Rescuing Abandoned Girls," since it was her husband who immediately benefited through examination success.[77] No didactic scenario could comfortably exist where a good mother was rewarded of her own accord, according to the strictures of the morality book genre. Although a husband's presence was not necessary to determine a daughter's death, as we saw in the example of the woman Ye, the sustenance of a daughter's life was impossible without his explicit support. One essayist against female infanticide acknowledged as much, writing, "Although the drowning of infants is the behavior of a vicious wife, this also stems from the husband's wishes. If the husband is determined not to drown it, the wife has no alternative but to go along."[78]

Only after death might a woman have the moral authority over her husband that she could not possess in life. A common figure in late imperial fiction, a ghost was sent back as a messenger for the living, warning them to repent and change.[79] A mother who had committed infanticide while alive, for example, could have a change of heart after suffering hellish torments in the afterlife. She could return in a dream to urge her husband to spread the word about retribution for infanticide:

> In Hangzhou there was a man named Chang whose wife was named Xu. She first gave birth to twin daughters, whom she drowned. Afterwards she became pregnant but did not give birth for ten months. Her belly was in terrible pain. She wanted to die but couldn't. In the sixteenth month, she gave birth to a monster, which had the head of a person and the body of a snake. Half of it remained in her womb. After suffering terrible pain for days, she died. The snake died too. The night she died, her husband dreamt that she sat in a tub of blood. The snake coiled around her body, biting her. The husband got mad and wanted to kill the snake. But his wife cried and told him to stop. "These are the two daughters that I drowned in the past. They returned as a snake to claim my life. I beg you to tell people everywhere, do not do what I did and suffer this misery."[80] (Figure 1.3)

This story of a female ghost returning to warn her husband fits the general description of ghosts in late imperial literature provided by Judith Zeitlin: "A ghost is a symptom of fatal blockage and congestion, a pathological return of something incomplete and unresolved."[81] Although the wife in this story is miserably punished, her husband lives to have a second chance. If a man who had earlier encouraged or permitted infanticide did change his ways and repent, he often experienced a reversal of fortune and eventually the birth of a son.[82]

Women, however, never got second chances, and their punishments were often painfully inscribed on a hypergendered body, at the very site of sexual reproduction. Mothers suffered from excruciating transverse or breech presentations in the womb, demonic offspring who refused to be born or painful sores erupting on the breasts, as in the next example.[83] In most of these punishment stories involving mothers, fathers made no appearance whatsoever: mothers suffered alone for their decision to commit infanticide. All of these stories of female exposure and punishment made for vivid visual tableaus, as in the following story:

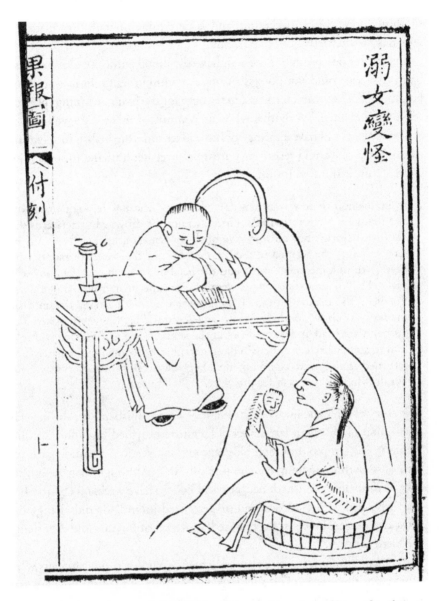

Figure 1.3. Morality book illustration of a man dreaming of his wife, who has died giving birth to a half-human, half-snake demon, as vengeance for previously drowning a daughter. His wife warns him to undo her past transgressions by exhorting others not to commit infanticide. Source: *Guobao tu* (1872), from the collection of the National Library of China.

In Zhejiang, Sui'an County, there was a woman named Liu. She first gave birth to two girls and drowned them both. Later, she gave birth to a son. She was so happy! One day as she was breastfeeding her son, he suddenly fell onto the ground. She saw two little girl ghosts, who latched onto her breasts and would not let go. Then she saw a horse-faced demon, holding a large sword, which he pointed towards her, saying, "These are the two daughters you drowned. Yama commanded me to bring them here to claim your life." Liu awoke with sore breasts. The next day, boils erupted on them. The pain was unbearable. Her whole body was covered in festering sores. Then she died. Her son also died because he had no one to breastfeed him.[84] (Figure 1.4)

Although it seems like the fate of unwanted daughters in all of these stories was only to be passive victims, this dynamic could be subverted, with a little supernatural help. An infant daughter, who in life was completely at the mercy of adults, gained the power to seek vengeance after her untimely death. With Yama's blessing, these unwanted daughters were sent back to the world as wronged souls (*yuanhun*) to demand retribution from their brutalizers, tormenting the living until an adequate punishment— usually the taking of another life—had been exacted.[85] Revenge not only granted the victim a chance to exact a painful retribution, it also gave an infant girl a voice—quite literally, the power of speech and the last word in the story:

A woman from Zhejiang, Qingtian County, drowned five daughters in a row. The sixth daughter lay sideways in her womb and would not come out. The pain cut like a sharp knife. Suddenly from the middle of her womb came the small voice of a child, who cried, "In your womb I took form five times, and each time you drowned me. Today I am once again in the form of a daughter, but I am afraid if I come out you will drown me again. It's better to die here in your womb, and end my life together with you." After these words, the woman wailed sorrowfully and died.[86]

Infanticide was not generally prosecuted as a crime in late imperial China, and it may have been this very lack of earthly punishments that made female infanticide into such a popular topic in the genre of morality books. These karmic tales of retribution would have been the only way that the weakest members of society—infant girls—could ever gain a just outcome against those who had so easily harmed them in life.[87]

Beyond the power of vengeance, an infant girl's only other means of persuasion was to plead with others to take pity upon her and protect her,

Figure 1.4. Morality book illustration of two ghost daughters biting the breasts of their mother, as vengeance for drowning them. The demon in the sky announces the mother's crime, while her son lies dead on the ground. Source: *Guobao tu* (1872), from the collection of the National Library of China.

articulating her helplessness as a kind of weapon of the weak. This popular rhyming song, written in the voice of a newborn girl, was attributed to the Boddhisattva Guanyin and frequently reprinted in morality books. Each stanza of the song implicated another member of the birth circle, as the girl appealed to all of those who had the power to prevent her early death: her father who might acquiesce to save her, her mother who might agree to give her up as a child bride, the midwife whose hands might be stilled, her brother who might take pity on his sister, and grandmothers and aunties who might urge restraint. In this remarkable presentation, the infant's physical form draws far less attention than the quality of her disembodied voice, which commands listeners from the start to "hear my song." Drawing upon a combination of logical reasoning, threats, cajoling and promises, these lyrics incorporate a range of emotional registers, each appropriate to the targeted audience:

Hear my song. Hear my song.
Hear me sing a song about wronged souls.
People who have daughters want to drown them.
How many wronged souls there are in the world!

Cruel father, cruel father.
A daughter is born and cries.
He does not allow her to be raised.
He is afraid that later she will be a burden to him.
Not knowing whether or not he will have children in the days to come,
Why shouldn't he have mercy on me now?
If one has a son without ambition,
He will lose the family money. How about that?
Please, sir, ask your conscience:
Isn't it a sin to harm my life?
Isn't it a sin to harm my life?

Cruel mother, cruel mother.
She is on her bed as the living Yama [in final judgment].
She is completely unwilling to raise me.
She says I should not be swaddled.
But really, even if the wraps are rags, they can be worn.
My future husband's family's clothes can keep me warm.
Even if I am taken to another family to be raised,
After I grow up I will still see you.
Please, lady, you are yourself a daughter, you see.
Your mother raised you and didn't complain.
Your mother raised you and didn't complain.

Good midwife, good midwife.
Why not save one more life?
One bucket of unfeeling water.
Carry it to the room to be the Messenger of Death.
This sort of midwife can bear to do this in her heart
And can bear to do this with her hands.
Seeing death, she doesn't save me and sits still.
Even when a hawk grabs young chicks,
Onlookers shout a few times.
I will go to the underworld and file a complaint.
You sat by and watched.
You sat by and watched.

Fact of injustice, fact of injustice.
Each and every household kills a person.
Daughters cannot speak
And can only cry, bewildered.
Aren't you afraid of heaven's anger?
The spirits are angry.
This kind of sin is very serious.
The gods Wenchang and Guangong have already written this,
Saying it to the mundane world, but no one listens.
I am urging those who study classics and know the rules
Examine your conscience.
Examine your conscience.

Good conscience, good conscience.
When your daughter was born you didn't let her live.
Aborting a life is serious.
A bloody fetus will go to the underworld court to file a case.
Today my four limbs are ready
And the six roots of sensation are complete [eye, ear, nose, tongue,
    body, mind].
But it is precisely the father and mother who kill the child.
Brother, if you can save me,
When your wife has a child I will take care of it.
If mother and father only wanted to raise you
Then where would your wife have come from?
Then where would your wife have come from?

I am suffering, I am suffering.
Just being born from my mother's womb I can't walk.
I open my eyes and cry.
When they see it is a daughter, they don't do anything.
In the room there are many aunties.

Why not urge my father to raise me?
Merciful granny burns some incense.
How can you just sit there and not open your mouth?
To say nothing of having glory at your door in the future.
Saving one person is greater than the morning stars.
Saving one person is greater than the morning stars.[88]

With regard to the practice of female infanticide in late imperial China, it is essential to consider how gender was a factor in a woman's decision-making, beyond the most obvious and immediate selection of daughters as victims. Women themselves were often complicit in ending the lives of their own daughters, but did so under complex and difficult circumstances. Giving birth to a son meant the possibility of future comfort and respect in the family, but daughters might have to suffer the same kinds of pains and miseries that a mother herself had endured. Moreover, the particular nature of the typical birth scenario as an all-female enterprise gave opportunities for women to influence each other's behavior—for both better and worse. Although it is not surprising that women would bear the brunt of the blame for female infanticide in genres authored exclusively by men, it is noteworthy that responsibility for infanticide was ultimately shared across a range of social actors, and not confined to the mother alone.

The question that remains to be addressed is that of male involvement. That the ghost of a drowned daughter might appeal to her father is not so surprising: after all, although a wife might decide to commit infanticide on her own, it would have been impossible to raise a daughter if her husband was opposed to the idea. But why would an infant girl appeal to unrelated male scholars, "those who study classics and know the rules"? What role did they play in the moral universe of female infanticide in late imperial China? If the first circle surrounding an infant girl involved childbirth and women in the inner quarters, then the second circle expanded into the outer world in which men moved, influencing public opinion about female infanticide. In Chapter 2, we will examine how male scholars worked against infanticide, through efforts at moral reform in their communities.

Reforming Customs

Scholars and Morality

Yu Zhi (1809–74), a schoolteacher from a village near Wuxi, in Jiangsu Province, lived in a time and place that called out desperately for succor. The devastating mid-nineteenth-century Taiping Rebellion (1851–64) began in southern China but quickly spread toward its cultural and economic centers south of the Yangtze River, including Wuxi. The rebellion eventually claimed the lives of some 20 million people. After it was finally put down by Qing troops in 1864, Yu Zhi wrote an illustrated book about the Taiping ravages, called *Jiangnan tielei tu* (The Illustrated Account of [Recent Events in] Jiangnan [That Would Make Even a Man of] Iron Cry). Set in forty-two illustrated panels with accompanying texts, the book was intended to drum up financial support for destitute war refugees by depicting the most horrific aspects of the Taiping destruction. It laid out the specter of death in its many guises: directly, at the hands of rebels and bandits, and indirectly, through starvation, disease and cold. Bandits lopped heads off of villagers, set fire to buildings, threw people out of their homes, raped women, forcibly conscripted young men and tortured villagers. Refugees drowned as they tried to escape over the river, or froze to death in the winter without adequate clothing or shelter. Survivors from the hands of the rebels were reduced to beggary, eating bark from trees or even eating human flesh.[1]

In the midst of this litany of suffering, Yu Zhi devoted one page to the problem of infanticide. It came after two other panels detailing how some had killed themselves rather than suffer starvation, and how families were reduced to selling their children. Here, infanticide was placed in a context of poverty, social dislocation and the uncertainty of war. Under such conditions, the act of infanticide was neither surprising nor unthinkable. The text accompanying the illustration included a short poem, italicized here, followed by Yu's essay and commentary.

ON HAVING NOTHING TO EAT AND THROWING A NEWBORN INFANT INTO THE WATER

Giving birth is normally a joyous matter. Why then throw [an infant] into the cold waves? To blame it is to extinguish reason and injure harmony.

Sorrowful feelings bottled-up inside are difficult to express to others. The heartbroken [mother] feels for her child, who is allotted a short fate. Its birth unfortunately coincides with the tumult of war. The mother does not know her own fate, so she says, "Go to the underworld first and wait for me."

Recently in every village there is the prevalent custom of drowning daughters, to the point where there are even those who drown their sons. . . . In these times today, those who have children old enough to carry in their arms often abandon them, to say nothing of a newborn crying and just arriving in the world. . . . Those with good hearts may wish to help, but they can only call out in vain; there is nothing to be done.[2]

Yu Zhi demonstrated a marked compassion for a mother committing infanticide during a time of war and hunger, while at the same time condemning the practice. The infanticidal mother of the text is heartbroken, not heartless: given the uncertainty of her own fate, the act of sending her child to an early death is presented as an act of mercy, not one of sheer cruelty. In the illustration, a mother lies on a bed in a broken-down hut, wiping away her tears, while another person dressed in patched rags, probably the father, is poised to drop the child into a nearby river (Figure 2.1). An old man also dressed in rags, with a good heart and wishing to help, stands next to him, shaking his finger and urging the father to refrain.

In Yu Zhi's commentary and illustration, the practice of infanticide was far from a private family affair, but a moral matter of everyone's business, even anonymous bystanders. The fourth wall was quite literally lifted from the family's ramshackle hut, so that what had been an intimate decision

Figure 2.1. Yu Zhi's illustration of a poor family during the Taiping Rebellion, forced by circumstances to commit infanticide. The wife in the hut has just given birth, while the husband is about to throw the newborn into the water. Nearby, an older man tries to stop him. Source: *Jiangnan tielei tu* (ca. 1864), from the collection of the C. V. Starr East Asian Library at the University of California, Berkeley.

made by women and their immediate families at the moment of birth was flung into the open, for all—particularly upstanding men in the community—to see and comment upon. Although Yu Zhi did not ignore the suffering and hopelessness of the mother and he appended comments on how to help poor pregnant women in disaster areas by providing food, clothing and cash subsidies, women's emotional experiences were not the focus of his writing. Instead, Yu shifted his attention to the old man in the foreground—a man, one imagines, not very different from himself (Figure 2.2).

This old man does his duty by stretching out his hand to stop the husband before he throws his newborn child into the water. But would other male scholars, the intended audience for Yu's words, do the same? Or would they pass by with their heads buried in their books? Wartime exigencies made the problem of infanticide particularly acute during and after the Taiping Rebellion, such that "there are even those who drown their sons," but poverty and lack of moral rectitude were even more enduring reasons that required continued assistance and constant vigilance from community-minded men.

In this chapter, we will examine how female infanticide was typically addressed by mid-nineteenth-century Chinese male elites, through the life and work of Yu Zhi. In the absence of sustained official or judicial actions from the imperial center to combat female infanticide, Yu Zhi's various endeavors against female infanticide, like those of his peers, were seen as a form of service to the community, falling within the context of Chinese philanthropy. Yu's central mission in life was to "exhort others to do good" (*quan shan*), guiding the moral behavior of the public at large. With regard to preventing female infanticide, this included staging moral plays, delivering public lectures, and writing didactic texts for children, as well as establishing relief institutions, such as foundling homes, and disseminating guidelines for these institutions. Although the core of Yu's message against female infanticide in his didactic works did not differ significantly from the lessons of cosmic reward and retribution found within the pages of morality books such as those examined in the previous chapter, Yu's writings form an exceptionally coherent body of work against female infanticide, demonstrating a sustained lifelong commitment to combating the practice.

However, there is an inherent tension in drawing attention to Yu's efforts in this regard: although he did much more than most to prevent female infanticide, the issue was far from his only or even his primary social concern.

Figure 2.2. Posthumous portrait of Yu Zhi. The caption at the top uses one of his alternative names, "Mr. Yu Xiaohui [literally, "filial and benevolent"] of Liangxi," while the note on the left side attributes the artwork to one of Yu's disciples. Source: *Zun xiaoxue zhai wenji* (1883), from the collection of the Peking University Library.

Many other causes, such as feeding the hungry or promoting the Confucian virtue of filial piety, were of at least equal if not greater importance. In the eyes of Yu Zhi and his fellow nineteenth-century moralists, the cultivation of virtue required a comprehensive approach. Preventing female infanticide and promoting filial piety, for example, were not separate and distinct issues, but part and parcel of the same complete package of virtue, ideally located in the same individual. Yu was therefore not what we might think of as an infanticide activist, reformer, expert or specialist—such a status did not exist in nineteenth-century Chinese society. Instead, the best description of his social role and function comes from his Chinese sobriquet, *Yu Shanren*, which can be translated as "Yu, Doer-of-Good-Deeds" or "Yu, the Virtuous One."[3]

REFORMING LOCAL CUSTOMS

Part of the difficulty of involving male scholars in the fight against female infanticide, according to Yu Zhi, was ignorance, plain and simple. "The custom of drowning daughters is quite widespread," he wrote, "but most scholars don't know about it. They always believe, 'This custom doesn't exist in my area.'" Although scholars often "closed their doors to study books, bragging about how they show concern for the people," he lamented, "little do they know that right outside their door, countless children are wailing, waiting to be saved throughout the day!"[4] At the same time, although the scholarly classes might be guilty of ignorance, Yu believed that ordinary, illiterate villagers, among whom "the habit of drowning daughters has become a custom," were most guilty of the deed itself. Numerous official edicts had been promulgated to prohibit the practice, but these flew too far above the heads of "foolish, common people," who could neither read nor understand their contents. In order to reach those at the lower end of the social spectrum, Yu advocated using "ordinary language . . . to make things clear and understandable," in the form of karmic retribution stories or folk songs.[5]

Although periods of war and natural disaster could increase the problem of female infanticide, it was most commonly understood by nineteenth-century elite men as a custom of everyday life, taking place in specific, local communities. In his writings, Yu Zhi, along with his contemporaries, most often used the term *su*, meaning "custom," "convention" or "common practice" (along with other synonyms, such as *xi*, "habit" or *feng*, "local custom/

practice"), to describe infanticide. Remarks about the local practice of female infanticide can be found in local gazetteers, which were informational
compendia detailing the geography, history, infrastructure, economy and
notable biographies of particular places, such as provinces, prefectures, subprefectures and counties, as compiled by relevant local scholars and officials.[6] If a specific gazetteer mentioned the practice of female infanticide, it
would be found under the section on "folk customs" (*minsu*), which also
provided details on special festivals, weddings and other unique, local phenomena, for example. Gazetteer references might not say more than a single terse phrase, such as, "It is a common custom to drown daughters here"
(*su duo ninü*).[7] When addressed in longer essays, female infanticide was often deemed a "vulgar custom" (*lousu*), or an "evil habit" (*exi*).

In the eyes of late imperial male elites and officials, female infanticide
was a regionally specific custom, and local officials spearheaded efforts to
eradicate it. Ming and Qing officials noted its particular occurrence in provinces south of the Yangtze River. A Ming dynasty official from Zhejiang
who served in Fujian, Song Yiwang, remarked, "South of the great river
[Yangtze] they are willing to drown their daughters. This destroys the harmony of heaven and earth."[8] The southern provinces of Zhejiang, Jiangxi,
Hunan and Fujian, along with the Jiangnan region, account for most of the
references to infanticide in Chang Jianhua's survey of Ming gazetteers.[9]
Likewise, references to infanticide appear most often in Qing gazetteers
from the southern provinces of Jiangxi, Zhejiang, Anhui, Fujian, Hunan,
Guangxi and Jiangsu, according to Feng Erkang's partial survey.[10] Although we are not able to make a precise count of rates of infanticide during the late imperial period in these areas, gazetteer references do at least
anecdotally support the general impression that infanticide predominated
in southern Chinese provinces.

The local custom of female infanticide was often linked to the incidence
of other undesirable local customs, particularly the economic burden of
extravagant bridal dowries. References to the burden of excessive dowries as
one of the main reasons for drowning daughters at birth can be found in
Qing gazetteers from Zhejiang, Fujian, Jiangxi, Hunan and Guangdong
Provinces.[11] Conversely, gazetteers noted that in areas where dowries were
reasonable, the custom of drowning daughters was less frequent. The importance of a properly sizeable dowry was not lost on any of the families
involved. As a Zhejiang official noted in 1825, "The groom's family regards

a generous dowry as an honor, while they will laugh at a skimpy one, to the point that the parents-in-law treat their daughter-in-law with love or hate depending on the size of the dowry."[12] A poor family in Jiangxi might be expected to spend on average several tens of *liang* of silver or more, and a wealthy family might be expected to spend several thousand or tens of thousands of *liang* of silver.[13] Moreover, a bride's family would need to continue to send gifts to the groom's family over the course of the marriage, on special holidays and celebrations, particularly after the birth of a son. Thus families might instead choose to save themselves a heap of future trouble by committing infanticide immediately after the birth of a daughter.

In contrast to local efforts, no empire-wide measures were ever implemented to end the practice of female infanticide. The Qing legal code, for example, did not explicitly treat neonatal infanticide as a punishable crime. The closest it came to doing so was in Article 319, which stated that parents or grandparents intentionally beating an obedient child or grandchild to death were to be punished by sixty strokes of the heavy bamboo and penal servitude for one year.[14] In practice, however, cases prosecuted under this article centered on the killing of an older or adult child, not newborns.[15] To be sure, at least some officials did hope to criminalize the practice of female infanticide. In 1772, a judicial official of Jiangxi Province, Ouyang Yongqi, requested imperial permission to prosecute those committing neonatal female infanticide by punishing them with sixty strokes of the heavy bamboo and penal servitude for one year—the very punishment prescribed in the Qing code for the killing of older children. Ouyang also believed that neighbors and relations who knew about the infanticide but did nothing to stop matters should be punished as accomplices.[16]

Without adequate judicial enforcement, it was more likely that heavenly, not earthly, punishments would still be the most effective. One anonymous Qing essayist recognized that when it came to the matter of infanticide, moral laws that governed all of human behavior proved less fallible than state law. "The Great Qing Code strictly prohibits a descendant from killing his parents and punishes this crime severely. Parents who kill a child without reason are also punished for this transgression. On such a scale, how can the drowning of a baby without reason be without blame? Sometimes it is possible to escape the law of the state. But the law of heaven does not miss even the finest needle."[17] It was not, he claimed, that infanticidal parents were not aware that their actions contravened heaven and reason, or that they did not know about the strictness of the punishments of the state laws. Instead, cases of infanticide often involved circumstances of extreme poverty, or the worry of having no male descendants to continue the family line.

PHILANTHROPY AS A WAY OF LIFE

According to his later biographers, everyone, whether they knew him or not, called Yu Zhi a *shanren* (virtuous person) because of his "love of righteousness and numerous charitable works, sounding out to those both south and north of the Yangtze River."[18] The explanation for his sobriquet underscored two central features in Yu's life: his geographic location and his orientation toward good works. The area below the Yangtze River delta, where Yu spent his entire life, was known as Jiangnan ("South of the River"). Jiangnan lay only a few meters above sea level and was interlaced with hundreds of rivers, lakes and streams. Jiangnan's wet climate encouraged agricultural productivity, which was itself the basis for other forms of handicraft industry. Throughout the late imperial period, the region was a rich economic and cultural center. Cities in Jiangnan, such as Suzhou, became centers for the highest levels of artistic achievement, and the region as a whole regularly supplied the empire with elite officials. Over the course of the late nineteenth century, the importance of Suzhou would be eclipsed by the burgeoning treaty port of Shanghai, which lay slightly more than seventy miles east at the terminus of the Yangtze River, where it flowed into the East China Sea.

What made Yu believe that he had an obligation to influence the moral behavior of others? To understand Yu's accomplishments in this arena, it might be best to begin with the single-most glaring failure in his life. Like so many before him, Yu had taken up a path of lifelong study, devoting his youth and much of his adulthood—two-thirds of his entire life—to passing the civil examinations in the hopes of obtaining an official position in the imperial government. Although Yu sat for the lowest level of local examinations five times, he never passed. Finally, at the age of forty-four, in 1852, he gave up the chase, lamenting the years he had wasted in the effort. His parents were dead and could no longer benefit from his examination success in any case: "I have let these months and years pass in vain. My own parents are now in heaven, without any such comfort. How could I flee from such a crime!"[19]

Despite his lamentations, Yu Zhi's examination failure, even at the lowest levels, was hardly remarkable. By its late Qing incarnation, the examination system winnowed hopeful male candidates in a series of ever more difficult and exclusive tests at the local, provincial and national levels, culminating in an examination at the imperial palace. Benjamin Elman estimates that after 1850, there were 2 million classically literate Chinese males attempting to pass local-level examinations, out of a total population of 450 million. At the next stage, approximately 50,000 to 75,000 candidates who had passed the local qualifying exams sat triennially for the provincial-level examinations. Of these candidates, only 1 percent to 3 percent would eventually pass, making them eligible for official appointments.[20] Although the civil examination system was still the most prestigious and direct path for a man to attain status and power in the late nineteenth century, in truth few aspirants ever came close to making it. Yu Zhi was far from alone either in his desire to join the ranks of officials or in his ultimate failure to do so.

The decision to turn from the examination path caused a change in heart in Yu Zhi. From this point on, according to his later biographers, "He stopped thinking about achieving office and instead focused solely on reforming customs and correcting people's hearts."[21] His biographers, comprising his students and admirers, may have exaggerated somewhat for dramatic effect: the urge to do good works was not really a new undertaking for Yu Zhi at age forty-four. Even before that fateful year, Yu's early adulthood reads like a roll call of mid-nineteenth-century Chinese philanthropic works: At twenty-six, he and two friends established societies to respect writing paper and preserve grain, typical philanthropic endeavors promoting Confucian virtues. At thirty-two, he wrote to officials to request funds to rebuild burst dikes and control flooding. At thirty-three, he set up a kitchen to feed rice porridge to the poor. At thirty-four, he started writing moral teaching texts for schoolchildren. At age thirty-five, he established a society to provide subsidies to poor families with newborn children to prevent infanticide. At forty, he collected more money to help build dikes burst by floods, and at forty-three, yet more money to rebuild a bridge.[22]

Philanthropy in late imperial China could be a respected alternative route to achieving local status and influence, in lieu of achievement in the civil examination system or material wealth in the form of landholdings. As Joanna Handlin Smith has described, philanthropy enabled "marginal figures who were of modest financial means and who lacked the degree-holding status . . . [to] wield moral authority to win cooperation from their community for worthy goals."[23] Although Yu Zhi would never become known for his elegant literary style or material wealth, he could and did manage to find a measure of social respect and meaning in his life through his numerous philanthropic works. On the other hand, had he actually been successful in his pursuit of a degree, he probably would have devoted more time and energy to traditional literary pursuits and had less time to spare for the cultivation of philanthropic works.

Yu shared with his contemporaries a deep and abiding belief in the power of words, both written and spoken, to inspire and transform society, a conviction made sensible in a male world centered on scholarship. Yu's own commitment to moral education was based on the pedagogical principles of the Song dynasty philosopher Zhu Xi (1130–1200), who had expounded on "Lesser Learning" (*xiaoxue*) as the requisite preparatory stage before "Greater Learning" (*daxue*). Lesser Learning comprised the study of practical etiquette and moral behavior in human affairs, such as "serving one's ruler, serving one's father, serving one's brother, and dealing with one's friends." Greater Learning was more philosophical and focused on "illuminat[ing] the principle behind these affairs."[24] Practice came before theory, just as Lesser Learning—for Yu Zhi shorthand for instruction in the rules of moral behavior—was the foundation for Greater Learning. Lesser Learning was such a central principle in Yu's life that one of his pen names was *Zun xiaoxue zhai* (Respecting Lesser Learning Studio), and his collected writings were issued under the title of *Zun xiaoxue zhai wenji* (Collected Writings of the Respecting Lesser Learning Studio).

Given the importance of moral education for a man like Yu Zhi, the publication and free distribution of morality books, with their unmistakable examples of good and bad behaviors, ranked highly as the method of choice in combating the pernicious effects of lowly customs, such as female infanticide. Morality books were idealized as having the most potential to change the behavior of the greatest number of people. Huang Zhengyuan, for example, who edited a 1755 edition of the morality book *Taishang ganying pian* (Treatise of the Most Exalted One on Moral Retribution), explained that this way of doing good spread through society like ripples on a pond. "There is more than one road to virtue," Huang wrote, "but none can compare to distributing morality books. By transforming one person, a morality book can go on to transform 10 million people. Spreading its teachings through one city, it can spread them through 10 million cities. By exhorting one generation to virtue, it can effectively exhort 10 million generations.

This is different from all other means of virtue, which do things one at a time in only one direction."[25]

Gui Zhongfu's preface to his popular 1741 essay against drowning daughters provided a perfect example of the multiplying effect of moral texts. As Gui explained, his exposure to female infanticide was not through personal experience, but mediated through another man's text. On his way to take an exam, he saw an anonymous essay against infanticide on the wall of an inn. He then copied and improved upon the language of the essay, but neglected to print and distribute it until a few years later, when he was reminded to do so by a friend who had received supernatural guidance from the god Wenchang. Upon finally completing this meritorious task, Gui passed the provincial exams and his wife gave birth to their eldest son the very next year. Later, Gui's son also passed the exams and was appointed to be a county magistrate, and Gui's friend was rewarded with an honorable mention in the provincial exams.[26] A subsequent morality tale extended the ripple effect of this virtuous behavior even further, by describing other scholars who copied, printed and redistributed Gui's essay once more, resulting in a cascade of karmic rewards for all.[27]

Morality books, in other words, not only had the potential to influence the behavior of the public at large; writing, printing and distributing them also could lead to karmic rewards for those who had a hand in their dissemination. Thus although Reverend Justus Doolittle, a nineteenth-century American Protestant missionary who spent fourteen years in Fujian Province, noted that morality books "exhorting people to preserve alive their female children" were frequently given away at examination sites, he surmised that this activity only reflected jaded attempts by aspiring candidates to garner the karmic reward of positive examination results. In Doolittle's opinion, their true purpose was "a selfish and personal one, terminating in the donor and his family—not a benevolent one, prompted by the desire to do good to others."[28] This purely instrumental attitude, which foregrounded the reward rather than the good deed performed, was even underscored in the morality tale about reprinting Gui Zhongfu's anti-infanticide essay. One scholar exhorts another friend, who has had no luck in producing a male heir, to take Gui's essay and "copy it well," adding, "I hope you will soon have a virtuous son."[29]

To take Doolittle's narrow view of morality book distribution, however, misses the point. Rather than gauging the genuineness of benevolent feelings, it is probably more helpful, as Joanna Handlin Smith suggests, to understand "how social, political and cultural forces constrained and guided . . . compassionate impulses or feelings of responsibility."[30] Whether one was motivated by dreams of examination success or more philanthropic impulses, the printing and distribution of morality books at examination sites was the definitive method for channeling one's efforts. At least in theory, the appearance of such printed material at examination sites did have the most potential to reach a broad and influential audience of male scholars. These candidates not only returned home to set standards of behavior within their own families, they also had status within their larger communities and might someday even serve as public officials, capable of instituting more far-reaching policies. Uplifting one's sense of self and fulfilling a perceived social need were not by any means mutually exclusive.

STAGING MORALITY

Yu Zhi's own most original contributions to the promotion of public morality were his so-called moral plays (shanju). For Yu, many of the most popular operatic plays of his time were also the most "depraved," leading village audiences astray.[31] Yu castigated Shuihu zhuan (Outlaws of the Marsh), a series of adventure tales involving a Chinese Robin Hood and his band of 108 Merry Men, for glorifying "thieves and bandits into heroes."[32] At the same time, he criticized Xixiang ji (Romance of the Western Chamber), a love story about a thwarted secret affair between a scholar and the daughter of a prime minister, for making "licentiousness appealing."[33] Yu called such operas "poison affecting people's hearts," and hoped that other gentlemen, "who shoulder the responsibility of guiding the world, will step up to advocate the reform of music, turning back the tide with their bare hands."[34] In truth, Yu Zhi's accusations of banditry and lewdness in cultural productions were neither original nor unique, as these dramas had been condemned by moralists throughout the late imperial period.[35]

However, Yu's suggested solution to the problem of depraved music was unusual. Around 1860, Yu issued his own collection of twenty-eight opera-plays in the Peking style, gathered under the title Shujitang jinyue (Music of the Day of the Near to a [Moral State] Hall). The title of the collection alluded to a story about the sage philosopher Mencius, who teaches the king of Qi about the instructive power of music. The king, somewhat embarrassed, admits that he prefers recent music over the rarefied music of the ancients. Instead of chastising him, Mencius replies, "If your Majesty's love of music were very great, [the Qi kingdom] would be near to a state of good government! The music of the present day is just like the music of antiquity, as regards effecting that."[36] Good music, in other words, could reform people's customs and lead to good governance. Yu hoped that his own moral plays might have this very effect. Yu explained that his plays were written with the "intention of urging the ignorant to pay attention," in a manner that was "easy to practice and easy for listeners to understand," using "simple and coarse" language.[37] He had no illusions that they were of any high quality: "I know very well that they are not refined or in good taste."[38]

In this collection, Yu included one play about the prevention of female infanticide, *Yuguai tu* (Illustration of Giving Birth to a Monster).[39] It staged a familiar combination of exemplary and execrable behavior, bringing to life the perpetrators, victims and saviors of infanticide. Two branches of the same family served as a model in contrasts. Zhu Sanlang and his wife, under the influence of his heartless mother, drown their newborn daughter, prompting her spirit to go to the underworld to seek revenge. Yama, king of the underworld, allows her to return as a monster, and she is reborn as a human-headed snake demon, killing Zhu's wife during birth. The snake-demon then kills their beloved only son and bites off the tongue of the mother-in-law. Meanwhile, Second Auntie, who is the kindhearted wife of Zhu's older cousin, tries to prevent Zhu from drowning his daughter at the start. Later, while picking mulberry leaves, Second Auntie rescues a new-born baby girl who has been thrown into a river, adopting the child as her own. A rich official soon follows auspicious signs to Second Auntie's front door, and requests the hand of their adopted baby daughter as a match for his own infant son. Better still, Second Auntie is rewarded with the birth of her own fine son, although she was originally fated to have none.

Audiences watching Yu's play on infanticide would have had ample opportunity to boo for a villain, laugh for a cowardly clown, cheer for a heroine or shiver with fear at a snake demon. The evil mother-in-law, the dreadful Old Lady Zhu, is the most contemptible of all the characters, snatching away her granddaughter to drown after the others are reluctant to do so, exulting, "If it weren't for me today, an old granny using her own two hands, how could this stupid girl have been sent running on her way to the underworld?" She gleefully sings, "This calculation is really grand. We save on food, save on clothes, and save on paying dowry. The next time there is another birth, we'll see who has what it takes! Only the old lady dares to put it into the water bucket."[40] Meanwhile, the girl's father, Zhu Sanlang, is little more than a spineless coward, hiding under the bed and shaking when the snake-demon emerges. To his partial credit, he is reluctant to drown his newborn daughter, holding her and sighing, "What a pale dumpling, a good daughter! How can I do this with my own two hands!"[41] The infant girl shows a fighting spirit of her own, when she returns as a ghost to the underworld to bring her case before Yama. She blames her grandmother, Old Lady Zhu, entirely, while more or less excusing her father for being a misguided tool: "Zhu Sanlang listened to his mother's words and didn't dare disobey her." Yama agrees, intending to spare the couple while punishing the mother-in-law: "Zhu and his wife were forced to do it on account of the mother. Usually they have filial hearts, and I saw that at the last moment he may have had some regret."[42]

It is likely that Yu Zhi's plays would have been staged for free on the occasion of temple fairs or festivals, coinciding with a town's market days. By the Ming and Qing periods, stages were often incorporated as a regular feature of temple architecture.[43] A village might collectively sponsor an opera performance for a special, once-a-year occasion by pooling resources to hire a traveling troupe.[44] An illustration from Yu's book on reconstructing Jiangnan in the aftermath of the Taiping Rebellion shows a sizeable crowd watching an operatic play, with the three actors and two musicians standing on the thrust platform above, while the audience crowds onto the ground below (Figure 2.3).

The characters onstage seem to be a poor filial son in patched clothes and his parents, to whom the son is serving tea. Mingling among the crowds are vendors selling snacks to eat, women seated at the left side of the stage, and even a child asking his mother for a treat. At the upper left, another idle viewer perches in the balcony, leaning over to get a closer look.

What might have been the audience's reaction to Yu Zhi's play against female infanticide? Would the audience have taken to heart the clear warnings against bad behavior, while being inspired to improve for the future? For his part, at least, Yu had no intention of letting audience members forget the overt moral purpose of his plays. In order to drive home the distinction between his own plays and other depraved plays, Yu even designed a set for a "Stage for Exhorting Morality" (Figure 2.4).

An audience could not easily forget Yu's didactic intentions with signs hung all around trumpeting the divide between good plays and evil ones. A paired couplet on either side of the stage read, "Nothing is greater than

Figure 2.3. Yu Zhi's illustration of a village opera performance. On the raised stage, a filial son seems to be serving his elderly parents tea. Two musicians accompany the performance, while the rapt audience enjoys the lively atmosphere. Source: *Jiangnan tielei tu* (ca. 1864), from the collection of the C. V. Starr East Asian Library at the University of California, Berkeley.

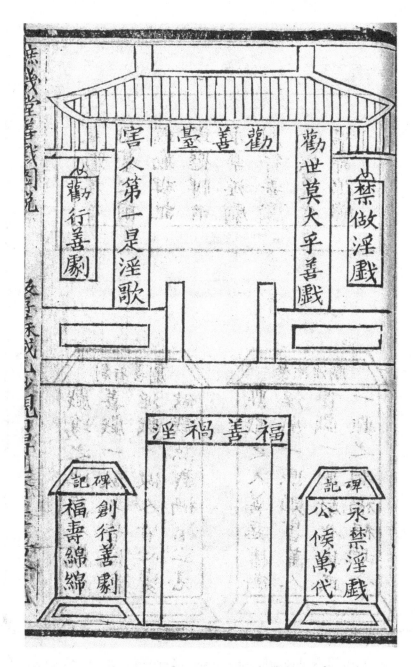

Figure 2.4. Yu Zhi's "Stage for Urging Morality" (*quan shan tai*), designed specifically for the performance of his morality plays. In the upper register, the outer hanging paired couplet reads: "Prohibit the writing of lewd plays." / "Urge the performance of moral plays." The inner paired couplet reads: "Nothing is greater than moral plays in reforming the world." / "Lewd songs are number one in harming people." In the

moral plays in reforming the world" and "Lewd songs are the number one in harming people." At the bottom of the stage, two tablets connected these positive and pernicious influences to rewards and retributions. "Banning lewd plays forever / Results in generations of high-ranking offspring" was echoed by "Creating moral plays / Results in continuous good fortune and longevity."

In spite of Yu Zhi's heavy-handed stage design, it is likely, as Andrea Goldman has suggested, that audiences gathered to witness "not necessarily the moral packaging but rather the dramatic excitement" of these free temple fair performances.[45] In the example of Yu's play against female infanticide, for example, one can imagine the thrill audiences might have had at seeing onstage the birth of the snake-demon, who upends the bedchamber, leaving mother and son for dead and mother-in-law mute, or the fear that might strike their hearts at the appearance of Zhu Sanlang's vengeful ghost daughter. Certainly by the early twentieth century, enthusiasm for Yu's plays had already been dampened by their overt moralizing tone. As literary scholar Lu Jiye put it in his 1935 study of Yu's works, "The more one puts on the face of defending traditional values, the more the audience will look distracted [and] then leave."[46] With regard to Yu's play on infanticide, it is unclear if it was ever performed in public. An unnamed subset of his moral plays was first performed in 1859, in Jiangying and Changshu, two towns in Jiangsu Province not far from his hometown.[47] Another report records performances of Yu Zhi's plays in Zhejiang in 1873, although again specific titles are not mentioned.[48] Opera expert Qi Rushan recalled that shortly after the turn of the twentieth century, sixteen of Yu's plays were still being performed, but these did not include the play on infanticide.[49] By the 1930s, only one of Yu's plays, which dealt with the topic of filial piety, continued to be performed.[50]

There is, however, evidence that Yu's other efforts at public exhortations did hit their mark, on at least two occasions when Yu delivered a village lecture (*xiangyue*) against the practice of female infanticide, first in 1858 and again in 1871. The village lecture system called upon local officials to deliver regular public lectures promoting the most common Confucian social values,

---

lower register, the tablet on the right reads, "Banning lewd plays forever / results in generations of high-ranking offspring," while the tablet on the left reads, "Creating moral plays / results in continuous good fortune and longevity." The sign over the lintel reads, "Good fortune and morality, misfortune and lewdness." Source: *Shujitang jinyue* (1880), from the collection of the C. V. Starr East Asian Library at the University of California, Berkeley.

such as filial piety, frugality, diligence, obedience and honesty, based upon a list of behaviors codified by the Kangxi emperor in the seventeenth century, and expanded by his son, the Yongzheng emperor, in the eighteenth century.[51] By the mid-nineteenth century, however, the village lecture had devolved into a rote ritual, involving monotonous recitation. According to one anonymous Western observer in Shanghai in 1847, "It was *reading*, and nothing more, in a rapid and distinct, but not very elevated tone of voice." Local officials themselves made no pretense of listening, using the occasion instead as a chance to gather together for tea and snacks. Meanwhile, the targets of the lectures, upstanding "scholars, soldiers, farmers, merchants and mechanics," were nowhere to be seen. Only those of the lowest classes of society, "vagrants, idle people who were loitering about the place, beggars, and truant boys," gathered to listen.[52]

Well aware that dispassionate and uninspired repetition could turn off a potential audience, Yu Zhi emphasized the critical role of the speaker himself in giving life and meaning to the words: "Everything rests on the way the words are delivered right at that moment. If we can undertake to do this with vigor, there is nothing that will not show some results. Under all of heaven, there is no person who cannot be changed. It is only a matter of having the sincere heart to move people."[53] Yu included an illustration of just such an effective village lecture in his book on rebuilding efforts in post-Taiping Jiangnan (Figure 2.5).

Yu himself recalled one notable occasion in 1858, when he was invited to deliver a village lecture in an area where female infanticide was widespread. He used "strong words" to urge the several hundred men and women in the audience to refrain from such behavior and returned the next year to the same area to deliver another village lecture.[54] After this second appearance, he met a man named Zhang, who described the effect of Yu's earlier lecture on one of his friends:

> After listening to your lecture, a friend and I walked home together. Because of your words, he sighed deeply. I knew it was because he had had so many children that he had in the past drowned a son. I took the opportunity to say, "Is it because you heard the village lecture that you know now to regret your past crime of drowning a child?" My friend said, "Yes, that's it. I didn't know about this principle to begin with. It was only because there were too many burdens. Anyway, other families drowned children, so I didn't think that it was worth making a fuss. Now it is too late to repent."[55]

Figure 2.5. Yu Zhi's illustration of a village lecture. The lecturer stands on the raised platform at the right, surrounded by a completely attentive village audience, while two officials listen from their positions in front of an altar. The two scrolls on display on the left read, "Filial behavior is exemplary" and "Moral integrity is exemplary." Source: *Jiangnan tielei tu* (ca. 1864), from the collection of the C. V. Starr East Asian Library at the University of California, Berkeley.

Zhang encouraged his friend not to give up, reminding him that Yu had said that people could atone for their past sins by urging others not to drown their daughters. Yu's lecture had definitely changed the man's behavior for the better, the man continued, because his friend had had a newborn daughter that very year. "Not only did he not dare to drown her," marveled Zhang, "he even loves her like a beautiful pearl! Isn't this all just because he heard you, sir, during that one lecture? He had previously drowned a son, to say nothing of a daughter! When you gave your village lecture, you saved a life."[56]

Yu was flattered and surprised at this outcome, explaining, "This event was really quite exceptional, and worth mentioning."[57] Despite the rarity of such audience feedback, Yu was convinced of the great effectiveness of the village lectures, optimistically envisioning countless others who had been similarly helped. Not only could moral lectures prevent female infanticide, they could also change all kinds of bad customs, and shape every kind of person: "Apart from this example, I don't know how many may have silently saved an infant. Moreover, how many might have heard the lectures and would have known thereafter to respect officials, be filial to their relatives, respect their elders, and be patient when facing hardship? [How many would have known] to stop killing and free captive animals, to cherish grain and writing paper, and to accumulate merit as good deeds? The positive effect of the village lectures is truly limitless."[58]

INFANTICIDE AS ONE MORAL PROBLEM AMONG MANY

Seeing the prevention of infanticide within the context of the entire spectrum of Yu Zhi's moral concerns allows us to get a better sense of its regular but limited place within his moral universe. In 1868, for example, Yu Zhi wrote a book targeted at teaching moral behavior to children, titled *Xuetang riji gushi tushuo* (Illustrated Daily Reader for Schools). In Yu's opinion, morality needed to be placed in front even of literacy as a goal: "I fear that if a child enters school and is taught to recognize characters without being taught how to be a good person, recognizing characters will simply be a tool to help him indulge in vice. This is not even as good as illiterate villagers who still know to respect the law and be disciplined."[59] Yu thus compiled in his reader 100 moral stories featuring positive and negative models of behavior for children to emulate and avoid, with the idea that a teacher would cover a few pages each day. Of these hundred stories, there were five tales dealing with female infanticide. Four of the tales detailed the rewards given to scholars and officials who made efforts to end infanticide, and the fifth story was essentially a much shorter version of Yu's anti-infanticide play, *Yuguai tu*.

If only five tales in Yu Zhi's reader dealt with female infanticide, then what types of behaviors formed the subjects of the other ninety-five stories? In a sense, all of them sprang from a central concern with the Confucian ideal of filial piety. The relationship of respect between parents and children was the root of all other human relationships, and therefore worthy of special emphasis. Harmonious family relationships—including those among siblings, between husbands and wives, and between married couples and their in-laws—extended outward to the clan, neighbors and the wider community. The implied order of these relationships provided a foundation for appropriate social behavior in all other arenas, which Yu painstakingly spelled out in his didactic writings, in innumerable examples of dos and don'ts. One should not be licentious or greedy. One should not get drunk, fight with others, take people to court, gamble or fritter time away on bawdy entertainments. Furthermore, one should be kind to beasts and preserve their life, and refrain from eating cows, dogs or frogs. One should cherish writing paper by disposing of it properly, live frugally and not covet money too much. Women should remain chaste; men should refrain from licentiousness. All should practice charity toward the poor, donating money, food and medicine to those in need.[60]

Indeed, in all of Yu Zhi's didactic works for children, infanticide appeared as but one single moral issue among many. A 1910 edition of *Xuetang riji* (Daily Reader for Schools) featured infanticide in six out of ninety-nine tales. In the 1865 edition of *Riji gushi xuji* (Continuation of Daily Stories), it appeared in only two out of fifty. The story of Yang Xiuzhen, the young woman who pleaded with her mother and grandmother to save the life of her infant sister, was the lone example dealing with female infanticide in Yu's 1872 compilation of filial stories for girls, *Nü ershisi xiao tushuo* (Twenty-Four Illustrated Stories of Filial Piety for Girls). An even shorter, early collection of nine illustrated tales from 1845, *Xuetang jiangyü* (Lectures for Schools), included no stories at all related to infanticide. Yu's collection of twenty-eight moral plays demonstrated the same diversity of topics; the prevention of infanticide appeared as only the tenth item on this list of play topics:

1.   Diligent farming
2.   Filial piety
3.   Love and respect for elder brothers
4.   Contributing to the maintenance of soldiers
5.   Modeling chastity for women and punishing adultery
6.   Teaching loyalty and filial piety
7.   Punishing the teaching of thievery
8.   Punishing the teaching of lewdness
9.   Cultivating the self to improve one's countenance
10. Punishing those who drown daughters
11. Warning against the private slaughter [of beef]
12. Cherishing grain
13. Cherishing writing paper
14. Freeing captive animals
15. Filial piety
16. Charitable relief
17. Punishing ingratitude
18. Celebrating virtuous wives and filial daughters
19. Warning against mistreating child brides
20. Punishing those who do not love and respect elder brothers
21. Punishing heretical beliefs
22. Reuniting families
23. Providing economic relief and rescuing babies
24. Punishing those who disrespect life and trick others
25. Prohibiting fighting and brawling
26. Warning against thievery
27   Distinguishing between good and evil; urging bandits to surrender
28. Prohibiting women from entering temples

What was the effect of including a single injunction against female infanticide among numerous other prescribed or proscribed behaviors? Did this diminish its importance, or mark it as an enduring moral concern, by reappearing in so many different works? Yu Zhi himself indicated no hierarchies or prioritized agendas, placing his stories and plays in no apparent order. On the one hand, the theme of saving infants or punishing infanticide found its way into all of Yu Zhi's didactic works—but on the other hand, so did stories about not wasting grain or establishing rice gruel kitchens for the poor. The prevention of infanticide, in other words, was a consistent but not necessarily special moral concern.

FOUNDLING HOMES AND INFANT PROTECTION SOCIETIES

Yu Zhi's efforts at community improvement were not limited to moral exhortation. Yu also was a proponent of an institutional approach to social welfare and wrote an extensive handbook on the subject titled *Deyi lu* (Record of Attaining [Goodness]). In it, Yu discussed instructions for establishing a wide range of charitable institutions, including foundling homes, infant protection societies, general benevolent societies, schools and societies for honoring writing paper and giving pointers for other philanthropic practices, such as how to save lives from fires, floods, famine or cold and how to feed widows and the elderly. The title of Yu's handbook alluded to a story from the Confucian classic, the *Zhongyong* (Doctrine of the Mean), in which Confucius remarks about an exemplary man, Hui, that when he "attained a certain goodness [*de yi shan*], he would clasp it firmly and never lose it."[61] The reference was an enjoinder to strive for and maintain the positive effects of moral works. Although Yu Zhi began writing the book in 1849, it was first printed only in 1869—perfect timing for a society in need of restoration after the Taiping ravages.[62] Again, Yu's philanthropic institution-building efforts were not unusual: in the wake of the Taiping destruction, there was a flurry of activity on the part of male elites, who desired to rebuild local communities by taking charge of a variety of social welfare and infrastructure projects, as Mary Backus Rankin has documented among Zhejiang Province elites and William Rowe has detailed for urban elites in the city of Hankou.[63]

Yu Zhi's proposed rules and regulations for establishing a community-sponsored foundling home (*yuying tang*) described in detail its general management, including its staff, finances and operational policies. If a foundling home were constituted as described by Yu Zhi, it would include a general director, an annual manager and monthly manager, a daily supervisor, two to four inspectors, a head nurse, wet-nurses and three or four cooks, who might also serve as doormen, general delivery men or scouts for more wet-nurses. Only a handful of the paid wet-nurses would live inside the walls of the foundling home itself; the large majority would be given a child to nurse in their own homes, outside of the orphanage. Wet-nurses living in the foundling home were to be given all their meals, as well as material supplements, such as a bed, mosquito net, blankets, clothes and a charcoal brazier. On festivals, they were to receive bonuses, such as noodles and cash. Outside wet-nurses were subject to regular inspections, to ensure that they were adequately feeding the child under their care and not privileging the care of their own children to its detriment.[64]

Besides setting up the system for basic sustenance of young children, the regulations also detailed specific attention to matters of their general well-being, health and education. Each baby was to be issued clothes, wraps, jackets, hats and socks throughout the year. The babies were also to be vaccinated annually for smallpox, and their hair was shaved twice a year (leaving a tuft of hair on the left side for boys, and a tuft of hair on the right side for girls). If a child became sick, it would be taken to the doctor, but if it should die, it was to be properly buried. Those under one year of age were to be buried in paper or a bag, and those buried after one year of age were to be buried in a wooden box. Both ages would have seven strings of paper cash burned as an offering, and during the Hungry Ghost Festival, monks were to be hired to chant sutras, and prayers and food would be offered for their souls. If a child was weaned but not adopted, it would be reared outside the home by a nurse and sent at age six to a community school if it was a boy, with the possibility for vocational education at age twelve, or arranged to be married at age thirteen if it was a girl.[65]

Yu's foundling home regulations specified not taking in children above three years of age, since the setup was designed to nurse infants only. The regulations were also clear about the relationship between the birth parents and their child. "When they desert an infant at the foundling home, their relationship with the child ends and the foundling home takes over." The birth parents should not try to reclaim the child if it had been adopted by another family. Adoptions were to be reported to the county officials, with a license given to the adoptive family and a copy kept at the foundling home. Before any such adoptions were allowed, families needed to be inspected, particularly those wishing to adopt a girl. Although boys could "become the son of the adoptive family and carry on the family line," without presenting any potential problems, girls might be resold into prostitution or taken for a concubine. To prevent these undesirable ends, the family had to prove its honorable intentions and report the adopted daughter's later engagement or wedding when she came of marriageable age.[66]

Did foundling homes operate successfully with such clockwork efficiency? By one measure, that of infant survival, nineteenth-century Chinese foundling homes had a fairly dismal record. In three separate examples, Fuma Susumu has calculated the death rate of infants as ranging from 31 percent to 39 percent for the Haining foundling home in Zhejiang Province from 1891 to 1893, from 48 percent to 50 percent for the Songjiang foundling home in Jiangsu Province from 1869 to 1870 and from 41 percent to 53 percent for another foundling home in northern Shanghai from 1888 to 1890.[67] Yet these death rates were comparable for foundling homes in other parts of the world in the eighteenth and nineteenth centuries. Angela Leung notes that infant mortality rates in the mid-eighteenth-century French foundling homes of Toulouse and Montepellier have been calculated at 53 percent and 60 percent, respectively.[68] By the early nineteenth century in Paris, according to Rachel Fuchs, foundling home mortality rates ranged from 20 percent to 30 percent.[69]

In part because of the high mortality rates in foundling homes, Yu's philanthropy handbook also included rules and regulations for a more innovative form of institutional relief for infanticide, known as the "infant protection society" (*baoying hui*).[70] Infant protection societies differed from more traditional foundling homes in that a child was never removed from its birth family. Instead, donations from local elites subsidized the maintenance of newborn children of needy families. Although Yu was not the first to think of this type of subsidy program for indigent families—back in the eleventh century, Su Shi had already called upon the wealthy to aid the poor to prevent infanticide—Yu's was perhaps the most successful systematic example to catch on in late nineteenth-century China, particularly in Jiangnan.[71] Yu established the prototype for the infant protection society near his hometown of Wuxi in 1843, in Qingcheng Village.[72] Under this assistance scheme, poor families within a radius of ten *li* who registered their newborn child could receive a subsidy of one dipper full of rice and 200 *wen* every month for five months. Only after such a period of time would the child be sent to a foundling home, if the parents really could not care for the child. The flexibility and extended reach of infant protection societies, argues Angela Leung, made them ideal for a society under reconstruction after a decade of Taiping destruction.[73]

The subsidy scheme's greatest intended advantage was that it fostered the development of natural, parental affection in the attempt to forestall leaving a child in a foundling home. Yu wrote, "If [the parents] keep their child, love will blossom. As the child grows bigger every day, their feelings of tenderness will deepen."[74] Elsewhere, Yu Zhi wrote that although parents might be frustrated and distressed at the outset, "After four or five months, the little child can already laugh and play. This attitude of delicate innocence makes it easy for people feel tenderness. The father and mother will be unwilling to abandon it then, and make the effort to raise it."[75] Once such an affectionate parent-child bond was established, surely no parent would wish to harm his or her own child. Infant protection societies, then, were set up to provide the necessary cushion of time and resources that poverty had eliminated. Angela Leung points out that these measures also strengthened traditional Confucian family bonds: "Not only was an infant's life saved, so was the completeness of the family."[76]

The benefits for newborn survival were also significant. One of Yu's explicit aims was to provide assistance to the poor in rural areas, who could not even afford to make the trip to a larger city where a foundling home might be located.[77] Moreover, when newborns from rural areas were transported to foundling homes, they were often only a few days old and had to travel over long distances. Many never survived the trip, or they got sick along the way. The care they received after arrival was not always optimal either: wet-nurses employed to feed these charges often had babies of their own to look after, and naturally treated their own children preferentially, feeding them more or giving them the clothing supplied by the foundling home for the foundling. One late Qing writer thus commented that infant protection societies were an improvement over foundling homes, since they could save both lives and money: birth mothers took better care of their own children than hired wet-nurses, and funds were not needed to build an actual building.[78] Yu Zhi claimed that the infant protection society established in Qingcheng, had saved the lives of 60 to 100 or more children during the ten years of the society's existence.[79] The research of Fuma Susumu has bolstered these claims, estimating that infant protection societies were on the whole more successful than local foundling homes in keeping children alive, with a mortality rate of 15 percent to 20 percent, which halved that of comparable foundling homes.[80]

Despite Yu Zhi's original intentions to prevent primarily *female* infanticide, the children saved by infant protection societies were not exclusively daughters. Of the children supported by the subsidies from the Shanghai infant protection society from 1874 to 1875, 90 were boys and 148 were girls.[81] Total abandonment at a foundling home, moreover, was still a more likely outcome for daughters rather than sons: females constituted 96 percent of recorded entries for the nearby Songjiang foundling home.[82] Still, the existence of infant protection societies was a net positive, and public officials eagerly promoted Yu Zhi's infant protection society plans. As early as 1846, the Jiangsu provincial governor circulated Yu Zhi's rules and regulations of the infant protection society within his own province and also to Anhui Province.[83] In the following year, the Zhejiang provincial governor circulated the rules within his own province, as well as to Fujian Province.[84] Twenty-five years later, Yu's plans still enjoyed official patronage. In 1872, Shen Bingcheng, the circuit intendant of the greater Suzhou area, invited Yu Zhi to establish the infant protection society in Shanghai.[85] Shen wrote to his provincial superiors again in 1873 to recirculate an expanded version of Yu's infant protection society rules and regulations.[86]

Still, even within the context of setting forth institutional guidelines, Yu did not miss the opportunity to emphasize the moral effects of establishing an infant protection society. Beyond the material help that an infant protection society gave to indigent families, an unanticipated consequence was the society's influence over the behavior of its contributing members, reminding them to perpetuate the preservation of daughters closer to home. Yu Zhi reported on just such a case involving his distant cousin Zhihong, a member of an infant protection society who lived in Suzhou and had had three daughters in a row. Upon bearing a fourth daughter, his wife attempted to drown it, but the eldest daughter ran to tell her father. Zhihong reasoned, "I contribute two *wen* to the Infant Protection Society almost every day. How can we behave like this?" He rushed home to fish his daughter out of the water so she would not die. When his wife had a fifth daughter, she was so angry she again tried to drown it, but Zhihong again refused: "My family donates money to help others save their infants. How can I then drown daughters in my own home?" His wife, wrote Yu Zhi, "could not disobey." Finally, two years later, the family had a son, which Yu Zhi reckoned was Zhihong's karmic reward for preserving the lives of his daughters.[87]

Yu cited another example, of a stubborn schoolteacher named Gu San-bao, who had two sons but had also previously drowned two daughters, fearing future burdens. After establishing the infant protection society, Yu told Gu about karmic retribution, and hoped to "move his heart, urging him to contribute one *wen* every day, in the hopes of partially atoning for his previous sins." Then, a year later, Gu suddenly told him, "My family cannot contribute one *fen*, even if we wished to." When asked for an expla-nation, Gu replied that they had had another daughter in his family, and because he had entered the infant protection society, they could not drown it. But now they needed all their extra money to raise their own daughter, and could no longer donate to the society. Yu smiled and answered, "Of course. Please do what is convenient. Though if you really have trouble rais-ing your child, you can always ask the Infant Protection Society for assis-tance." Chastened, Gu also laughed and replied that it had not yet come to that, even though he still believed his daughter would become a burden in the future.[88]

Although Yu Zhi gained a reputation as a *shanren* and spent his life do-ing good works, did his works actually do any good? Only a few examples, such as those of Zhihong and Gu Sanbao above, attest to Yu's personal ef-fectiveness in preventing female infanticide, and all of these accounts come from Yu's own hand. By the karmic measure of rewards and retributions most familiar to other nineteenth-century Chinese, Yu's numerous good deeds to prevent infanticide—putting on moral plays for villagers, writing didactic works for children, giving village lectures and establishing infant protection societies—never quite yielded their promised fruits: Yu neither enjoyed examination success nor had any sons of his own. By the time of his death, at age sixty-six, he had one nephew, who served as his adopted heir, and three married daughters.[89] But if Yu was disappointed in his fate, he never let on. He never mentioned his own daughters directly in his writ-ings, but perhaps he treasured them, never begrudged them their dowries and appreciated their care for him in his old age, as so many of his morality books admonished. Or perhaps he was an eternal optimist and never gave up hope for the morality book miracle of a fine son, even as he and his wife grew frail with old age.

At the same time, Yu did enjoy some small measure of renown for his efforts, as his moniker *Shanren* attests. In his later years, Yu was awarded a number of minor honorary official titles and emoluments, all tied to his service as a public educator.[90] What is perhaps more important than the outward success of Yu Zhi's life is the realm of possibility that his life course represented in a post-Taiping era. Yu Zhi, a man with no degrees, mediocre abilities and a fairly narrow mindset, was able to craft a life of meaning in the late nineteenth century by devoting it entirely to moral education in all of its written and oral forms. His work may or may not have done much to change any customary practices, but what mattered to his contemporaries were the sincerity of his effort and the seriousness of his purpose. All of Yu Zhi's ideas emphasized an individual's proper place and comportment within family and society, remaining well within the confines of main-stream Confucian precepts. Men, women and children all had their pre-scribed roles. Understood only superficially, such pedantic prescriptions for behavior could seem hollow, repetitive and endless. But taken on a deeper level, these ideas represented the outward expression of ideal human rela-tionships, imbued with a sense of propriety. Every person had the potential to change for the better, if only he or she would try.

Yu Zhi's lifelong commitment to moral education made sense in the context of his local community and his peers. But the sum total of his vi-sion and values was less well-equipped to deal with the arrival of foreign armies, missionaries and traders on China's shores in ever greater numbers throughout the late nineteenth century. In 1866, at the age of fifty-seven, Yu was invited by the circuit intendant Ying Baoshi to serve as a principal of the *Guang fangyan guan* (lit., "Institute for the Propagation of Area Lan-guages"), a new educational institution in Shanghai, set up three years earlier to teach French and English to young Chinese boys.[91] In the wake of the Second Opium War (1856–60), which China had lost at the hands of allied Anglo-French forces, the need for Chinese translators of Western languages had been made painfully clear during treaty negotiations, and the language school was part of efforts by Westernizing officials, such as Li Hongzhang (1823–1901), to unravel the secrets of Western military tech-nology and science.[92]

Although the primary reason for creating this new school was to pro-mote Western learning, Yu's single noted contribution to this enterprise was to hearken back to Chinese tradition by insisting upon enshrining Zhu Xi's principle of Lesser Learning as an essential teaching at the school. Accord-ing to his chronological biographers, Yu was "worried that people would forget the foundation" of Lesser Learning, which was listed as one of the school's ten curricular standards in 1870, ahead of foreign languages and other Western technological subjects.[93] Yu's fastidious attention to moral education, above and beyond all else, demonstrated how little he understood the scientific and political preoccupations of these foreign interlopers. Moral exhortation may have been the unshakeable foundation upon which he had built his entire life, but it was easily overlooked by Western observers who came to write the next chapter on the story of female infanticide in China.

THREE

Seeing Bodies

Experts and Evidence

Herbert A. Giles (1845–1935), a long-serving member of the British consular service in China in the nineteenth century and a prominent Sinologist of the early twentieth century, was never one to shrink from a fight. In his obituary, he was remembered as a "ruthless controversialist," "always furiously taking sides no matter right or wrong."[1] His pugnacious style served him well in stirring up some measure of excitement in the North China branch of the Royal Asiatic Society (NCBRAS) in Shanghai, where he served as branch president in 1885. In an attempt to revive what he considered a "moribund" society, Giles instituted a series of symposium-style meetings, where numerous short papers of differing opinions were delivered on one subject.[2] The subject for the May 1885 meeting was the question of the prevalence of infanticide in China, an issue Giles would encounter so many times in his long Sinological career that he eventually declared himself "heartily sick of this subject."[3] Yet that evening his interest was still fresh. According to Giles, the question before the group was not *"Does Infanticide exist in China?"*—the affirmative of which participants could "take for granted"—but "To what extent does it prevail here in comparison with other countries of the world?"[4]

It may come as some surprise to a twenty-first-century reader that there would have been any debate at all about the comparative extent of infanticide in China, but in the nineteenth century, infanticide was considered a serious problem *within* Great Britain, France and the United States, not a problem confined to Asia alone.[5] Britain in particular seemed to undergo an "epidemic of child murder" in the 1850s and 1860s, with frequent newspaper stories on scandalous cases.[6] So-called baby-farming incidents were rife, in which women were paid a minimal and insufficient fee to "care for" another's unwanted or illegitimate child, often ending in its neglect and eventual death. This situation in Britain was deemed serious enough to warrant the passing of the Infant Life Protection Act in 1872, which required those hired to care for more than one infant at a time to register their homes with authorities.[7]

To the gentlemen of the Royal Asiatic Society, then, more than mere curiosity was at stake in determining an answer to the question of the prevalence of infanticide in China. Underneath any such assessment lay an implicit judgment about the barbarity or humanity of Chinese civilization as a whole, as compared to Western society. Margaretha Weppner, for example, a British woman who spent two years traveling around the world in the late 1870s, was appalled by the abandonment of Chinese children in Shanghai. Yet she was similarly shocked by the easy access to abortions available in New York City. Although she condemned "heathen mothers" with their "benighted notions," she paused long enough to wonder, "But are we free from blame, we people of the *civilized* world, who point with scorn and pity to the heathen"?[8] As Jennifer Holmgren has suggested, the capacity nineteenth-century Westerners demonstrated for detecting infanticide in China may well have had more to do with "concern about the extent of the practice in European society" rather than "Chinese reality." She argues that the "Western mind in the latter part of the nineteenth century was more or less programmed to discover the presence or absence of the social evil of infanticide in other societies."[9]

Until now, most historians writing about infanticide in China have used nineteenth-century Western sources directly, as just more evidence of its existence.[10] But doing so ignores the fact that such evidence is fundamentally of a different order than the Chinese sources on infanticide that had preceded. Although Chinese sources were almost exclusively couched in forms and language preoccupied with morality and local acts of philanthropy, intended solely for the exhortation of Chinese audiences, nineteenth-century Western sources on Chinese infanticide were written as exercises of "scientific" investigation, with the general purpose of informing European and American audiences about the cultural mores of an exotic land. Infanticide was regarded as one of any number of distinct Chinese cultural markers that required endless commentary from nineteenth-century Western writers, along with Chinese eating habits, dress, language, treatment of women, religious practices, sanitary habits (or lack thereof), moral character and so on. Discussing female infanticide in these textual excursions to China was as inevitable as a trip to the Great Wall would become for later visitors.

In asking the question of prevalence, Western writers shifted concern away from the moral outcomes for Chinese adults perpetrating or preventing infanticide, who had been both the subjects and targets of native exhortatory writing, and emphasized instead the physical bodies of Chinese infants as victims. Finding, describing and finally counting Chinese infant corpses seemed to be a critical way to measure the actual prevalence of infanticide in China, relative to Europe. One major obstacle, however, hindered these efforts: given the intimate and hidden nature of infanticide as an act generally taking place within the confines of Chinese homes and within the even more restricted female sphere of birth, curious Western men had an even lower likelihood of seeing an infant corpse than their Chinese male counterparts. Conclusions about the practice of infanticide could therefore be based only on circumstantial evidence, all of which was subject to interpretation and debate, including the visual examination of infant burial sites, secondhand estimates of rates of infanticide by Chinese men and women, and the profusion of Chinese morality books that mentioned the practice.

Although the members of the Royal Asiatic Society may have fancied their meeting as a kind of scientific debate on the prevalence of infanticide in China, in actuality, both sides shared more fundamental assumptions about the practice than they did differences.[11] Regardless of their stated positions, all the debate participants demonstrated an unshakeable confidence in a scientific approach to infanticide, based on the fundamental practices of description and enumeration. Moreover, by constructing and taking part in such a forum, all of the participants implicitly believed themselves fit to render judgment on the question of prevalence, even if they never stirred beyond the comfort of their library chairs or could not speak a word of Chinese. Finally, all saw the utility of this comparative civilizational model, and the place of infanticide as a representative indicator within it. None of the debate's participants envisioned a different possibility, one that would have come naturally to a nineteenth-century Chinese man like Yu Zhi. Although Yu recognized that infanticide existed in his local community and he did his utmost to combat it, the practice took its place as only one single behavioral node in a complex, living human web, and an even vaster moral universe. Infanticide was never a test case on which to hang or pardon all of Chinese civilization.

SINOLOGICAL EXPERTISE

An informational enterprise was always a part of Western presence in China, beginning with the efforts of Jesuit missionaries in the late sixteenth century. Although their primary goal was to convert China's elites to Christianity, the early Jesuit missionaries never attracted more than a limited number of Chinese to renounce their age-old beliefs for a new, foreign faith. As one scholar has remarked, although the Jesuits "failed in their mission to interpret Christianity to the Chinese, they were brilliantly successful in interpreting China to the West."[12] Beginning in 1703, popular collections of Jesuit letters, acquainting Western audiences with the manners and customs of China and other strange, distant lands, were published under the title of *Lettres édifiantes et curieuses* (Edifying and Curious Letters). Over the next three quarters of the century, the Jesuits in Paris published thirty-four volumes in the series, a third of which focused on China. Subsequent editions were published in the late eighteenth and mid-nineteenth centuries, assuring the popularity of the Jesuit letters for new generations of readers.

The letters, written by various Jesuit missionaries to their superiors, friends, patrons and scholars back home, touched on hundreds of different topics. Everything about China, from its modes of governance and systems of belief to its flora and fauna to the finer points of appreciating its porcelain and music, was a subject for discussion. Many of the Jesuit fathers were extraordinarily erudite and immersed themselves in the study of Chinese classical texts. The letters they sent home, selected and heavily edited by Church fathers in Paris, were highly appealing to European audiences, sharing with them "the images and perfumes of another planet."[13] Eventually, however, the Jesuit mission in China was challenged by opponents inside and outside the country alike. Beginning in 1724, the Yongzheng emperor had all but a handful of Jesuit missionaries working in the capital expelled from China, forcing them to retreat to the foreign enclaves at Canton and Macao on the southern coast. The Jesuits were dealt an even more serious blow in 1773, with Pope Clement XIV's suppression of the Society of Jesus in much of Europe, resulting from domestic political pressures to curb Jesuit influence.

To a great degree, the Royal Asiatic Society and other similar nineteenth-century scholarly societies inherited the mantle of Western investigative science in China, initiated by the Jesuits in the eighteenth century. At its inception in Shanghai in 1857, the goal of the Shanghai Literary and Scientific Society (rechristened the North China Branch of the Royal Asiatic Society in the following year) had been to assist and encourage amateur scholars living in China to bring their collective skills to bear in the massive task of generating knowledge about China in all of its aspects. Members devoted themselves to investigating Chinese history, literature, institutions, schools of thought, language, geography, plants, animals, people and customs, in studies that were read aloud at regular meetings and published in the society's journal. The society later established a library and a museum in Shanghai, to further the research efforts of its members. As stated in the society's inaugural journal issue, scholars at home in the West needed the assistance of those on the ground in China, "who can form an estimate of the institutions of the empire from personal observation,—and who can investigate at the fountain head all that bears upon the physical, intellectual, and moral condition of this countless population. This is a work beyond the compass of any single individual."[14] The North China Branch shared this larger mission of knowledge production with other branches of the Royal Asiatic Society, which itself had begun in India in the early years of British presence there, as part of a collective imperial scientific enterprise.[15]

Herbert A. Giles and the other gentlemen of the NCBRAS in Shanghai in 1885 represented this late nineteenth-century world order. Of the branch's 181 members, more than half were British, followed by another third who were German, American or French, and a minority from other European nationalities, along with two Japanese members.[16] There were no Chinese members and no female members of the society, although women were in the audience of those listening to the symposium itself. That the members even found themselves in China in the first place had everything to do with the larger forces of empire and trade: almost three-quarters worked for the consular services of various nations or as customs agents or merchants, and the remainder were support professionals of one kind or another, including doctors, engineers, lawyers, professors and journalists. Only eleven of the NCBRAS members were missionaries, and all of these were Protestants, marking a distinct absence of any Catholic missionary involvement.[17] Any number of cities around the world at the time could have boasted amateur scientific societies with similar memberships—male, Anglophone, secular and white.[18]

Scientific work produced in China did not stay there, any more than the men themselves did. Their work filled libraries and lecture halls back home, expounding on the minutiae of Chinese history, language and culture, or sought broader audiences with titles that emphasized expertise born out of long years of exhaustive study, such as the Reverend Arthur Evans Moule's *New China and Old: Personal Recollections and Observations of Thirty Years* (1891). Others parlayed linguistic skills honed in China as consuls or international members of the maritime customs service into second careers as academics in Britain and America. The 1885 NCBRAS members included the China-nurtured scholars Herbert A. Giles, future professor of Chinese at Cambridge University (1897–1937); Thomas Lowndes Bullock, future professor of Chinese at Oxford University (1899–1915); Frederick Hirth, future professor of Chinese at Columbia University (1902–17); and John Fryer, future chair of the Oriental Languages and Literatures department at the University of California, Berkeley (1896–1914).[19]

At their May 1885 meeting, the gentlemen of the Royal Asiatic Society brought together all the evidence they could gather regarding the prevalence of infanticide in China. Nine men, arguing on both sides of the question, mentioned the great quantity of Chinese moral tracts, illustrated wall posters, or proclamations from local officials against the practice. Frederic Hirth, a German deputy commissioner of customs in Shanghai, even brought in a sample of an anti-infanticide moral tract printed in 1873, reasoning that their popularity proved the prevalence of the problem: "There must be some trouble and expense in preparing and publishing them, and I cannot imagine that they should have no other purpose than the amusement of the public."[20] A few referred to secondhand encounters with Chinese eyewitnesses, such as William Cooper, British consul in Ningpo, who had previously lived in Swatow (Shantou) with his family from 1864 to 1865. There, the family's amah (nursemaid) told his wife that she had killed three of her own children at birth "by their mouths and nostrils being stuffed with the tinder of burnt cotton rags, because she and her husband were then too poor to bring them up; and that she herself had assisted at the death of several other women's female infants." In spite of her confession, though, Cooper refrained from condemning her actions: on the contrary, he added that she was a "strong, active, good-tempered woman," who "proved an admirable servant."[21]

One form of evidence, however, trumped all other sources, and was cited more frequently than any other type. These were writings from other Westerners on the practice of infanticide in China, previously published in other contexts. No fewer than ten different Western sources were cited in the course of debate and discussion, often including the precise bibliographic detail of publication date, volume or issue. Interestingly, the content of what was cited differed little from the personal observations recounted by the Royal Asiatic Society members. The very fact of publication, however, seemed to lend these other utterances a degree of scientific authority that the members' own impressions lacked. During the discussion, for example, E. B. Drew, chief secretary of the imperial maritime customs, drew attention to the fact that his own knowledge of the subject was thin, and he professed his reliance on a previously published work by Samuel Wells Williams titled *The Middle Kingdom* (1882). Drew joked that he had planned to "palm off Dr. Williams's opinions as his own. However, his conscience got the better of him, and he would acknowledge where he got the information."[22] Ironically, Williams's comments on infanticide were themselves cribbed from another Western source, an article by Protestant missionary David Abeel about the practice of infanticide in China, examined later in this chapter.[23]

More than producing any decisive conclusions about the practice of infanticide in China, the ultimate result of the Royal Asiatic Society debate was to reinforce the underlying structure of Sinological expertise upon which the whole scientific enterprise was based. The role of "expert" was reserved for these self-styled Western Sinologists alone: such a title would never have applied to a nineteenth-century Chinese man such as Yu Zhi, even if he was more familiar with Chinese practices and customs related to infanticide, because Yu was interested in perfecting a well-rounded vision of moral virtue, not subject mastery. This enclosed system of citation, illustrated by the comments of the NCBRAS meeting participants, codified a narrow subset of ideas on the topic of infanticide through continual repetition and transmission. Often one Western text on infanticide in China referred to another Western text on infanticide in China, and so on, in an endless chain. The more frequently an idea was repeated, moreover, the more it gained heft as a permanent and real fact.

BURIAL PRACTICES

By far the most convincing proof of infanticide for many Westerners lay in the visual sightings of abandoned infant corpses in China. Father François Xavier d'Entrecolles (1664–1741), a Jesuit missionary in Peking, described in a 1720 letter to a European patroness how priests and native Christian converts had stumbled upon abandoned infants, discarded in a box beside a river, buried alive in a case, or even being devoured by wild animals. One priest walking on a remote path walked into "a pig holding a child between its teeth, which it was ready to devour. He pursued the animal, and removed its prey. The child, all bloody, still gave signs of life. It was baptized, and shortly thereafter flew away to heaven."[24] Another Jesuit missionary, Father du Baudory, wrote in 1722 from Guangdong Province, "Nothing is more ordinary than seeing [infants] floating down the river, or carried away by the current."[25] A Swedish chaplain, Olof Torén, who traveled around Asia with the Swedish East India Company in 1751, also remarked on having seen "several children floating on the water" in the vicinity of Canton during his brief stay there.[26]

Although the visual evidence of infant corpses was undeniably stark and arresting, conclusive interpretation of the meaning of such evidence was murky at best. There was no doubt that Western eyewitnesses had seen decomposing corpses of infants, but what, precisely, did these bodies prove? Were exposed infant bodies evidence of intentional infanticide, as most Westerners assumed, or merely the evidence of minimal burial practices? Abandoned infants found alive might well be tantamount to attempted infanticide, since exposure would in most cases have led to death. But what about infants who were already dead when found? Were these also cases of exposure, or might they have died of other causes? If they had died earlier, had they been intentionally killed, or had they died of disease or illness, only to be disposed of carelessly? There was a strong desire to make such visual evidence count, but it was nearly impossible to determine parental intent from the sighting of infant corpses alone.

Although great effort was expended on ritual formalities of burial for adult family members in China, infants or young children generally did not merit the same ritual care. For those wishing to demonstrate the appropriate forms of respect for the dead, Zhu Xi's *Family Rituals*, written in the twelfth century, was the paradigmatic prescriptive text on burial rites during the late imperial period.[27] Zhu Xi's chapter on funerals took up almost half of the book, specifying the appropriate preparation of the body for burial, the honoring of the deceased and the proper mourning clothes to be worn or actions to be performed by the living, ranked by degree of relationship to the deceased. The prescribed lengths of mourning were shortened for those who died below the age of nineteen, and shorter yet for those younger than eight. As for the burial or mourning of infants, Zhu Xi offers only one brief remark: "Those who do not live three months are not wept over."[28] The absence of a standard mourning period for a young infant may seem somewhat harsh to readers today, accustomed as we are to much lower levels of infant mortality. It is important to note, though, that mourning rituals were in large part about an individual's incorporation into the realm of venerated ancestors, and not merely a measured outlet for survivors' grief. In this schema, very young children, even if beloved, would never be accorded the same honor and status as full-fledged adult family members, since they would never have any descendants of their own and represented the end of a family line.

Children's burial in late imperial China was often little more than a "systematic throwing away" of the corpses, in the words of J. J. M. de Groot (1854–1921), a Dutch consular official who lived in China for eleven years and later became a professor of Chinese in Leiden and then Berlin.[29] In his monumental study of Chinese religious and funerary practices, published from 1892 to 1910, de Groot highlighted the minimal attention given to children's corpses, which seemed to Western eyes haphazard and uncaring:

> [Children's] corpses are placed in a jar or a poor wooden box, which a workman unceremoniously carries on his shoulder, or in some other way, to the open country, together with a hoe to dig the grave pit. No relations escort him on his way. At best the sorrowing mother sees him out into the street, giving vent to her grief by piteous wailing, and loudly protesting against her child's leaving her. The corpse is buried anywhere at a depth of a few inches, and the rest of the earth heaped up over it. Within a short time the dust

returns to dust, or, as is very often the case, the remains are devoured by dogs and crows. No property in the ground is secured, nor is any attention paid to the spot afterwards. Many babies are not buried at all, the urn or box being merely set aside in the open country, where it likewise soon falls a [sic] prey to birds and starving dogs.[30]

Chinese public initiatives to care for abandoned children's corpses were very often an extension of initiatives to care for living children in foundling homes. Huang Liuhong (fl. 1651–93), a seventeenth-century Chinese official, included in his famous magistrate's handbook, *Fuhui quanshu* (A Complete Book Concerning Happiness and Benevolence), a section on how to establish a foundling home, along with instructions on the public collection of abandoned children, both living and dead. Live children were to be collected for the foundling home, and dead children were also to be brought back for proper burial in a "wholesome place," in order to show "equal compassion" for both.[31] Huang recommended dividing the city into four quadrants, and having one or two men assigned to each section, taking a wheelbarrow, mounted with a frame, to collect any children found. Huang's arrangements for the care of unwanted children so impressed Father D'Entrecolles, the Jesuit priest who had described how one of his brethren had seen a Chinese child being devoured by a pig, that the priest sent a lengthy translation of sections of the work to his patroness in 1720, enthusing, "I thought that you would be glad to see some extracts of a Chinese book that fell into my hands recently. You will find in it sentiments of a natural compassion with regard to exposed infants & other unfortunates . . . which will inspire you with respect for the sages of China."[32]

The first orphanage in Peking, established around 1662, seems to have implemented this collection and burial practice at some point in its history, probably after 1724, when the orphanage was brought under imperial sponsorship under the Yongzheng emperor.[33] Father Jean Joseph-Marie Amiot, who had spent more than four decades as a missionary in China, was also favorably impressed by the benevolence of the Chinese government in its system to collect unwanted children from families in the capital. Amiot described the burial process in detail, in a letter from Peking in 1777. Five bullock carts were driven around the north, south, east, west and central parts of the city, to collect both living and dead infants. Living children were taken to a foundling home, "where there are doctors, caretakers, wet-nurses, supported by the Emperor at the expense of the state, and mandarins to attend to decency and good order." Dead children were consigned to a crypt and "covered with some lime to consume their bodies promptly." Every year, officials came to build a funeral pyre for any of the remaining corpses, reducing them to ashes. Monks were invited to say prayers for these children, and the next day, after cooling, the ashes were taken to a river or creek to be released.[34]

A different Chinese philanthropic initiative to bury children's corpses seems to have emerged in the nineteenth century, perhaps as part of other charitable efforts to bury the corpses of indigent adults.[35] The building of a so-called bone-collection tower (*jigu ta*) is described in at least one Chinese historical record as an act of public charity. One such tower was erected in 1805 in Xinfeng, Zhejiang Province, by a group of men who, like Yu Zhi, "wanted to do good deeds." The record describes the difficulties their predecessors had in accomplishing such a task: "When they occasionally saw unburied corpses, they were saddened, and wished to have them covered. But either they were too poor and did not have the ability to do anything, or they had the ability but had no land, or they had the land but others thwarted them. Thus, there were many who had the desire to do a virtuous act, but time and again were stopped halfway." No doubt these potential do-gooders would have been obstructed by uncooperative landowners, who would not have welcomed an inauspicious gravesite of abandoned corpses neighboring their properties. Finally three men, Yuan Zaishan, Tang Yuanxiang and Cai Tingfang, managed to donate money, purchase land and build a series of three bone-collection towers for the burial of exposed skeletons and corpses: one for men, one for women and one for children. Others in the village also donated to the project, and three local pawnshops provided funds annually to pay for the collection of exposed corpses and the performance of religious rites to release souls from their suffering.[36]

De Groot, in his study of Chinese funerary practices, described bone-collection towers as small, pagoda-like structures of brick and stone, "some five metres in diameter . . . either round, polygonal or square . . . with a tiled roof" that served as common gravesites for infants. "Corpses are to be dropped in through a window-like aperture, from which the winds, birds and bats are warded off by a square wooden shutter. . . . [They] have no doors, never being entered by living man, and because doors might enable voracious swine, dogs and rats to intrude." Inscriptions on an attached stone slab, such as "Pagoda or Tower for hoarding up bones" (*jigu ta*) or "Place of resort for infants" (*haier guisuo*), made clear that these were for the deposit of dead infant bodies. Another slab might list the names of local philanthropists, "virtuous men who, out of compassion with the countless infant souls doomed to suffering because of their bodies being mercilessly abandoned by their parents to decomposition in the open air, defrayed the expenses connected with the erection of the building."[37]

Did such charitable practices and built structures merely collect bodies that would have otherwise been disposed of indifferently, or did they, as so many Western travelers asserted, encourage the destruction of newborn infants? What in Chinese had been known as *jigu ta*, or bone-collection towers, came to be known in English as "baby towers," where innocent babes, alive or dead, might be cast away by cruel Chinese parents. During a visit to China in 1919, the famed novelist and sometime travel writer W. Somerset Maugham told the story of a chance stroll, probably while traveling in Fujian Province, to see the "sights of the town," when he wandered outside the city wall and came across a hillside studded with graves:

> A trodden path led to a little tower and I followed it. It was a stumpy little tower, ten feet high perhaps, made of rough-hewn blocks of stone; it was cone shaped and the roof was like a Pierrot's hat. It stood on a hillock, quaint and rather picturesque against the blue sky, amid the graves. At its foot were a number of rough hewn baskets thrown about in disorder. I walked round and on one side saw an oblong hole, eighteen inches by eight, perhaps, from which hung a stout string. From the hold there came a very strange, a nauseating odour. Suddenly I understood what the queer little building was. It was a baby tower. . . . The odour was the odour of putrefaction. A lively little boy came up to me while I stood there and made me understand that four babes had been brought to the tower that morning.[38]

Maugham's experience was fairly typical. Whether by chance or on purpose, an encounter by a curious Western visitor with a baby tower always resulted in images of arresting visual and visceral impact. The baby tower assaulted the senses—eyes, nose and stomach—as well as Western sensibilities.

Some foreign eyewitnesses might be lucky enough to see the actual corpses of infant bodies, but only if they happened to go at the right times. George Wingrove Cooke, a China correspondent for the London newspaper *The Times*, described how he was taken to see the baby tower near Shanghai by the British vice-consul during his trip there in 1857–58. He asks his host about the source of a "more than usually pestilential stench" which seems "to radiate from that decaying pepperbox-shaped tower." The two men walk closer and the consul encourages Cooke to peep right in: "Look through that rent in the stonework—not too close, or the stream of effluvia may kill you. You see a mound of whisps of bamboo straw. It seems to move, but it is only the crawling of the worms. Sometimes a tiny leg or arm, or a little flesh-less bone, protrudes from the straw. The tower is not so full now as I have seen it; they must have cleared it out recently." When Cooke asks whether the baby tower is a "cemetery or a slaughterhouse," the consul explains, "The Chinese say it is only a tomb. Coffins are dear, and the peasantry are poor. When a child dies, the parents wrap it round with bamboo, throw it in at that window, and all is done. When the tower is full, the proper authorities burn the heap, and spread the ashes over the land."[39]

In spite of his host's description of the efforts of Chinese public officials to deal with the infant corpses of the poor, Cooke openly condemned the structure as an "invitation to infanticide."[40] Henry Auchincloss, an American visitor to Shanghai, writing in 1864, considered baby towers to be "among the most hideous spectacles to be met with in a heathen land" and "openly inviting . . . the most unnatural and heartless of murders."[41] Mary Isabella Bryson of the London Mission in Wuchang wrote in 1885, "If the little one is a girl, the parents are not always particular to ascertain if it is quite dead or not" before dropping it into the tower (Figure 3.1).[42]

Constance Frederica Gordon Cumming was similarly convinced of the evils of baby towers during her visit to Ningpo, described in her 1886 trav-elogue, where she saw the body of one infant "stuck fast" in the window and other corpses scattered on the ground.[43] W. Somerset Maugham was certain that live children must be abandoned during his visit in 1919 by the detail of the string that emerged from the baby tower window: "Why, if the person who brought the baby, parent or grandmother, midwife or obliging friend, were of a humane disposition and did not care to let the new-born child drop to the bottom (for underneath the tower was a deep pit), it could be let down gently by means of the string."[44]

But it was unclear from their testimony whether any of these writers had seen live children abandoned or not. Other Western visitors remained en-tirely unconvinced that living newborns were ever dumped at the towers. John Scarth described his visit to the Shanghai baby tower, sometime be-fore 1860. Although the tower was "piled to the top with bodies" and "the infants were wrapped in mats or old clothes . . . there was nothing to lead to the belief that they were thrown there alive, or that they had been killed." Moreover, he noted that at the foot of the tower "remains of small fires were

Figure 3.1. Illustration of a Chinese man throwing the wrapped body of a child into a baby tower. In the accompanying text, the author notes, "If a Chinese baby dies, no loving hands prepare it for its grave. A piece of coarse matting is tied around the tiny body, and it is carried to a little tower erected outside most cities, with little openings like windows, but without doors. All that is left of baby is thrown in through one of these openings, and falls into the pit below the tower. If the little one is a girl, the parents are not always particular to ascertain if it is quite dead or not." Source: Mary Isabella Bryson, *Child Life in Chinese Homes* (1885), from the collection of the Moody Library at Baylor University.

visible, showing that offerings had been made" to the deceased through the burning of paper money. If the children had been heartlessly abandoned, he reasoned, why show this type of care for their souls?[45]

What seemed far more certain than the circumstances of infant death was the feverish grip that the built form of the baby tower itself held on the imaginations of numerous nineteenth- and early twentieth-century Western visitors. Henry Auchincloss, who had visited Shanghai in the 1860s, remarked that although ponds or rivers might be more common sites where "babies are daily drowned like puppies," "they do not affect the mind with such a horror as these palpable structures, erected with the best skill of their architects for this express purpose. The water closes over the murdered infant, and no trace of the crime remains; but here is a tower—a high tower— with deep foundations, filled with the bones of murdered babes that have been accumulating for generations."[46] Pictures of baby towers were commonly reproduced in travel narratives, reflecting this shiver of simultaneous repulsion and attraction (Figure 3.2).[47]

Baby towers were often also featured in guidebooks for foreign tourists throughout the late nineteenth and early twentieth centuries, as "one of the points of interest" in Chinese cities, such as Chefoo (Yantai in Shandong Province), "where the bodies of undesirable girl babies were thrown by parents," or Shanghai, where even the former location of the baby tower, destroyed in 1864, was pointed out as one of the sights along a "favourite evening drive" out of town.[48] To be sure, some Western visitors did recognize that their imaginations may have played a more active role in filling these public burial receptacles with live children than Chinese parents. Writing about a visit to China before 1919, Mary Ninde Gamewell was forced by a local missionary to readjust her sense of what exactly she had seen. A subsequent visit rendered the purpose and even existence of these burial sites even more ephemeral:

> A few years ago in Nanchang I noticed small oblong boxes painted blue nailed here and there to walls at the side of the streets. I was told that they were public receptacles for babies. At once I looked at them with new interest and all sorts of sad scenes presented themselves to my imagination.
>
> "I suppose that the little things die very soon after they are placed in the box?" I remarked pensively to the longtime missionary who was my companion.
>
> "It is not likely that a living baby is ever left in one of these boxes. No, nor a baby that has been put to death," she said, anticipating my next question.

Figure 3.2. Photograph of a baby tower in Fuzhou. In the accompanying text, the author notes, "When a baby dies, and the parents are too poor to give it a decent burial, they drop its poor little body into one of the openings in this tower. A Guild of Benevolence charges itself with the task of clearing out the tower every two or three days, burying the bodies with all religious rites and ceremony." Source: Mrs. J. F. Bishop, *Chinese Pictures: Notes on Photographs Made in China* (ca. 1900), from the collection of the Pollak Library at California State University, Fullerton.

"It is not customary to buy coffins for infants, so the little dead bodies are laid in these boxes to be carted away and buried by the city."

When in Nanchang recently I looked in vain for the baby boxes. They had all disappeared.[49]

COUNTING BODIES

If physical bodies of Chinese infant victims were not readily available as evidence, then another potential method of measuring the prevalence of infanticide was through statistical enumeration. Theodore Porter has described quantification as a "technology of distance" in his study of objectivity claims in Western science: "Since the rules of collecting and manipulating numbers are widely shared, they can easily be transported across oceans and continents and used to coordinate activities or settle disputes. Perhaps most crucially, reliance on numbers and quantitative manipulation minimizes the need for intimate knowledge and personal trust. Quantification is well suited for communication that goes beyond the boundaries of locality and community."[50] The enumerative approach to infanticide greatly appealed to the 1885 Royal Asiatic Society members as the most scientific way to settle the question of prevalence. Unfortunately, however, even basic statistical information was unavailable. Frederick Hirth, a German deputy commissioner of customs in Shanghai, suggested that in the port of Amoy (Xiamen), where female infanticide was believed to be prevalent, it might be possible to track the "scarcity of women" but "unfortunately, we possess no statistics regarding the distribution of sexes in the population of Amoy."[51]

Just as a lack of bodies had not prevented Western observers from "seeing" corpses, neither did a lack of statistics prevent Western travelers from deriving their own estimates of the rate of infanticide in China. One of the most frequently cited observations came from the pen of John Barrow (1764–1848), a member of the first British diplomatic mission to China in 1793. His main motivation for enumerating infanticide was to compare China unfavorably to the ancient Greeks and Romans and contemporary Europeans. China could not compete in civility with either the European past or present. Barrow admitted that infanticide did exist in Europe, but it was due to the shame of illegitimate birth rather than cultural barbarity. Barrow asserted "with confidence, that a British cottager, however indigent, would divide his scanty pittance among a dozen children, rather than consent to let some of them perish." Even in poverty the Chinese had no real excuse for their crimes. Barrow dismissed the work of Chinese foundling hospitals, sniffing that "they are on a small scale, being raised and supported by donations of individuals, and their continuance is therefore as precarious as the wealth of their charitable founders."[52] Barrow, whose visit to China was primarily limited to Peking, drew upon the comments of a Jesuit missionary to support his calculations regarding the rate of infanticide in the whole Chinese empire:

> The number of children thus unnaturally and inhumanly slaughtered, or interred alive, in the course of a year, is differently stated by different authors,

some making it about ten and others thirty thousand in the whole empire. The truth, as generally happens, may probably lie about the middle. The missionaries, who alone possess the means of ascertaining nearly the number that is thus sacrificed in the capital, differ very materially in their statements: taking the mean, as given by those with whom we conversed on the subject, I should conclude that about twenty-four infants were, on an average, in Pekin [*sic*], daily carried to the pit of death where the little innocents that have not yet breathed their last are condemned without remorse. . . . This calculation gives nine thousand nearly for the capital alone, where it is supposed about an equal number are exposed to that of all the other parts of the empire.[53]

Barrow later acknowledged that some of the children found abandoned may have been stillborn or may have died of causes other than abandonment in infancy. This would adjust his estimate by half to about 4,000, "according to the rules of political arithmetic."[54]

Barrow's offhand reference to "political arithmetic" gestured toward the late seventeenth-century work of William Petty (1623–87), whose nascent iteration of political economic thought argued for the quantified reckoning of the value of all things, including people. From this, the concept of "statistical thinking" would eventually emerge in the nineteenth century, developed to aid the state in its measurement of all types of social phenomena.[55] Petty had explained that "instead of using only comparative and superlative Words, and intellectual Arguments," he desired "to express [himself] in Terms of Number, Weight, or Measure." The truth of his numbers, he claimed, could be easily verified, and if they were found false, they were "not so false as to destroy the Argument they are brought for; but at worst are sufficient as Suppositions to shew the way to that Knowledge I aim at."[56] Barrow could easily have concurred with such sentiments: should his estimates of the rates of infanticide in China overshoot in magnitude, they still flew in the proper direction.

Later Western visitors to China attempted to derive a rate of infanticide using data from native informants rather than from foreign missionaries. These later Western accounts, though, were no less damning of Chinese cultural propensity to the practice. David Abeel (1804–46) was an American Protestant missionary who spent the better part of 1842 and 1843 in the southeastern coastal province of Fujian. Having previously worked in regions populated by overseas Chinese, including Batavia, Singapore, Bangkok, Malacca, Macao and Hong Kong, Abeel waited for an opportunity to make evangelical headway on the continent. The end of the First Opium

War gave him this chance, and while residing in Fujian, Abeel made inquiries into the extent of female infanticide in two of its counties, Quanzhou and Zhangzhou. Although Barrow's figure had relied upon the estimates provided by other foreign missionaries, Abeel's survey was the first to query native informants. Listing some of the districts within each county, Abeel noted the number of different towns and villages within each district from which his informants had come, along with the average estimated rates of infanticide (Tables 3.1 and 3.2).

Significantly, Abeel did not personally see any act of infanticide or infant corpses, nor did he make any attempt to do so. Indeed, Abeel's lack of intimate access to Chinese families was turned to his advantage: relying

TABLE 3.1

Average Estimated Rates of Infanticide Within the Districts of Quanzhou County, Fujian Province, Provided by Chinese Informants, ca. 1843

District	Number of towns and villages represented	Average estimated rate of infanticide
Tong'an	40	One-tenth to seven- or eight-tenths, or 10 percent to 70 or 80 percent, Averaging nearly four-tenths, or 39 percent
Anxi	8	Between one-fourth and three-tenths, or Not far from 30 percent
Jinjiang	6	Not more than 16 percent
Hui'an	4	Not more than 16 percent
Nan'an	7	More than one-third, or Just 36 percent
County total/average	*65*	*Less than a quarter*

TABLE 3.2

Average Estimated Rates of Infanticide Within the Districts of Zhangzhou County, Fujian Province, Provided by Chinese Informants, ca. 1843

District	Number of towns and villages represented	Average estimated rate of infanticide
Longxi	18	More than one-fourth, less than three-tenths
Zhangpu	6	One-fourth
Nanjing	4	More than one-third
Haicheng	Several	Between one-fifth and one-fourth
Zhangtai	Limited	Same as proportions last given
Pinghe	Limited	Same as proportions last given
Zhao'an	Limited	Same as proportions last given
County total/average	*More than 28*	*Less than a quarter, or 25 percent*

upon quantitative estimates alone meant that his final results could be compared, tallied and averaged, yielding a picture of the behavior of the population as a whole, rather than just a handful of families. "One-fourth," "seven-eighths" or "thirty-six percent" offered a sense of security, a solidity that indicated clear results. This firmness of fractions and perfection of percents, suggested more than a century earlier by Petty, continued to attract Abeel and his contemporaries as a better "approximation to the reality" than other, more imprecise means.[57]

However, Abeel's attempt to quantify the extent of infanticide was hardly foolproof, as he himself admitted. His method was simply to ask Chinese men whom he happened to meet, some "hundreds of persons of all classes," their place of origin and their estimate of the rate of infanticide there. These were "opinions rather than facts," and Abeel recognized that these data and the means by which they had been obtained could not "secure entire accuracy." His explanation of his methods also highlighted his own influence over the responses given by his subjects, depending on the way in which questions were posed or on the ensuing conversation. His respondents gave their "individual impressions . . . according to the shape of my question." For those who were reluctant to "acknowledge what many of them know to be a barbarous custom," "a little conversation has generally dismissed their reserve and brought them to a candid expression of their belief." When estimates of the rate of infanticide varied in the responses of individuals from the same place, Abeel averaged their responses to determine a representative number. Likewise, he averaged the estimated rates of infanticide from numerous villages and towns to obtain the estimated rate within a single district.[58]

Abeel's numbers, in other words, were based entirely on anecdotal evidence, stories of the Chinese men with whom he had spoken about infanticide. For Abeel, however, this "independent testimony of men of all classes from nearly every section of the country" demonstrated that all were guilty of the crime. The poor had only "paltry reasons" for their actions, but the rich schemed with "heartless calculations." The results were the same, whether Abeel spoke with literati in the provincial capital taking civil examinations, Chinese military officers or villagers who confessed to killing their own infants. Foundling hospitals did exist, he noted, but were simply few and far between. Abeel's strict missionary perspective left no room for sympathy. Infanticide was an "exhibition of heathenish cruelty" from a Chinese "heart ignorant of its relations and obligations to the true God, destitute of natural affection, and perfectly alive—and alive only—to its worldly interests."[59]

Adele M. Fielde, an American Protestant missionary who spent ten years in Swatow (Shantou) in the southern coastal province of Guangdong from 1873 to 1883, offered another quantitative survey of the practice of female infanticide by asking her fellow female missionaries around China to query native female congregants about the practice. She received replies from nine different cities around the empire, in both the north and the south. Fielde reported that the responses, combined with her own queries of her own congregants, revealed that 160 Chinese women, all over the age of fifty, had given birth to a total of 631 sons and 538 daughters. Although 366 of the sons, "or nearly sixty per cent.," had lived beyond ten years, only 205 of the daughters, "or thirty-eight per cent.," had lived beyond ten years.[60] Although none had ever killed a son, the women had reported killing 158 of their daughters, with one woman confessing to killing eleven children. Fielde shared with Abeel an overwhelming desire to render anecdotal evidence with statistical certainty. Yet even Fielde's foreign missionary informants cautioned that these results were not necessarily reliable. The resident missionary woman at Tung Cho, near Peking, said the results "could not be used as representing the percentage of infanticide in this region. To say that four women in twenty-five destroy their female offspring would be untrue. I do not believe that one in a hundred does so, counting all classes, even the beggars."[61]

Like Abeel, Fielde backed her quantitative evidence with more arresting qualitative evidence, stories recorded from female Christian converts. In these conversion stories, infanticide figured primarily as a sign of heathenish ignorance, from a time before the woman had adopted Christian values. One woman, "Treasure," who gave birth to three daughters, then a son, then another daughter, explained that of the girls, she kept only the eldest daughter, who died at the age of nine. "All the other daughters were put into a hod and thrown alive into the river, one each year. My husband got a chair-bearer to carry them off and drown them. I did not feel sorry when the little girls were carried away, and did not cry. I was vexed because they were not boys, and I did not want them, and I hoped to have sons the sooner if I did not keep the girls. I had not then heard of God, and I did not think that what I did was wrong."[62] Another woman had three sons and six daughters, but "cast away" three of the daughters, "as no one kept more than three girls. . . . I did not then know, as I now do, that infanticide is a great sin."[63] Through these tales of redemption, readers could be in turn horrified by the number of daughters killed and encouraged by the ameliorative effects of Christian conversion. Fielde concluded that "poverty and superstition" were the main causes of infanticide, and Christianity would end the latter, "leading parents to depend on God, not on male descendents, for comfort in the life to come."[64]

TEXTUAL EVIDENCE

Since the significance of foreign eyewitness evidence seemed uncertain and statistical evidence was scanty and unreliable, as a final resort Western scholars turned to textual evidence about the prevalence of infanticide, supplied by the Chinese themselves. Gabriel Palatre (1830–78), a French Jesuit missionary based at the Zikawei mission complex in Shanghai, was the author of the most comprehensive and exhaustive study of Chinese infanticide of the nineteenth century, *L'infanticide et l'Oeuvre de la Sainte-Enfance en Chine* (Infanticide and the Holy Childhood Association in China) (1878) (Figure 3.3).

Palatre envisioned his task as representing the prosecution in a courtroom trial, with the French reading public as judge and jury. The book was essentially a massive collection of written documents, running 300 quarto pages, which Palatre considered to be a "dossier" of evidence.[65] As befitting a legal case, Palatre labored to make it airtight, leaving no room for equivocation. This was to be as comprehensive a selection of evidence as he could gather: quantity, not quality or reader comfort, mattered most. "Perhaps one will wonder why we amassed so many documents, when a few would have been enough to demonstrate the truth of our thesis. To this we respond, it is the truth as science, and repetitions are necessary for them to penetrate the spirit. If we only quoted two or three documents, you would then find men ready to argue that this shortage does not constitute a definitive proof of the facts in question. . . . This painful work was to be made once and for all, in order to prevent spite from clinging to some paltry objection in the future, due to the small number of quoted documents or the exaggerated consequences drawn from some."[66]

In his foreword to Palatre's study, another Jesuit missionary, Aloysius Pfister, explained that one of the central conundrums of proving the prevalence of infanticide in China was that foreigners had never seen any infant corpses: "Tourists, maritime officers, attachés of embassies, traders, missionaries alike have spent long years in the Far East and affirm never to have seen the body of an infant thrown into the road."[67] Yet Catholic missionaries repeatedly claimed to have saved thousands of infants year after year in China. Where then did all of these children come from? Palatre

KIANG-NAN (Chine). — R. P. Gabriel PALATRE, de la Compagnie de Jésus, mort à Zi-ka-wei
le 11 août 1878; — d'après une photographie (voir p. 362).

Figure 3.3. Engraved obituary portrait of Gabriel Palatre,
embellished with his signature. Source: *Les Missions
Catholiques* (July 25, 1879), from the collection of the
Northern Regional Library Facility.

himself relied upon the accounts of Chinese intermediaries, converts to Catholicism who were able to see into spaces where foreign eyes could not pry. He described the sheer folly of disbelieving what Chinese eyes had seen:

> What would be the astonishment of the Chinese, if, at the moment when they presented the priest with the exposed infants which they had gathered, or those which had been given to them, he dared to utter some phrases to prove to them his difficulty in believing that all of these infants had been exposed, because he saw them neither in the place where they were picked up nor in the hands which brought them! "Father," these Chinese could respond, dumbfounded by the same argument, "do not preoccupy yourself too much that you have not seen, that is not the question. For we, we have seen, and the best proof we could give to you, is that we bring you these infants, which you can see at your orphanage."[68]

If foreign travelers and missionaries could not "see" the bodies of abandoned Chinese infants, then Palatre would render them visible by laying down a thick, inky blanket of Chinese texts: the outlines of countless dead infant bodies curled underneath would then be revealed. Palatre wanted to allow Chinese writers to speak for themselves, relying on their native authority to prove the prevalence of infanticide. The bulk of his evidence came from original Chinese sources, which were translated into French and presented in the first five chapters of the book, classified as (1) official proclamations, (2) Buddhist and Taoist writings, (3) Confucian writings, (4) Chinese newspapers and (5) popular imagery. Altogether, Palatre included sixty-seven separate Chinese entries, taken from fourteen books and five newspapers. Moreover, transcriptions of the original Chinese texts appeared in a seventy-four-page appendix (Figure 3.4). He also included seventeen illustrations from morality books against infanticide, along with six illustrated broadsheets.

Why did Palatre feel it necessary to include the original Chinese texts in a lengthy appendix, when the majority of his audience of French readers would not have been able to read Chinese? After all, the inclusion of Chinese required considerable extra effort and made it prohibitively expensive to print and distribute the book in Paris. Two hundred copies were eventually printed in Shanghai at the Zikawei mission complex, through a lithography process that allowed for the reproduction of both illustrations and non-Latin scripts.[69] The original Chinese texts certainly protected Palatre from accusations of fabricating evidence. But the inclusion of Chinese original texts indicated more than just a concern for accuracy and completeness. The lengthy Chinese appendix made an immediate visual impact on a European reader, all

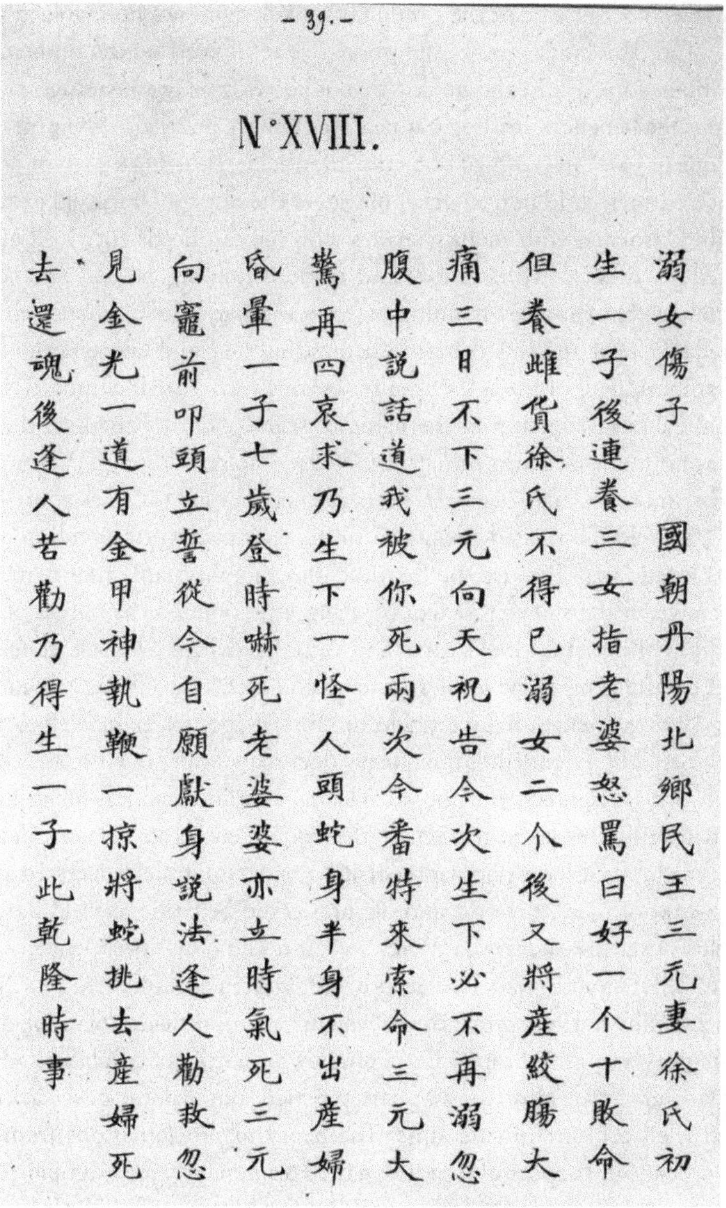

N˙XVIII.

溺女傷子

國朝丹陽北鄉民王三元妻徐氏初

生一子後連養三女指老婆怒罵曰好一個十敗命

但養雌貨徐氏不得已溺女二个後又將產絞腸大

痛三日不下三元向天祝告今次生下必不再溺忽

腹中說話道我被你死兩次今番特來索命三元大

驚再四哀求乃生下一怪人頭蛇身半身不出產婦

昏暈一子七歲登時嚇死老婆婆亦時氣死三元

向竈前叩頭立誓從今自願獻身說法逢人勸救忽

見金光一道有金甲神執鞭一掠將蛇挑去產婦死

去還魂後逢人苦勸乃得生一子此乾隆時事

Figure 3.4. Excerpt of a Chinese morality tale copied in the appendix of Palatre's study. Source: Gabriel Palatre, *L'infanticide et l'Oeuvre de la Sainte-Enfance en Chine* (1878), from the Widener Library at Harvard University.

the more so because he or she would most likely not have been able to read a word of it. This stark visual impression was reinforced by the numerous illustrations copied into the book. Anyone looking at these strange pictures without the benefit of reading Chinese would have puzzled at their meaning: only one or two even seemed to depict infanticide, showing a man or woman about to drop a child into a bucket of water. The rest contained old men with beards consorting with monks, snakes with human heads entwined around women's bodies, scowling horse-faced demons holding cudgels and chains, beasts with human faces standing before a man at a desk, a man being devoured by a tiger and tiny demons surrounding men and women (Figure 3.5).

Combining all of these Western obsessions with visual, enumerative and textual evidence together in the name of science, Palatre mapped the incidence of infanticide across the entire Chinese empire. Although Palatre called Chinese morality tales "legends" (*légendes*), as opposed to "stories" or "histories" (*histoires*), he treated them as a uniform dataset corresponding to real world locations.[70] Because the first line of a morality tale often named the hometown of the story's protagonist, Palatre pinpointed the names of these villages within actual prefectures and actual provinces. Palatre concluded, based on the geographic locales in morality tales, that Chinese documents proved the existence of infanticide in thirteen out of eighteen provinces, which could be extended, if missionary documents were to be considered, to fifteen out of eighteen provinces.[71] Placing this information alongside the population figures given in 1812 by the Jiaqing emperor, Palatre calculated that for a total Chinese population of 360,279,597, infanticide affected at least 300,568,323 of them.[72] Words and pictures could be made to yield numbers, the elusive statistical data that were the best testament to prevalence.

But what exactly had Palatre proven? Did the abundance of Chinese texts and illustrations prove the prevalence of infanticide there, or merely its ubiquity as a moral topic? Every single Chinese source Palatre had cited was written in an effort to stop the practice, but Palatre never acknowledged their anti-infanticide aims. The flurry of proclamations from Chinese officials in support of building native orphanages, for example, merely illustrated his larger point: "In speaking ceaselessly of building [orphanages] it is thereby proved that no one hastens to do so."[73] Palatre found in his Chinese evidence precisely what he aimed to find, copious textual and visual proof of the prevalence of infanticide. Had he been able to dig a little deeper, though, Palatre might have discovered a curious feature of many of the texts he cited. Palatre singled out only two Chinese authors by name in

serpent, et elle tomba immédiatement sans connaissance; son fils, âgé de sept ans, mourut aussitôt de frayeur, et la vieille belle-mère rendit le dernier soupir. Le père de famille se précipita alors vers le dieu du foyer, se prosterna la face contre terre, fit un voeu et promit qu'à l'avenir il exhorterait ses compatriotes

漓女傷子

En noyant ses petites filles, une femme donne la mort à son propre fils.

à sauver les enfants. Il vit alors apparaître un Esprit éclatant de lumière, couvert d'une cuirasse d'or, et qui, la main armée d'un fouet chassa le serpent et le mit en fuite. La femme Liu étant morte, puis revenue à la vie par la trans-migration, exhortait tous ceux qu'elle rencontrait. Elle devint ensuite mère d'un fils. Ce fait s'est passé sous le règne de Kien-long.» 1.
On aperçoit dans cette gravure un vase, dont il est facile de deviner l'u-sage à la vue des jambes qui le surmontent; on le remplit d'eau et il sert alors à noyer les enfants. Ce mode d'infanticide est le plus ordinaire. 2.

1. 孶堂日記 Kio-tang-je-Ki, page 38. Édition de Sou-tcheou, 7e année de Tong-tchi. Voir Pièces justificatives, n° XVIII.
2. Le P. Gotteland, missionnaire au Kiang-sou méridional, où est située la ville de Tan-yang, écrivait en 1845, " Ici on a un mot particulier pour exprimer la ma-nière horrible, dont on fait périr les enfants naissants : iam modom, noyer le vase

---

his study, one of whom he called "Liang-Ki-Koei." Palatre considered Liang-Ki-Koei to be a scholar (*lettré*), and elsewhere called him a moralist. Without seeing the corresponding Chinese characters, one could imagine "Liang-Ki-Koei" to be a Chinese name, where Liang would be the surname and Ki-Koei the given name. What Palatre had no way of knowing was that this person, whom he called "Liang-Ki-Koei," was none other than Yu Zhi, the Wuxi schoolteacher discussed in Chapter 2.

The two names are nothing alike, so where did the name "Liang-Ki-Koei" come from? After one examines the preface to one of Yu Zhi's books, the mystery is laid to rest. Palatre had correctly read the first three characters of what was printed: "Liang-Ki-Koei" is simply the French transliteration of one part of a much longer Chinese attribution, *"Liang xi hui* ["Liang-Ki-Koei"] *zhai shi ji yu ji yun shan fang."* Palatre did not seem to realize that *Liangxi* is the name of a place, and *Hui* is part of the pen name, *Huizhaishi* (Man of the Concealed Studio).[74] This complete pen name can be translated as "The Man of the Concealed Studio of Liangxi, written in Residing in Clouds Mountain Studio." In fairness, Palatre should not be chided for not knowing the true identity of Yu Zhi, since literate Chinese of the time often had many different pen names, and rarely used their given names on their own writings. Yu Zhi himself wrote under a variety of names, including *Liancun* (Lotus Villager), *Huizhai* (Concealed Studio), *Jiyun shanren* (Man Residing in Cloud Mountain) and *Zun xiaoxue zhai* (Respect Lesser Learning Studio). Still, even a basic understanding of Chinese ought to have been enough to recognize that *Liangxi* was a location, not the first two characters of an individual's name.

Since Palatre had no idea that this person whom he called "Liang-Ki-Koei" was actually Yu Zhi, he also did not realize that of the fourteen different Chinese books he quoted on the subject of infanticide, four of them came from Yu Zhi alone.[75] Most likely Palatre came across all of these books of Yu Zhi because they were practically neighbors in the Jiangnan region. Palatre reported that he found an 1872 edition of *Xuetang riji gushi tushuo* (Daily Reader of Illustrated Stories for Schools) "in Shanghai in the garden of the pagoda of the Tcheng-hoang-miao [Cheng Huang Miao, a local temple], from the bookstore of morality books, I hoa-tang [Yi Hua Tang]."[76] As for the other texts he cited, Palatre appears to have asked missionaries in other parts of the country to send him any materials on infanticide that they could find, yielding a small collection of volumes held today in the storage facilities of the Zikawei Library, now under the auspices of the Shanghai Municipal Library.

Although Palatre had carefully separated his Chinese sources into distinct doctrinal chapters—writings from Buddhist and Taoists versus those from Confucians—both of these chapters contained books written or compiled by Yu Zhi. Palatre's imposed sectarian divisions, which made sense to a nineteenth-century French Jesuit, as part of a much greater Catholic mission in China that included Franciscans, Lazarists, Dominicans and general Paris Foreign Mission missionaries, made little sense in Yu Zhi's lived world. The system of karmic rewards and retributions may have had its origins in Buddhist and Taoist texts, but examination success would have spoken to this-worldly, Confucian concerns. A man like Yu Zhi could and did embrace all of these social values as part of the same holistic system. Moreover, in the original Chinese sources, the overt motivation of the texts was one of moral exhortation. Although pictures were provided alongside some of these moral tales so that even an illiterate audience might benefit from didactic lessons, illustrations never appeared alone, but moral tales often did. Words, not pictures, were of central importance.

By bisecting the original Chinese sources, placing their eye-catching illustrations in the body of his book, while relegating the Chinese text to the appendix, Palatre tore apart the comprehensive social fabric of the Chinese original. This divided textual and pictorial treatment allowed later Western experts to disrupt even more thoroughly the moral trajectory of the original Chinese sources. Rather than connecting readers in time and space to a universe of cosmic rewards and retributions, Palatre's flattened versions reduced the Chinese originals to two dimensions. Now text related to text and image related to image in singular interpretive planes, and their purpose was no longer to warn Chinese readers about the karmic consequences of infanticide. Instead, these texts and images served to condemn the mores of Chinese culture while titillating the curiosity of Western audiences, for whom the exoticism of the content would have been the most striking message.

THE AFTERLIFE OF *L'INFANTICIDE*

Palatre's study of Chinese infanticide later became known as *the* reference work on the subject for China cognoscenti in the West. Old China hands, professional scholars, medical doctors and religious groups confirmed Palatre's expertise by repeatedly citing his work. At the 1885 Royal Asiatic Society meeting, for example, R. A. Jamieson, an American surgeon, referred to

Palatre as one of the "best authorities" on Chinese infanticide and his work as "proof of the existence of infanticide."[77] In Paris that same year, Léon Lallemand published a general history of abandoned children and cribbed his chapter on China entirely from Palatre's study.[78] Lallemand copied only the text, but other scholars were more enamored of Palatre's illustrations. Members of the 1885 Geographical Society of Lyon in France listened to a report from a medical doctor, Éduoard Chappet, on Palatre's work as an important contribution to an understanding of China's population and territory, which included four illustrations from Palatre's book.[79] In 1902, another French medical doctor, J.-J. Matignon, wrote a book titled *Superstition, Crime et Misère en Chine* (Superstition, Crime and Poverty in China), and, along with chapters on suicide, self-immolation of Buddhist monks, eunuchs, foot-binding and pederasty, included a chapter on infanticide and abortion, which drew heavily from Palatre's work and included several of his illustrations.[80] As late as 1914, Herbert Giles, resident curmudgeon and Sinologue of Cambridge University, refuted Palatre's work on Chinese infanticide as an exaggerated account, but still included four of its "horrible pictures."[81] All of these writers included copies of Palatre's Chinese illustrations alone, while omitting the translations of the accompanying didactic stories.[82]

The most striking example of this excision of Chinese images from Palatre's work comes from a lavishly illustrated exhibition catalog from Rouen around 1884. The pictorial exhibition was the brainchild of Father Adolphe Vasseur, a French Jesuit missionary who had also worked in the Zikawei mission complex, directing its atelier of religious images, which was part of the vocational training of its orphaned Chinese boys. Palatre's study was prominently displayed in the exhibition space, and the catalog explained its importance: "This album, in quarto-size with three hundred pages, contains in French and Chinese, one hundred imperial edicts, proclamations of viceroys and provincial governors, and twenty-four images of popular contemporary propaganda. All of these declare that it is necessary to oppose this *general habit, which exists in a great number of the provinces*, of getting rid of children at any time that their parents are not pleased [original emphasis]."[83] The illustrations from Palatre's study were then reproduced in the catalog, in a miniature storyboard of Chinese infanticide (Figure 3.6).

The pictures included one-line captions in French but did not include any Chinese texts or any longer explanations of the stories they represented. The illustrations were literally reduced to a uniform collection of visual in-

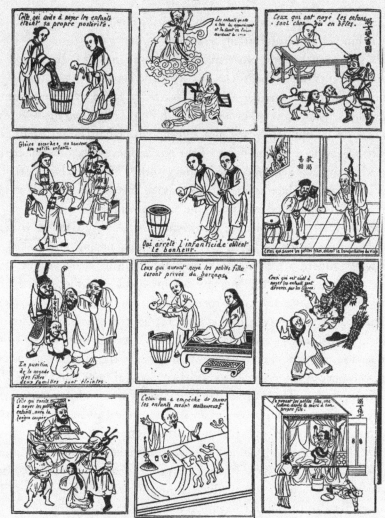

Sujets tirés des livres illustrés Bouddhistes et Taoïstes, pour détourner le peuple de l'infanticide.

Figure 3.6. Page of miniature illustrations copied from Palatre's study in Adolphe Vasseur's exhibition catalog. Each image represents one morality tale against infanticide. The French text at the bottom of the page indicates, "Subjects have been taken from illustrated Buddhist and Taoist books that discourage people from infanticide." Source: *Un orphelinat chinois de la Sainte-Enfance à l'exposition internationale d'imagerie de Rouen et l'infanticide en Chine prouvé à M. Tchen-Ki-Tong par ses compatriotes* (ca. 1884), from the collection of the Bibliothèque nationale de France.

formation on Chinese infanticide, eviscerating any moral context and leaving behind only cultural strangeness.

But perhaps the most evocative and literal *re-vision* of Palatre's work appeared in an 1885 series of articles by Charles de Harlez, a celebrated Belgian scholar of Oriental languages at the University of Louvain. In a French-language scholarly journal of his own founding, *Le Muséon: Revue Internationale*, de Harlez condensed and summarized large chunks of Palatre's study, reprinting verbatim many of the pieces of evidence that Palatre had already translated into French in his own work.[84] However, French translations alone would once again not suffice. Like Palatre had done before him, de Harlez also included excerpts in the original Chinese (Figure 3.7).

Yet de Harlez did not have the privilege of a native Chinese writer at hand, and probably provided the copy himself, having undertaken the study of Chinese only two years earlier. The resulting characters, although they are formally adequate, are ugly and inelegant—clearly the work of an unskilled nonnative novice. In one excerpt, the cited Chinese text ends abruptly and nonsensically in midsentence. In other places, de Harlez miscopied words, transposed their order or missed entire lines of text. Few of his readers, though, may have known any better: the meaning of the content was once again less significant than the visual impression of the characters themselves. De Harlez's article gained an even wider audience when a slightly revised English version appeared in *The Dublin Review* in 1892, although the Chinese copied text was dropped.[85]

De Harlez's ungainly Chinese handwriting makes an immediate impression on a modern reader of Chinese, as powerful as any made by Chinese morality tale illustrations on nineteenth-century French audiences. This learned Belgian Orientalist, regarded as an expert of the time, wrote in a hand worse than an earnest schoolchild's. His clumsy Chinese handwriting makes a wonderful visual metaphor for the cultural translation of knowledge about infanticide in China as it moved to the West. This is ostensibly Chinese writing, copied from Chinese sources, and published in an academic journal—in other words, Chinese knowledge taken from the Chinese themselves. But this "Chinese" source has been selected and reproduced by a French missionary in Shanghai, and copied once more by a Belgian scholar in Louvain, and printed once again in Dublin. The result, although it retains a certain resemblance to the Chinese original, grew only more skewed and haphazard with each copy, moving further and further from its original form and context.

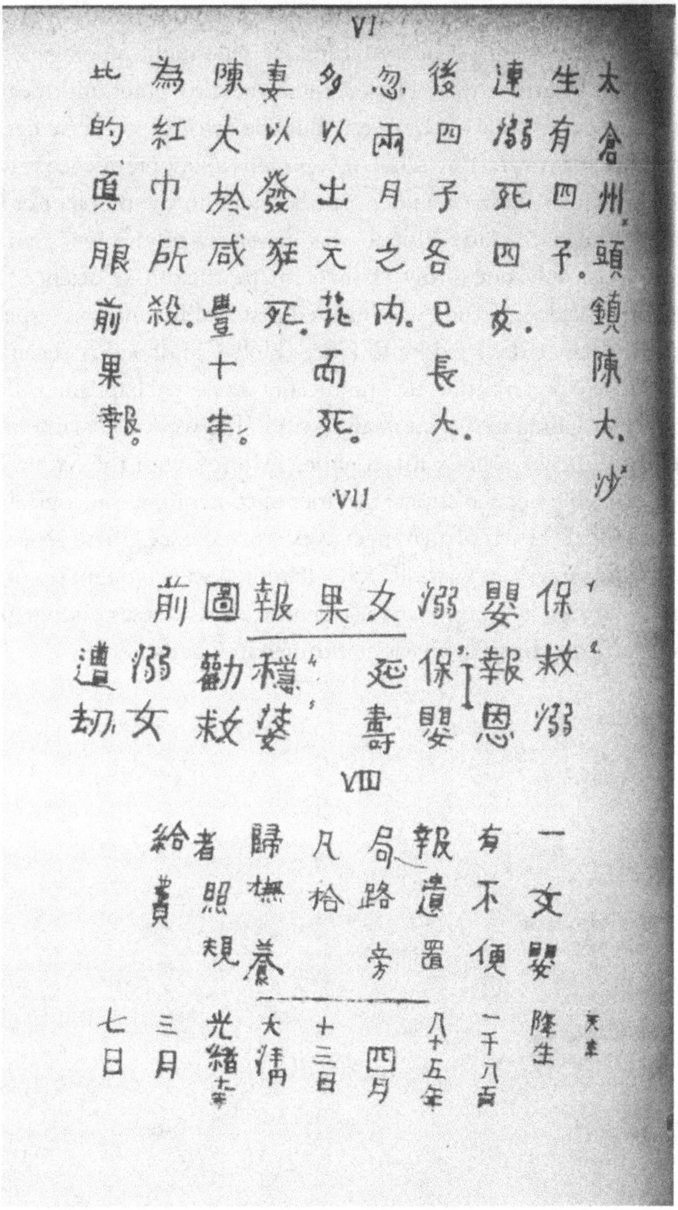

VI

太倉州頭鎮陳大沙．生有四子女．連溺死四女．後四月之內．長大．忽兩以子各巳⋯⋯多以出元花而死．妻大於咸豐十年．為紅中所殺．比的頁眼前果報．

VII

保救溺　嬰報恩　溺　保嬰延壽　女穀婆　報勸救　圖溺女　前遭溺劫

VIII

一文嬰隆生　有不便　局路遺置　凡拾路旁　歸撫養　者照規　給費

一千八百　八十五年　四月　十三日　大清　光緒　三月　七日

Figure 3.7. Page of handwritten Chinese excerpts printed in Belgian Sinologist Charles de Harlez's article on infanticide, copied from Palatre's study. Source: Charles de Harlez, "L'infanticide en Chine," *Le Muséon: Revue Internationale* 4, no. 4 (1885), preceding p. 429, from the collection of the British Library.

In this chapter, we have traced the transformation of perceptions of female infanticide in nineteenth-century China, as self-taught Sinological experts, such as Giles, Palatre and de Harlez, interpreted its proof and meaning for scholarly audiences back in the West. But the spirit of scientific debate that had framed these contrasting scholarly opinions about prevalence was not the only way in which Western audiences responded to the problem of Chinese infanticide. Indeed, Palatre himself was driven by motivations that were at heart religious, only outwardly clothed in the rhetoric of science. Palatre's study of infanticide in China was inspired first and foremost as a spirited defense of the Oeuvre de la Sainte-Enfance (Holy Childhood Association), the Catholic charity organization that financially supported baptismal efforts and orphanages in China and around the world. The work of Palatre and other nineteenth-century Catholic missionaries involved with the Sainte-Enfance aimed at engaging not the critical faculties of contentious Sinological experts, but the passionate hearts of a younger Western audience. These generations of European and American Catholic schoolchildren were brought up to pity the multitudes of poor, little, unwanted (and heathen) Chinese children, inspiring the heroic acts of Christian charity examined in Chapter 4.

FOUR

Saving Souls

Missionaries and Redemption

A child lucky enough to find a place in the audience of the central music hall in Quebec City one evening in May 1872 would have seen a wonderful sight: 3,000 children were jammed in the space, eagerly awaiting the lecture of a French Jesuit missionary, Father Adolphe Vasseur (1828–99), who had recently returned from a six-year period of service in Nanjing and Shanghai. The children waved a riotous mass of white, blue, yellow, green and pink banners, all painted with the same four Chinese characters, *yu xian zhu rong*, a translation of the Jesuit motto, "Ad Majorem Dei Gloriam" ("To the Greater Glory of God"). Two more gigantic banners with Chinese characters in gold hung on either side of the stage, while at the center stood an ornate painting of the Virgin Mary, with a wax doll of the baby Jesus at her feet, his arms outstretched to the audience. The wax baby Jesus was surrounded by a solemn honor guard, formed by eight children, half of them dressed as ordinary Quebecois children and half of them dressed as "improvised" Chinese children. A chorus of fifty more children was arrayed around the entire tableau. Meanwhile, Father Vasseur had himself appeared onstage in the "typical dress" of a Chinese scholar, including a long robe covered by a short mandarin jacket and collar, a belt, white stockings and cloth shoes. His ensemble was topped by a skullcap that even had a long queue made of black silk sewn into it. The meeting was memorialized with a photograph of Vasseur, cradling the wax doll of the baby Jesus and surrounded by some of the honor guard, in their Chinese dress and with their Chinese banners (Figure 4.1).[1]

This fantastic visual spectacle was called forth by the intractable problem of infanticide in China, which inspired millions of distant benefactors, including these children of Quebec, with a deep sense of pity. Vasseur's lecture attested to both intense curiosity about Chinese customs and popular religious fervor for the Catholic missionary cause. In the first part of his lecture, Vasseur addressed the many basic questions that he knew his audience wished to have answered: "What do they wear in China? How do they greet each other? How do they eat, travel, play, study, write, and recite their lessons and prayers?" Vasseur obligingly described a Chinese man's queue and a Chinese woman's bound feet, the respectful greeting of the kowtow, and the common method of traveling in a wheelbarrow pushed along by a porter. He explained that when eating a meal in China, no spoon, fork or knife was used, only two chopsticks of ivory or bamboo. The meal itself substituted rice for bread, tea for wine and cooking oil for butter. He even taught the children how to count out loud to ten in Chinese. This led him to the second part of his lecture, devoted to the need for Catholic missionary activity in China, because the number ten, he explained, looked exactly like the sign of the cross when written in Chinese.[2]

For as much as this gathering of 3,000 faithful Quebecois children cheered his heart as a missionary, Vasseur noted, he was even more moved by the gathering of "millions of little children of China," who had been "sent to heaven" by the Oeuvre de la Sainte-Enfance (Holy Childhood Association).[3] The Sainte-Enfance was a Catholic charity, originally established in 1843 by a Parisian bishop with the express purpose of saving the souls of heathen children, in particular the abandoned children of China. In this chapter, we will examine how the Sainte-Enfance took up Chinese infanticide as a humanitarian cause célèbre in the mid-nineteenth century, transforming evidence about the prevalence of infanticide in China into calls for Christian charity among Catholic schoolchildren in Europe and North America. As an institution, the Sainte-Enfance linked Euro-American schoolchildren to their counterparts in China, encouraging the first group to act as benefactors for the second through regular donations.[4] Collected funds were used to support missionary efforts to gather and baptize abandoned

" Aimez-le bien celui qui vous a tant aimés, travaillez à le faire connaître, aimer
et servir par tout l'univers ! "

Figure 4.1. Photograph of Father Adolphe Vasseur, surrounded by Quebecois
children, all dressed in Chinese garb for Vasseur's lecture about the work of
the Sainte-Enfance in China. The boys are carrying banners inscribed with
the Jesuit motto in Chinese, *yu xian zhu rong* ("To the greater glory of God").
Father Vasseur cradles a wax doll of the baby Jesus in his arms. The caption
below the photo directs Catholic schoolchildren to work hard in the name of
Christ and the Sainte-Enfance: "Love Him well who has loved you so much;
work to make Him known, loved and served by the whole world!" Source:
*Iu-Chien-Tchou-Iom: Trois entretiens illustrés sur la Chine donnés à Québec,
Avril 1872 par le R. P. Vasseur, S. J., Missionnaire Apostolique en Chine,
Directeur de l'Oeuvre Chinoise de St. Luc pour la Propagation de la Foi* (1872),
from the collection of the Shanghai Library Bibliotheca Zi-ka-wei.

children, eventually raising those who survived as Christians in missionary orphanages.

The textual and visual materials produced by the Sainte-Enfance in the nineteenth century are prime examples of what Thomas Laqueur has called the "humanitarian narrative," a mode of relating that arose in Europe during the eighteenth and nineteenth centuries, whereby "details about the suffering bodies of others engender compassion," a sentiment which in turn invokes a "moral imperative to undertake ameliorative action."[5] For sociologist Luc Boltanski, humanitarian narratives center on the presentation of "distant suffering," or suffering occurring in some distant location.[6] The humanitarian narratives of the Sainte-Enfance foregrounded the suffering bodies of abandoned Chinese children, by depicting the numerous dangers that awaited them in an uncaring, alien environment. These textual and visual presentations relied heavily on a foundation of cultural exoticism and difference, imagining the distant land of China to be at once quaint and threatening. Together, words and pictures evoked strong emotions of pity, horror and anger among the young members of the Sainte-Enfance, compelling them to do their utmost to bring such distant suffering to an end. After framing the significance of the sacrament of baptism within the Catholic faith and providing a brief background on the establishment and operation of this pontifical charity, this chapter will focus on the strategic presentation of nineteenth-century Sainte-Enfance propaganda, designed especially to appeal to the eyes and ears of children.

THE SACRAMENT OF BAPTISM

Catholic theology regarding the sacrament of baptism was several centuries in the making. Christ himself had explained the necessity of baptism, saying, "Unless a man be born again of water and the Holy Spirit, he cannot enter into the kingdom of God" (John 3:5). Modeled after John the Baptist's original baptism of Christ, the sacrament itself required three things, according to a decree from Pope Eugenius IV in 1439: the material element of water for ablution, the proper form of the words uttered (e.g., "I baptize thee in the name of the Father and of the Son and of the Holy Spirit") and an appropriate person to perform the baptism in the spirit of the Church.[7] Usually this ministrant was a priest, but when deemed necessary could be a layman or woman, or even a nonbeliever in life-threatening situations, provided the baptism was performed with the form and intention of the Church. At its most essential level, baptism granted remission from both original sin, the condition into which all humans were born since the fall of Adam and Eve from Paradise, and actual sin, which a person actually committed in his or her own life. Baptism also granted remission from all punishment resulting from sin. Moreover, since all of the other sacraments—communion, confession, confirmation, marriage, ordination and extreme unction—were dependent upon the foundation of baptism as the first of the sacraments, it was an essential introduction to an individual's life within the Church.

The theological question as to what would happen to newborn infants who died before being baptized was still open to debate in the nineteenth century. The early medieval philosopher St. Augustine had held a firm position on the matter, affirming that due to original sin, any unbaptized child would be barred from salvation, suffering (but of the mildest form) in hell for eternity.[8] Other theologians, such as Thomas Aquinas, softened the strict Augustinian stance, and argued that although unbaptized children would never attain salvation, neither would they be punished; instead, they would be suspended in limbo, lingering forever between eternal beatitude and the punishments of hell.[9] The precise fate of unbaptized infants thus remained an open theological question. In the eyes of many nineteenth-century Catholics, the only way to be absolutely certain of an infant's salvation was to baptize it as soon as possible after birth. Otherwise, an early death would leave the child to linger in limbo for eternity, or worse yet, to suffer eternal damnation.

So strong was this belief in the necessity of infant baptism for eternal salvation that there were several documented cases in nineteenth-century Brittany, a traditional stronghold of French Catholicism, of women accused of infanticide who had still insisted on first baptizing their newborns. Marianne Bourbé, for example, had in 1851 brought along a bottle of holy water before giving birth in secret, as a local newspaper in Rennes reported, with "the evident intention of preparing eternal life for him before giving him a physical death." In another case from 1825, Jeanne Brunet had secretly given birth and baptized her newborn son twice, both immediately after its birth and the next morning: "I made the sign of the cross over him, and poured the water over his head while saying these words in Breton: in the name of the Father, the Son and the Holy Spirit. . . . I used cold holy water, as it was in a small bottle at the head of my bed." Unfortunately for Brunet, judicial officials felt that her effort to baptize the child was proof that it had been born alive, and thus was a piece of damning evidence of her own culpability in its death.[10]

Catholic parents no doubt desired the expedited baptism of their own children, but what of the children of nonbelievers? Most theologians here agreed with Aquinas, who wrote in the thirteenth century that no Christian had the right to baptize such a child against the will of its non-Christian parents.[11] According to a nineteenth-century French study of baptism, there were three notable exceptions to this rule: if the child was old enough to ask for baptism for himself, if the child was in imminent danger of death or if the child had been abandoned and was no longer under parental care.[12] Based on these last two points, then, abandoned Chinese children could offer an excellent opportunity for acts of Christian grace, if they were found on the verge of death. Catholic missionaries sent to China in both the eighteenth and nineteenth centuries seized every opportunity to "redeem" such unwanted infants, with increasing urgency from one century to the next.

In 1720, Father François Xavier d'Entrecolles (1664–1741), a Jesuit stationed in Beijing, wrote a letter to a wealthy English patroness to thank her for her generous contributions toward this baptismal project. Her money supported the work of several Chinese catechists, whose "principal function" was to go every day in search of babies abandoned by their impoverished parents on the streets in order to baptize them. They also accompanied Chinese doctors and "infidel midwives" on their house calls, in the hopes of baptizing yet more newborns, before they might be drowned on the spot. D'Entrecolles and his colleagues had gone so far as to recruit a Buddhist monk to assist them, "forcing, to some extent, the demon to cooperate with the salvation of souls." By paying the monk a monthly fee, a catechist was allowed to enter a temple in one of the largest and most populous quarters of the city, in order to baptize the exposed infants who had been brought there each day. In this way, the Chinese catechists could gather "five or six thousand infants purified by the waters of baptism" each year.[13]

Another Jesuit, Father du Baudory, described the similar efforts of his Chinese catechist in Canton in 1722. Rather than tailing Chinese doctors or infidel midwives, du Baudory had his catechist go straight to the collection point of the Chinese orphanage itself, taking advantage of the fact that a Chinese catechist could enter but du Baudory, as a European man, could not. When a child there neared death, a message would be sent to the catechist, who lived nearby. The catechist would then be allowed to baptize the child in the nick of time, taking care "to write down the names of those he baptized, and those who died after baptism." The costs were negligible, requiring only the support of the catechist, "some presents" to the orphanage's doctors and directors, payments to the two people who warned the catechist and something for the wet-nurse who carried the child to be baptized. Altogether it was no more than twenty taels, or five francs. "For such a trifling sum . . . ," du Baudory wrote, "one has the consolation of placing every year a great number of infants in heaven." In this manner, the souls saved slowly mounted. Du Baudory kept even more careful records than d'Entrecolles, and could detail the increase in baptisms from year to year: 136 in 1719, 114 in 1720, 241 in 1721, and already 267 in 1722, with the possibility of reaching 300.[14]

The baptism of the children of infidels was not without its own risks and difficulties. In order to be efficacious, baptism needed to be performed before death, or at the point of death itself, *in articulo mortis*. This complicated the sacrament of baptism in a context with nonbelieving parents. If one waited too long and a heathen child died before baptism, then the opportunity for salvation was lost. If one baptized too soon, however, and the child survived, there was the risk that infidel parents might somehow return to claim the child, or other infidel parents might adopt it, rendering the overall purpose of salvation null and void. In order for baptism to remain efficacious, a baptized child should be brought up in accordance with Christian teachings, which meant that it would have to be raised in a Christian family ever after. Maximizing the number of souls saved and minimizing complicating circumstances related to the intentions of infidel parents meant that baptism *in articulo mortis* was the sweet spot, which both guaranteed eternal salvation and guarded against reversion. As Father du Baudory explained, his method of baptizing children near death in the Chinese orphanage posed these exact theological difficulties:

> Though one only baptizes dying infants at the hospital, it is probable that not all die after receiving baptism, and there are some who escape death. In this case, what becomes of them? If they pass into the hands of infidels, the grace of baptism is useless to them: marked by the blood of the Lamb, it is difficult for them to profit from this grace, since apparently they will never know its price. This is a great disadvantage, I admit, but it is not without remedy. The catechist and I have an exact list of baptized infants and of those who die after the baptism. From time to time, we examine this list, and if there are some who recover from their illnesses, the stewards, who

also have their names, are informed not to give them to infidels who would come to ask for them. We take care to remove them from the hospital and place them in Christian homes.[15]

The theology of baptism necessitated further arrangements for a surviving child's care, to avoid the looming specter of reversion. Pope Pius VI emphasized this point once again in 1775, telling missionaries expressly *not* to confer baptism on the child of infidel parents, even if the parents asked for it, unless it was certain that the child would later continue to be raised as a Christian and not revert to infidel beliefs.[16] Continuing care in the eighteenth-century Jesuit mission meant placing a baptized Chinese child in a Christian family to be raised; later, in the nineteenth century, this meant placing a child in a Catholic orphanage, where it would receive the appropriate religious education. Rather than seeing this continuing care beyond baptism as an extra burden, though, this theological necessity could be used to the Church's advantage. By saving, baptizing and rearing unwanted Chinese children to adulthood, it would be possible, according to the nineteenth-century founder of the Sainte-Enfance, to create an indigenous army of Christians to spread the message of salvation in China, making those infants "who live into the instruments of salvation for their own brothers."[17] A program of baptism could thus become the cornerstone for building the entire edifice of the nineteenth-century Catholic mission in China.

THE ESTABLISHMENT OF THE SAINTE-ENFANCE

The Sainte-Enfance had been the brainchild of a Parisian Catholic bishop, Mgr. Charles Conte de Forbin-Janson (1785–1844). Established in 1843, shortly after China's defeat in the Opium War and the forced opening of five treaty ports in China to foreign traders and missionaries, the Sainte-Enfance had as its goal, according to its 1872 membership booklet, the rescue and redemption of the souls of the "multitude of children born of infidel parents" who would otherwise be destroyed "by the thousands and hundreds of thousands, either in the waters of rivers and the abysses of the sea, or by the teeth of dogs and pigs."[18] In Forbin-Janson's opinion, nowhere was the problem of infanticide more severe and intransigent than in China. Although he had never been to China himself, Forbin-Janson had heard about the problem of infanticide there from other European missionaries, and it was the plight of heathen Chinese children that most inspired him. A seminary friend described how, even as a student, Forbin-Janson was obsessed about serving as a missionary in China: "He rarely mentioned the subject without becoming heated at the thought of the immense harvest which the baptism of little abandoned children offered to his zeal! He was always talking about it, indiscriminately to everyone and everywhere."[19] The precarious fates of Chinese children animated the public campaign of the Sainte-Enfance, particularly in the first three decades of its existence. The central aim of the group was to save heathen children's souls, "to open the heavens to the greatest possible number of these unfortunate beings through baptism."[20]

Forbin-Janson was certainly not the first to profess a great desire to convert the infidel Chinese—his missionary predecessors had been trying to do so for more than a century. His real contribution was establishing a "special and distinct" source of funding to enable missionaries to carry out their work.[21] The operation of the Sainte-Enfance, originally designed to benefit the infidel children of China, would be made possible through the regular membership donations of Catholic children, mostly Europeans and North Americans. Children were envisioned as both benefactors and beneficiaries through this arrangement: "The Sainte-Enfance has been established exclusively for Children: it calls on Christian children of all the parts of the world to save infidel children, in honor of the Holy Childhood of Jesus and in its likeness. Children are thus of the first rank; they are its premier and principal members."[22] Each member of the Sainte-Enfance was expected to donate one *sou* (equivalent to five *centimes* or pennies) per month. This emphasis on young children was integrated into the rules and regulations of the charity itself. First-class membership in the Sainte-Enfance was limited to children under the age of twelve who had been baptized in a Catholic church. Those older than twelve were considered second-class members. After the age of twenty-one, adults were expected to join the Propagation de la Foi (Society for the Propagation of the Faith), the original Catholic mission charity after which the Sainte-Enfance was modeled, which gathered subscriptions from adults to support the general work of overseas missionaries.[23]

Forbin-Janson's greatest stroke of genius, though, was his characterization of the relationship between European children and their pitiable Chinese counterparts. Rather than emphasizing the financial relationship between benefactors and beneficiaries, Forbin-Janson encouraged the members of the Sainte-Enfance to serve as distant "godfathers and godmothers" to these "poor infidel little children," in essence "regarding them as their own, giving them proper names, and in this way placing them under the protection of a patron saint."[24] Beyond the theological implications of opening the gates of the Kingdom of God to the baptized child, the sacrament also brought a child into a spiritual network of human relationships, by giving him or her a set of godparents, who were to sponsor the baptism and support the child's spiritual education and development. In centuries past, one of the major roles of the godfather had been to choose the baptismal name of the infant. One of the first questions during a European baptismal ceremony was to ask of the godparents, "What name do you give this child?"[25]

Because of the number of European children involved, however, each Sainte-Enfance member would not automatically receive his or her own Chinese godchild. Instead, for every sixty *centimes* contributed, a member of the Sainte-Enfance would have a chance to name one Chinese child in a lottery. The children were assured that all Sainte-Enfance names would not be indiscriminately mixed together, but that from every series of twelve members, three names were to be drawn, ensuring that each group had provided "three godfathers or three godmothers."[26] The natural corollary to this lottery system was that the more money a child raised, the more chances he or she would have to name a Chinese child. And since a French child might have four or five given names, there were plenty of names to choose from: "Ordinarily, each member will put in the ballot box one of the names which were given to him at baptism, or the name of a saint to which he has a special devotion."[27] It was not just centimes that mattered; it was the centimes of every François, Berthe, Jean-Louis or Marie-Claude, which were destined for a tiny Chinese equivalent.

The success of the Sainte-Enfance in raising funds was thus built upon the religious fervor and devotion of young children. In nineteenth-century France, with its multiple popular sites of Marian devotion, such religious precocity was not unusual. Several famous sightings of the Virgin Mary in nineteenth-century France were attributed entirely to the visions of children or teenagers. The most famous of these, Bernadette Soubirous, was fourteen when she saw the Virgin Mary in 1858, in a grotto near her home in Lourdes. Sightings of the Virgin Mary at La Salette in 1846 and in Pontmain in 1871 were also the visions of shepherd children.[28] Although these popular religious responses reflected the spontaneous visions and yearnings of young Catholic faithful, often in rural peripheries of France, the work of the Sainte-Enfance emanated directly from the center of Church power in Paris. As an institution, the Sainte-Enfance could channel and direct youthful religious fervor into ways that financially supported the Church's broader overseas missions.

By personalizing its appeal to Catholic schoolchildren, through tokens of membership and the chance to name Chinese children, the Sainte-Enfance managed to swell its ranks and achieve marked financial success. At its start, the Sainte-Enfance was primarily a French organization, established and led through its headquarters in Paris. In 1846, only three years after its inception, the Sainte-Enfance raised almost 100,000 francs, 86 percent of which came from France alone.[29] The Catholic missionaries it supported worldwide were also by and large French. In the 1890s, two-thirds of all Europeans working in Catholic mission groups and twenty-eight of forty-four Catholic missionary congregations were French.[30] Gradually, over the course of the late nineteenth century, the organization grew more diverse and international in both the sources and recipients of its contributions. By 1875, the Sainte-Enfance raised more than 2.1 million francs, with less than half the budget coming from France.[31] Other large contributors included the Catholic children of Germany, Belgium, Italy and the Netherlands. As the membership of the Sainte-Enfance diversified, so too did the beneficiaries of its support: China received 71 percent of the total allocation for missions in 1846, but only 38 percent of the total allocation by 1900.[32] Although the children of China were still featured occasionally as poster children for the organization, the comfort given to abandoned children now blanketed the whole world.

Back on the ground in Asia, the growing financial support of the Sainte-Enfance allowed Catholic mission groups in China to increase dramatically the numbers of children baptized year by year. One Jesuit publication from 1926 graphically represented this steady rise in the number of children baptized every year in the Jiangnan Vicariate, superimposing a photograph of four caterwauling Chinese babies on the graph (Figure 4.2). The number of children baptized had risen from about 2,000 in 1848 to about 12,000 in 1872, all the way to a high of 48,000 in 1917.[33] The article credited the success of the baptismal program to its Chinese converts, who as designated baptizers could cover more ground than missionaries working alone. The ever-higher number of children baptized was not only overt proof of the efficacy of all of those *sous* from the Sainte-Enfance in Europe, it was also

La Ste Enfance.

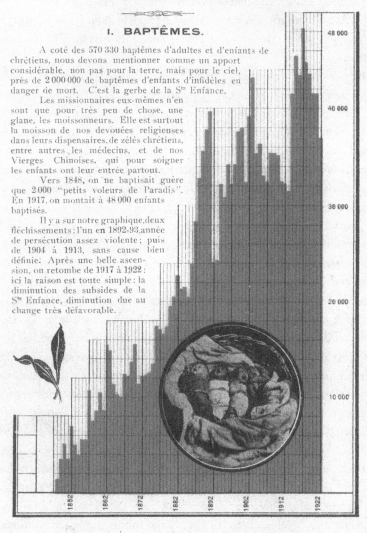

I. BAPTÊMES.

A coté des 570 330 baptêmes d'adultes et d'enfants de chrétiens, nous devons mentionner comme un apport considérable, non pas pour la terre, mais pour le ciel, près de 2 000 000 de baptêmes d'enfants d'infidèles en danger de mort. C'est la gerbe de la Ste Enfance.

Les missionnaires eux-mêmes n'en sont que pour très peu de chose, une glane, les moissonneurs. Elle est surtout la moisson de nos dévouées religieuses dans leurs dispensaires, de zélés chrétiens, entre autres les médecins, et de nos Vierges Chinoises, qui pour soigner les enfants ont leur entrée partout.

Vers 1848, on ne baptisait guère que 2 000 "petits voleurs de Paradis". En 1917, on montait à 48 000 enfants baptisés.

Il y a sur notre graphique, deux fléchissements : l'un en 1892-93, année de persécution assez violente ; puis de 1904 à 1913, sans cause bien définie. Après une belle ascension, on retombe de 1917 à 1922 : ici la raison est toute simple : la diminution des subsides de la Ste Enfance, diminution due au change très défavorable.

Figure 4.2. Graph of annual baptisms in the Jiangnan Vicariate from 1847 to 1922. The accompanying text explains that close to 2 million "infidel children in danger of death" were baptized during that time. Source: Louis Hermand, *Les étapes de la mission du Kiang-nan, 1842–1922: Chine* (1926), from the collection of the School of Theology Library at Boston University.

by far the most numerically successful program of the nineteenth-century Catholic mission in China. The number of children baptized in Jiangnan, for example, far outstripped the number of adult baptisms, which barely rose above 1,500 per year.[34] Catechumens, or non-Christians receiving religious instruction for eventual membership in the Church, remained below 4,000 per year until 1892.[35]

Forbin-Janson's brilliant idea for a charity organization, then, converged along several different points. It was modeled after the Propagation of the Faith in that it set up a system for regular donations, but called upon the precocious religiosity of young children, giving them an individual, spiritual relationship with Chinese children. It collected money *and* it couched this collection in spiritual terms, marking its success one *sou* and one soul at a time. Yet it was a form of religious participation that had a formal place within the Church hierarchy and filtered down from its top officials, instead of bubbling up spontaneously as in the Marian visions of poor nineteenth-century children in the peripheries of France. Finally, as it grew, it became a consciously international Catholic group, with participation from Catholic children around the world.

A SHORT SAINTE-ENFANCE CATECHISM

The international membership of the Sainte-Enfance was brought together through the print medium of the *Annales de l'Oeuvre de la Sainte-Enfance*, a bimonthly journal that reprinted inspiring letters from Catholic missionaries around the world, as well as letters and writings from both child members and adult supporters of the Sainte-Enfance. By 1872, the *Annales* were published in seven European languages, including French, English, German, Spanish, Italian, Flemish and Portuguese.[36] Within the pages of the journal, children learned not only about the activities of overseas missionaries, whom their contributions supported, but also about the sacrifices made by other Catholic children, just like themselves, to give to this great cause. Although such outlays for printing the journal could be expensive, Sainte-Enfance leaders realized that these costs were offset by "the ardor which it thus maintains within Association."[37]

One issue of the *Annales* in 1860, for example, included a short catechism written by the curate of Our Lady of Châteauroux in the Indre department of central France, explaining the work of the Sainte-Enfance. Presented in the traditional format of a series of questions and answers, and phrased in simple language that a young child could easily understand or even memorize, the unnamed curate's catechism provides us with a clear vision of how the problem of infanticide in China and its proposed solution were presented to nineteenth-century French Catholic schoolchildren. The curate described how he had read it aloud during a mass in January 1860, producing "quite an impression" on the children in his own parish.[38] The catechism, he boasted, had assured the complete success of subsequent fundraising efforts for the Sainte-Enfance. Its structure emphasized the three basic goals of the Sainte-Enfance: saving the lives of "abandoned infidel children," procuring for them the "grace of baptism," and bringing them up with a "Christian education."

The catechism begins with basic questions and answers concerning the motivation and purpose of the Sainte-Enfance, to save the countless, abandoned infidel children in China. The problem of infanticide in China was framed as one of both culture and religion. Parental cruelty and governmental indifference were identified as the main culprits; both issues stemmed from pagan beliefs and ignorance of the Catholic faith:

Q: What is the Oeuvre de la Sainte-Enfance?
A: It is an association of Christian children for ministering to one of the greatest miseries that exists in the world.

Q: What is this misery?
A: It is that poor children born to idolatrous parents, in peril of dying by the thousands without having received baptism, are abandoned or exterminated by their cruel parents.

Q: Is this true?
A: This should be impossible, without a doubt, but it is nothing but very true.

Q: In which countries in the world are these horrors committed?
A: At the ends of Asia, particularly in the immense empire of China. There, a profound contempt reigns for these poor little children. They are thrown entirely alive into the streets and into the rivers. Horses trample them underfoot, dogs and pigs devour them, and people are not disturbed at all.

Q: But is there no one to prevent these crimes?
A: No. These parents believe they have the right to kill their children. It is the custom over there. The government lets them and these malicious parents take advantage of this ungodly unconcern on the part of their government.

Q: Where does all of this wickedness come from?
A: Alas! They do not know Our Lord Jesus Christ; they do not worship the true God. They are idolatrous; they have not heard of the gospel of charity. They do not love the infant Jesus, no one has ever spoken to them of the Very Holy Virgin.

Q: Can children like us prevent these barbarities?
A: Yes, that is the goal of the Oeuvre de la Sainte-Enfance.[39]

In the space of seven short questions and answers, the catechism moves from defining the aim of the Sainte-Enfance as addressing the problem of infanticide in heathen countries to identifying China as the world's worst offender. The problem was particularly acute in China because it linked the "cruelty of the savage state . . . with the immorality of an old civilization."[40] The logic of this sequence of questions and answers implicitly suggests that a solution to the issue must be imposed from the outside, since indifference reigned within, thus opening a space for the charitable activity of foreign Catholic missionaries, supported by Catholic children.

Having established the roots of the problem and the need for an external solution, the catechism then discusses how Catholic missionaries and their native catechist assistants roam around the countryside looking for abandoned Chinese children to save. Most critically in this segment, the catechism notes that Chinese children were not only found abandoned along paths and rivers; they could also be purchased directly from their greedy parents, who would rather sell them than raise them.

Q: But how can one deliver these unfortunate children from death?
A: Some Christians scour all the paths, going down hedges and rivers, and when they see a little abandoned or exposed child in the water, they gather it up and take it with them . . .

Q: Oh! Are these little children pitied?
A: Their parents are miserly as well as cruel. They love money and quite often they exchange their children for a few *sous*.

Q: Can one buy these children?
A: Yes, one can, and this is also what the Oeuvre de la Sainte-Enfance does.[41]

The language of the marketplace thoroughly infused many missionary descriptions of acquiring children in China. As Henrietta Harrison has described, the day-to-day operation of orphanages supported by the

Sainte-Enfance in China often involved them in the "market for children" there, since missionaries frequently gave small sums of money to those who collected children and brought them to the orphanage.[42] The sums were small for Europeans, but they could be a good day's wage for a Chinese laborer.[43] An 1847 letter from a Jesuit missionary near Shanghai, Father Théobald Werner, describes how young girls would bring children to his fellow priests, eagerly detailing the prices paid for each child: " 'He cost me 209 *sapecs* (one franc); his mother preferred to throw him out rather than give him away for less.' 'This one,' said another, 'Was a bit cheaper because I had already bought the previous one, and on the understanding I would be charged even less for the next ones.' "[44] At the other end of the transaction, the idea of "purchasing" a Chinese child in order to save it was repeated so often in Sainte-Enfance literature that it shaped the attitudes of Sainte-Enfance contributors in Europe, who came to see a helpless Chinese child, as Henrietta Harrison suggests, as a kind of desirable "consumer item."[45] Chen Jitong (1852–1907), the military attaché to the Chinese embassy in France, wrote in 1884 that an old woman on the streets of Paris had once pointed at him from behind and said, "Here is a Chinese: who knows if it was not my own *sous* that purchased him?" Fortunately, he joked, she did not "quite have her title deed in order. Otherwise I undoubtedly would have had to pay interest on her *sous*. For shouldn't all good actions [in French, a pun for shares of stock] be repaid?"[46]

Immediately after collecting or purchasing unwanted Chinese children, the first order of business was to baptize them, so that if they died they could escape the fate of limbo and enter the gates of heaven. Should any baptized child survive, the next duty was to provide the child with a Christian education. According to the catechism, this meant that infants would even be suckled at the breasts of Christian women working as wet-nurses before the infants were moved to orphanages and cared for by the gentle ministrations of French Catholic missionary women. The children would be given a basic education and vocational training, but most importantly they would learn to love Jesus Christ as savior. Eventually, once they grew up, these former orphans would themselves someday serve as the bedrock of conversion efforts among other Chinese, yet untouched by grace:

Q: But after they have been taken in, what do they do with them?
A: Then they give them the right to be children of God. They are made Christians through baptism, and they obtain the happiness of heaven, if they die after baptism.

Q: But if these children live, what happens then?
A: They are entrusted to Christian wet nurses, then a little later they are gathered in the orphanages, governed by the good Christian women who have come especially from France, who have gone by the seas and have made a journey of more than two thousand leagues to come and look after and raise these poor children.

Q: What is an orphanage?
A: It is a house where one provides for orphans. There are little children there, like in foundling homes, there are those who are a bit bigger, as in the schools, and there are those bigger yet, as in the shops of workers. The latter are apprenticed. They learn a trade to make a living. Above all, they learn to love Our Lord Jesus Christ. They become in this way the true servants of God, Christian workers and godly. Later they will be among the pagans, like so many torches in the darkness.[47]

The final and most important component of the catechism was its description of the supporting role that young members of the Sainte-Enfance could take in order to help with missionary efforts to baptize, raise and educate unwanted children in distant lands like China. There were two components to their support. First, children were to give a monthly contribution to the Saint-Enfance. The catechism gave explicit instructions about how much, when and to whom such contributions should be given, as well as how those funds would then be redistributed. Second, children were to say a daily prayer for heathen children all over the world. In cases where children were too small to undertake these actions on their own, their mothers were to help them:

Q: What should one give when one is a member of the charity?
A: One gives one *sou* per month. One gives especially his heart and his little prayers for the poor little infidel children.

Q: What is the prayer that one should say?
A: One should say every day an *Ave Maria*, and add: *Holy Virgin Mary, pray for us and for the poor little infidel children*. When the children are too little to say this prayer themselves, their mamas can say it in their place . . .

Q: To whom should one give this little subscription every month?
A: Small children who go to school can give it to their teachers, and they can give it to the parish priest. Mothers whose children do not yet go to school can give their small sums to their parish priest, or to another priest

who is in charge of receiving all the resources for the charity in the city. All of these funds are sent to the diocesan council or the central council in Paris, to be distributed to the places where there is a need.[48]

Some children (or more significantly, their parents), though, might doubt the efficacy of such small sums of money. Or a skeptical parent might ask, why should the pennies of French schoolchildren be sent off into the great blue yonder, when there was already such a great need for charity at home? The curate's catechism also addressed these points directly, in order to alleviate such concerns. The donation of one *sou* per month was purposely small, in order to allow for children of all socioeconomic backgrounds to participate: "We wanted poor children to be able, along with rich children, to be members of this beautiful Association of the Sainte-Enfance, and become benefactors for children infinitely more unfortunate than themselves." At the same time, although each child's individual contribution was very tiny, taken collectively, even these pennies could save millions of Chinese souls: "All these little *sous* will make up quite a sum, which will be distributed to orphanages where poor little children of cruel pagans are taken in." Finally, to address the question of sending contributions abroad as opposed to using them for charity at home, the catechism explained that there were already many good Christians undertaking these efforts in "Christian countries," where "charity is not lacking." The greater need was for the "hundreds of thousands of children among the idolatrous who have a body and soul like us, for whom Jesus Christ died, who are our brothers and sisters, and who will perish if we do not help them." Suffering was worst, in other words, in distant pagan countries, which had no relief for such problems without the interceding efforts of foreign missionaries.[49]

SEEING THROUGH THE EYES OF CHILDREN

The leadership of the Sainte-Enfance was savvy enough to realize that the best way to address children was through pictures rather than words, taking care to "not neglect any means of speaking to their eyes in order to grab their attention."[50] Visual lessons for Catholic schoolchildren took their most tangible form in illustrated devotional cards, given to each new Sainte-Enfance member upon completion of a full year's subscription. The cards were printed in a number of different European languages. All of the engraved nineteenth-century versions shown below include blank spaces for the new member's name and his or her date of entry into the ranks of the Sainte-Enfance. Each card also includes a biblical verse from the story of Moses, himself a near victim of infanticide. At the time of his birth, the Pharaoh of Egypt had decreed that the sons of all Hebrews were to be thrown into the Nile River. Moses' mother raised him in secret, but when he was three months old, she was forced to send him down the river in a basket. The Pharaoh's daughter finds the basket, and Moses' sister, who has been watching the events unfold, runs to ask the Pharaoh's daughter if she would like a Hebrew nursemaid for the child, bringing back her own mother. The Pharaoh's daughter then promises Moses' mother that if she nurses the child, she will be rewarded, saying, "Take this child away, and nurse it for me, and I will give thee thy reward" (Exodus 2:9). Likewise, by caring for discarded Chinese children, European Catholic children could be rewarded with God's grace.

As the curate's catechism had instructed, the first stage of salvation in the unfolding drama of unwanted Chinese infants was the physical act of gathering their bodies, either by collecting them from the rivers, streams and by-ways of the empire or by purchasing them from Chinese parents. One membership card shows a small Chinese boy, whose queue is just visible trailing down his back, carrying an even smaller, inert baby to the outstretched arms of an awaiting nun, while her companion sister lovingly cradles another infant in her arms (Figure 4.3). At the second nun's feet, a pig lurks in the underbrush, having just been denied the tasty morsel of a drowning child. In the background, a missionary stands in a boat holding yet another babe in arms, trawling for more bodies. (The popularity of depicting Chinese babies floating in rivers on Sainte-Enfance membership cards may have served as a visual reminder of the ur-story of Moses' abandonment and subsequent rescue.) A second card illustrates a set of Chinese parents having apparently just sold to the missionaries their own child, now placidly resting in the ample lap of a nun (Figure 4.4). Another Chinese man carrying a child on his back climbs the hill in the background, apparently headed for same purpose.

Although both cards depict the various ways that Chinese children were collected by missionaries, the contrast in the two scenes could not be made plainer: the nun on the first card stretches out her arms in an act of Christian mercy, awaiting the nearly lifeless body of an abandoned infant; the Chinese parents on the second card stretch out their hands in a blatant act

Figure 4.3. Late nineteenth-century Sainte-Enfance membership card, depicting abandoned Chinese infants being rescued from a river by two nuns, assisted by a small Chinese boy. Note the pig lurking in the bushes and the archetypal junk in the background. Source: Author's personal collection.

CACHET DE LA SAINTE ENFANCE.

ACCIPE PUERUM ISTUM ET NUTRI MIHI
EGO DABO TIBI MERCEDEM TUAM. [Ex. ch. 2, v. 9.]
REÇOIS CET ENFANT ET NOURRIS LE POUR MOI.
JE TE DONNERAI MOI-MÊME TA RÉCOMPENSE.

a été reçu membre de l'Association de la
St. Enfance, le

Figure 4.4. Late nineteenth-century Sainte-Enfance membership card, depicting an unwanted child being purchased from its Chinese parents by a priest in exchange for a few coins.
Source: Author's personal collection.

of greed, awaiting the metallic clink of a few coins in exchange for their own child. The focal point of each scene reinforces the underlying message. In the first card, both the young boy and the standing sister gaze toward the gentle countenance of the nun with outstretched arms, whose enormous wimple draws the viewer's eye to contemplate her central role in the act of rescue. On the second card, the focal point is the exchange of money for flesh, as the Chinese father holds out his hands awaiting payment from the priest. Here, the Chinese parents have cast their eyes downward (the better to display the slant in their eyes?), as if in eager anticipation of the payment, while the priest seems unable to bring himself to witness this display of greed. He turns his own eyes heavenward, while the nun too casts an admonishing glance at the exchange.

The second stage of salvation was the all-important act of baptism, after which a dying child's soul might ascend to heaven. In one membership card illustrating a baptism scene, the same Chinese parents who have sold their child seem to have undergone a transformation by way of Christian conversion. A Chinese man and woman stand in the exact same positions and poses, but now they are dressed as a native nun and a native priest, lovingly assisting as a child is baptized by a Jesuit father (Figure 4.5). Another baby awaits baptism in the arms of a maid in the background, while two small Chinese boys, probably themselves rescued orphans, serve as acolytes. Instead of focusing on an exchange of money, all eyes now are riveted by the pouring of holy water over the infant's head, part of the sacrament that would miraculously transform the quality of the child's soul. Even if a child did not survive after baptism, there was now no need for sadness or lamentation. Another card shows a different group of Chinese men and women, probable Christian converts, along with a European missionary, kneeling in awe as they look heavenward at the baby Jesus himself, surrounded by a chorus of angels, as he waits to embrace the souls of more Chinese infants, one of whom is sprawled on the ground (Figure 4.6).

The third stage of salvation was that of Christian education, should a Chinese child survive infancy. This educational program of the Sainte-Enfance is depicted by an image of a group of Chinese orphan children, kneeling in front of a priest and an altar, during mass (Figure 4.7). The priest serves as the conduit of God's luminous grace, his whole body bathed in light from heaven, demonstrating faith in action once more. Yet the most visually curious feature of this image is the neat row of queues hanging

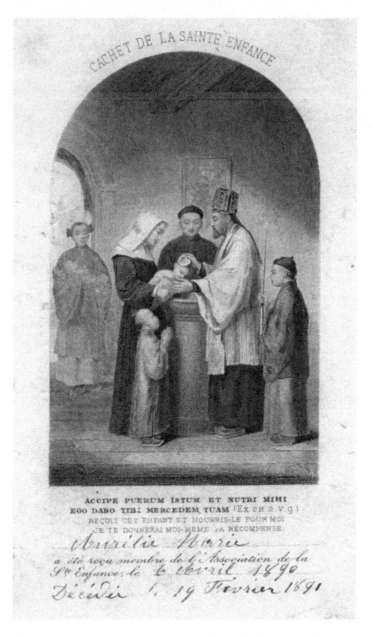

Figure 4.5. Late nineteenth-century Sainte-Enfance membership card, depicting the baptism of a Chinese child. Note the queue of the Jesuit priest performing the baptism. Source: Author's personal collection.

Figure 4.6. Late nineteenth-century Sainte-Enfance membership card, depicting the baby Jesus in heaven, surrounded by a host of angels, waiting to welcome the soul of a dead Chinese infant into his open arms. A group of Chinese Christian converts and a European priest look on in awe. Source: Author's personal collection.

CACHET DE LA SAINTE ENFANCE.

ACCIPE PUERUM ISTUM ET NUTRI MIHI
EGO DABO TIBI MERCEDEM TUAM. [Ex. ch. 2. v. 9.]
REÇOIS CET ENFANT ET NOURRIS LE POUR MOI,
JE TE DONNERAI MOI-MÊME TA RÉCOMPENSE.

a été reçu membre de l'Association de la
S.te Enfance, le

Figure 4.7. Late nineteenth-century Sainte-Enfance membership card, depicting a Jesuit priest leading a group of Chinese boys and girls in prayer during a mass. Note the visual prominence of the boys' queues. Source: Author's personal collection.

down from the head of each kneeling boy. In this scene, as well as many of the other membership cards, the artist has deliberately chosen to depict the boys from behind, the better to show off this most distinctive Qing dynasty male hairstyle. In the baptism scene, even the Jesuit priest sports a false queue, such as Father Vasseur wore in his lecture to schoolchildren in Quebec. Other visual cues of cultural difference and exotic location include slanted eyes, conical straw hats and flowing robes on native men and women in the foreground, as well as palm trees, pagodas and junks in the background. Each reference wordlessly reminds viewers of the supposed setting of all of these scenarios in the distant land of China, where infanticide reigned.

The final stage of the Sainte-Enfance salvation story was the action required on the part of the Catholic European schoolchild. In this final example of a membership card, a European girl stands on a chair in order to place her coins into the collection box, guided under the watchful eyes of her mother (Figure 4.8). Both the sweet, innocent charity of this child and the genuine maternal devotion of her mother contrast markedly with the scene of distant suffering in the background. There, a Chinese man, perhaps himself a father, is in the midst of throwing away an unwanted child. A missionary tries to stop him by pulling on his arm and offering him a bag of money for the child's life. Another unwanted baby crawls piteously on the ground, clinging to the priest's vestments. The connection between the action in the foreground and the action in the background was direct and unmistakable. By placing her penny into the collection box, this young European girl could personally prevent the killing of Chinese babies by their parents, aiding the work of Catholic missionaries there. In this single image, the Sainte-Enfance tied together all of the necessary elements for a humanitarian narrative, including both the source and cause of distant suffering, as well as visual instructions on how to prevent it.

Above all else, the Sainte-Enfance membership cards make manifest the physical bodies of unwanted Chinese children, the debated existence of which so preoccupied Western Sinological experts in Chapter 3. These illustrations neatly solved the problem of missing Chinese infant bodies: even if decomposing corpses could not be found in baby towers, the bodies of Chinese infants could easily be imagined and depicted at every different stage of rescue, from collection to baptism to Christian education. Not only that, these illustrations articulate how the abandoned physical bodies of Chinese babies would find care and comfort in the literal bosom of the Church: the

Figure 4.8. Late nineteenth-century Sainte-Enfance membership card, depicting a European girl making a donation to the charity with the assistance of her mother. In the background, a priest restrains a Chinese man from throwing away a child, enticing him with a bag of money. Source: Author's personal collection.

posture of the infants and the way they are lovingly cradled by the nuns in the first two collection scenes immediately call to mind iconography of the infant Jesus in the arms of the Madonna. Along with making manifest the bodies of Chinese infants, the rendering of each scenario also details the critical role of tireless European missionaries and faithful European schoolchildren in recovering these bodies.

The images the Sainte-Enfance presented to Catholic schoolchildren made a deep impression on young minds, at least in the case of Francisque Sarcey (1827–99), a Parisian journalist and drama critic, who recalled seeing similar pictures during his childhood. Sarcey, an outspoken anticlerical critic of the perceived powers and privileges of the Catholic Church, wrote a series of articles in the republican daily newspaper, *Le XIXe Siècle* (The Nineteenth Century) in 1875, criticizing the Sainte-Enfance for duping innocent schoolchildren and their mothers into contributing to the bulging coffers of the Church with exaggerated reports of infanticide in China.[51] Sarcey recalled that during his childhood communion classes, the priest would often distribute images of Chinese children suffering horrible fates. One image in particular, a "scene of massacre in China," remained lodged in Sarcey's memory. It featured "a line, illuminated by the most beautiful ochre, symbolizing the Yellow River. On the edges of this cursed river, multitudes of little children swarmed, while dirty pigs tore through to devour them. I imagine there was supposed to be in a corner somewhere some missionary or angel to save these unfortunate creatures from the pigs' teeth. But here my memory is muddled, and it is impossible for me to recall this part of the image."[52]

For Sarcey, the pigs played a central role in this drama of fleecing French schoolchildren and their mothers. "It is a known fact, certain and incontestable," Sarcey asserted, that "these little Chinese abandoned to pigs have served more than once and still serve to rouse the sensitivity of our children and their mothers, in order to engage them by compassion with these famous alms of one *sou* per week, which day after day swell into the millions."[53] As far as Sarcey was concerned, this solitary *sou* sat at the very heart of the matter. In his childhood recollection, he acutely realized that the only way to stop all of this suffering was to take action, by contributing money to the greater cause of the Sainte-Enfance:

> Oh! Those pigs! Those savage pigs! Those raging pigs! My imagination had been overrun by them! I saw them in my dreams, foraging through clusters

of small naked bodies, which crossed a yellow ochre river! What burning faith I had in the pigs at that time! I would have readily shouted to them from the depths of my heart:

Wicked pigs, stop what you do!
Show them grace! Here is my *sou*![54]

Whereas Sarcey has long rejected the religious lessons of his youth, he vividly recalls the "burning faith" with which he believed in the story of the ravaging pigs. The power of the pigs, as both the real and the symbolic cause of bodily suffering, overturned all other considerations, both religious and pecuniary. One can imagine Francisque, the small boy, thrusting his *sou* into the snout of a raging pig, bringing it into quiet submission: magically, it trots away.

What stuck so vividly in Sarcey's childhood memory was the yellowness of the river (and presumably the people), as well as the horrible piles of children being eaten by pigs—the provocative twin allure of the exotic and the terrifying. Although the child Francisque may have been comforted by the actions of the missionaries in saving these innocent children, the adult Sarcey rejected any symbols of Catholic salvation, claiming not to recall these other prominent features. Captivated by his memory of the pigs, Sarcey asked his readers if anyone could send him a copy of the image that had so impressed him as a child. He was, however, never able to locate an exact replica, although he later found and described two other similar examples from the Sainte-Enfance. One showed a "tangle of little children lying on top of one another" and "two ghastly snouts rushing toward this heap of naked bodies," while "a horribly fat pig runs away on all its legs." The other included a bishop holding a child in his arms, while a little girl "beats back a frightful pig with her hands, which is hurtling itself on the body of a baby, sprawled out on the ground." Meanwhile, in the distance, "you see a Chinese man, dressed all in purple, who is holding by its feet a small infant, naked as a worm, head down, which he is shaking as if he were a cook draining a chicken."[55]

But none of the images Sarcey found as an adult could compare to the power of the picture in his childhood imagination. Perhaps that should come as no surprise, for the pigs had only ever existed with such terrible urgency in the mind's eye of his childhood. When we consider the membership cards of the Sainte-Enfance today, the pig seems to be more part of a bucolic, pastoral scene, snuffling at the babies with gentle curiosity rather than fearsome rage (see Figure 4.3). Yet to note this disparity is less to fault

Sarcey with intentional exaggeration or a shoddy memory (although he may have succumbed to both) than it is to draw attention to the motive power of those images, as he remembered them. Time had redrawn the lines and erased certain elements of those early childhood pictures, but Sarcey was still left with the deep impression of pity, fear and righteous indignation, which were all wrapped up in the helpless bundle of the Chinese child. The truth of the situation on the ground in China mattered little, when it came to the hearts and minds of Catholic schoolchildren in Europe and North America: the emotions they felt, and the humanitarian actions they were so moved to take, were only all too real.

PERFORMING CHARITY AND VENGEANCE

Beyond looking at images of distant suffering, European children had the chance to perform and even embody the suffering of unwanted Chinese children in the many plays featured in the *Annales*. The plays were occasionally written by child members, and others were offered by adult associates of the Sainte-Enfance, such as local diocesan directors. Children performed the plays at special Sainte-Enfance masses or fêtes, held annually by churches large and small. In the first two decades of the publication of the *Annales*, the plays emphasized the charitable work of children in France, dramatizing their empathy and passion for the cause of Sainte-Enfance. In later decades, the dramatic action shifted to China, where the lives of unwanted Chinese children, alongside their villainous birth families and their virtuous Catholic rescuers, were imagined and performed on the stage. By the time of the late nineteenth century, the dramas turned attention to other international regions, particularly Africa, mirroring the expansion of French colonial interests and the internationalization of the organization itself.[56]

Like the didactic plays written by Yu Zhi, these plays of the Sainte-Enfance are not subtle. Their underlying message is clear. In order for French children and missionaries to play the heroic saviors of unwanted Chinese children, the cultural wantonness and wickedness of Chinese parents served as an essential backdrop. European children were to be moved to pity and inspired to action, on behalf of helpless, abandoned Chinese children who suffered at the hands of their cruel and indifferent birth families. The audience's sympathy is meant to rest entirely with either the generous European children or the victimized Chinese children, whose families have abandoned them out of greed or intolerance for their physical disabilities. These plays for children contain clear-cut examples of virtue and villainy, with no room for pity for destitute Chinese parents, who felt driven to abandon or kill their children.

The plays set in France were situated in its remoter, most fervently Catholic, rural regions. There, the children of working-class families could have much to teach the children of the urban bourgeoisie. In one play from 1860, two young brothers from the city, Joseph and Emmanuel, are spending their vacation gathering plants for their collection in the mountains of Savoy, a region in the French Alps, annexed to France only that year. The brothers meet two young local shepherds, André and François, who are of a similar age, twelve and thirteen. André and François are looking for the lost mother ewe of one of their baby lambs. (The stage instructions helpfully indicate that "if no real lamb is available," one can "make one from wood or cardboard, and imitate the plaintive bleating of the little animal and its mother ewe.") In a flash, André suddenly connects the little lamb without a mother to the little children "in a country very far from here, where their barbaric mothers abandon them, exposed along the roads or in the rivers, where they perish before their very eyes." "You are speaking," Emmanuel exclaims, "of the poor little Chinese!" The shepherd boys explain to the city boys that they are members of the Sainte-Enfance, and that they have recruited many other members to join it.[57]

The city boys are impressed, wondering how they have done so in such a thinly populated, mountainous region. François explains: "When I happen to meet a child from our village or the neighboring village, I ask, 'And you, are you a member of the charity of the little Chinese?' If he responds, 'No,' well, then! I don't wait another minute, and ask him and his parents, again and again, so that willingly or unwillingly, I get them to give me his name . . . and one *sou* per month." He also asks the parents of newborns in the village to enroll their children in the association. The city boys are so impressed by the devotion of the shepherd boys that they convince their father to give their new friends money to buy another ewe. Miraculously, just as soon as he does, the lost ewe returns of its own accord, and the group decides to donate the money to the Saint-Enfance instead. The play closes with the two mountain shepherds singing about little lambs and little Chinese children: "In another land, / There, very far from our hamlets, / *How many other little lambs / Have lost their mothers forever!*"[58]

Equating abandoned Chinese children with helpless, wild creatures was a recurring theme in these short plays. In another play set on the coast of

Normandy, Rosalie, the ten-year-old daughter of a fisherman, learns about the children of China, cruelly abandoned by their indifferent mothers. She is overcome by emotion and gushes, "If the country of China were near the coast of England . . . I would say to our father, when he goes there to fish, 'Take me papa, I beg you!' . . . Then while my father and the other seamen go fishing for fluke or herring, well then, I would go down to shore and run quickly to China. There, I would take my own turn to fish for the little children exposed on the roads. Oh, such beautiful fishing! Then I would gladly put them into my apron and bring them quickly back to our boat! . . . But it is a little too far . . ." Another friend assures Rosalie that even if she cannot get to China herself, missionaries could go in her place. The girls then proceed to collect fish that fall onto the docks, having escaped boats' nets, in order to raise money for the Sainte-Enfance. Plays such as these promoted the idea that the bodies and souls of Chinese children were ripe for the taking, randomly strewn about the byways of the empire.[59]

If these early plays staged the innocence and devotion of French children to the cause of the Sainte-Enfance, then later plays performed the opposite extreme, illustrating the victimhood of Chinese children and the cruel villainy of their parents. "Sin-a-li, the Orphan Boy of Zi-Ka-Wei" (1862), "Maria Siao, the Blind Girl of Kiou-kiang" (1870) and "Sio-tsia, the Orphan Girl of Pen-choui" (1877) all shared a similar fate of having been cruelly abandoned by their birth families at the age of ten or eleven, only to be saved by Catholic nuns and priests.[60] Sin-a-li's parents have died, and his greedy uncle is too miserly to spend money on his food, so he is left to starve in the woods. Dahe Siao, the daughter of an official in Kiou-kiang, suddenly goes blind, prompting her unfeeling and un-Christian mother to sell her off to a trader of human flesh, since she is now useless and cannot be married. Likewise, Sio-tsia breaks her leg, which a Chinese doctor falsely claims cannot be healed, such that her mother decides to have her thrown into a ditch, after having her beaten with a cane. These Chinese guardians are verbally as well as physically abusive, calling their children every possible epithet, from "lazy" and "useless" to "piece of furniture," "viper," "disgusting little monster" and even more colorfully, "vile crocodile" or "ignoble hippopotamus."[61]

None of these children are actually without family to care for them. They have all been abandoned by still-living parents or guardians. Why? In the first place, the role of the suffering Chinese child never changes in the course of the drama: he or she is always the helpless victim, whose innocence comes to embody the epitome of religious devotion, once in the care of the Catholic orphanage. Other Christian characters remain just as stout, brave, good and obedient at the end of the plays as they do at the beginning. Dramatic action of any kind, therefore, demands that a villainous Chinese parent make an appearance. Only the transformation of the heathen Chinese parent gives an opportunity for religious redemption. In the second place, because the Chinese guardians in the plays were not dead, that meant they had undeniably rejected their own children. The Catholic orphanage could then fill an essential role as savior of last resort. Alternative circumstances of abandonment that were not so clear-cut might raise uncomfortable questions. If, for example, a child was sold by its parents to an orphanage due to poverty and not for lack of parental affection, a later change in fortune might have them return to exercise their legal rights to reclaim their child, meaning that the child would once again find itself among heathens. This concern was so palpable that non-Christian Chinese family members giving up a child at a Catholic orphanage were later required to sign contracts, formally stating that they were "breaking off relations" with their child and would never return to reclaim it.[62] In staging Sainte-Enfance plays for schoolchildren, these more complicated (and realistic) scenarios had to be scrupulously avoided.

These plays may have dramatized the rescue of Chinese children from infanticide, but they also served a broader didactic purpose in justifying French imperial involvement in nineteenth-century China. The play about Sin-a-li was published in 1862, only two years after joint Anglo-French forces had marched on Peking and destroyed the Summer Palace at the end of the Second Opium War. The victory for the Western allies resulted in the signing of the Peking Convention, which among other stipulations forced China to open its interior to foreign missionaries and pay indemnities to Britain and France. The Sin-a-li play takes place within the unspoken context of this larger military confrontation. After Sin-a-li is abandoned in the woods near Shanghai, he is soon "adopted" by a French sergeant, who happens to be bivouacked with his military company near the Zi-ka-wei mission complex—although no explanation is given for the presence of the sergeant and his company on Chinese soil. The sergeant takes Sin-a-li to the Catholic orphanage for boys at Zi-ka-wei, paying generously for Sin-a-li's school fees and upkeep out of his own pocket.[63]

The dramatic tension rises when Sin-a-li's evil uncle returns to the orphanage to demand money from the missionaries. He demonstrates both naiveté and greed, convinced that because the missionaries are European, they are therefore rich, and will pay him well to take his nephew back. He cackles, "This won't be the first time that a Chinese teaches a European a thing or two! . . . I will let him see that a child of the Celestial Empire is not afraid of the dog of a European!" The uncle's boastful cultural pride is quickly burst, though, when he is tricked not once but twice, first by a group of orphan boys, friends of Sin-a-li, then by the protective French sergeant. Both parties play upon the uncle's ignorance of the French language, making him out to be a fool and a coward. The orphan boys get Sin-a-li's uncle to put on a dunce's cap (in French, *bonnet d'âne*, literally, "cap of an ass") by convincing him that the French have a magical cap that, when worn, allows the wearer to find that which has been lost. In order to find his donkey (which has been hidden by the sergeant), the uncle puts on the cap, but when he opens his eyes, he sees nothing. The boys, however, tell him that they can all see the ass. That's impossible, the uncle insists. The boys fetch a mirror and tell him to look in it, and he finally gets that the joke is on him.[64]

A more serious and lasting lesson is meted out by the French sergeant, who returns to accuse Sin-a-li's uncle of cheating French soldiers the previous year, having sold them what he claimed was tobacco, which later turned out to be only the leaves of beetroots. The sergeant declares that a person who sells troops bad tobacco can be charged as a poisoner, and he reads aloud authoritatively from a soldier's manual—in French—to bolster his claim. (In truth, however, the lines the sergeant reads just describe how to polish the buttons on one's military uniform.) Should the uncle still harbor any doubts, the sergeant uses the threat of violence to clarify his meaning: "I'll cut off your ears to make you hear better, you miserly prig!" The bluster is enough to scare Sin-a-li's uncle straight: he signs an official statement renouncing all his familial rights over the boy, and hands over all his money to the sergeant in order to compensate for the bad tobacco. The sergeant's final demand is that the uncle must pay for a fine dinner for himself and his French comrades-in-arms. "If you treat us like kings, with lots of good wine," says the sergeant magnanimously, "I will spare you from the gun and a shooting." As sole consolation, the uncle is allowed to keep his donkey.[65]

The specific fate of Sin-a-li's uncle mirrored the fate of China itself, in the aftermath of the Opium Wars: a recalcitrant Chinese population could be forced to give up sovereign rights, pay indemnities and sign legally binding treaties to that effect, all through the threat or use of state violence. The shared aims of French missionary and military might are made manifest when, at the end of the play, a ship from France drops anchor in Shanghai. It arrives bearing 1,000 francs and a box of toys, contributed by French schoolchildren in the name of the Sainte-Enfance, all destined for the orphan boys at Zi-ka-wei; it will depart with the French sergeant and his troops, bringing them back to France.[66] Whereas Sin-a-li's uncle requires the threats of the French military to teach him a civilizing lesson, the Chinese guardians in the other Sainte-Enfance plays are led in the right direction by the gentler influence of French missionaries: thanks to their good intentions and holy works, both the mothers of Sio-tsia and Dahe eventually convert to Christianity. Might not the Chinese masses someday do the same?

BAPTISM ON THE GROUND IN CHINA

The images of countless Chinese children could be celebrated as the potential sites of so much Catholic grace in the pages of the *Annales*, on the face of membership cards or in performances on the stage. The actual fate of abandoned Chinese children on the ground in China, however, was far more sobering. In 1853, Mgr. François-Xavier Danicourt, Vicar Apostolic of Zhejiang Province, sent a letter to Sainte-Enfance officials in Paris, which included a list of children baptized in four different locations in the towns of Ningbo, Jiaxing and Zhoushan, in approximately the past sixteen months.[67] This baptismal list, handwritten neatly in Chinese characters on red tissue paper, contained the names of 316 Chinese children, along with, in most cases, the date and location of baptism and the corresponding date of death.[68] As Mgr. Danicourt had explained in an earlier 1851 letter about baptismal efforts in Ningbo, there were a number of methods of finding Chinese children to baptize. One was to use a small network of Christian families to baptize abandoned children placed in the care of local families by Ningbo's own Chinese foundling home, numbering around 200 on any given day. The manager of the local foundling home happened to be Christian, and she and the handful of other Christian families took care to baptize all infants who died there. Another method was to baptize children through the Catholic foundling home in Ningbo, which had only just been established in 1849. It was much smaller, however, than the Chinese foundling home, and only twenty-six children were cared for there.[69]

Not surprisingly, girls made up the great majority of the baptismal list, as they were more likely to be abandoned, with 270 names, or 85 percent of the list, and boys were in the distinct minority, with 46 names, or 15 percent of the list. Yet what is far more striking than the sex of the children baptized is their eventual fate. Out of all of the 252 children listed whose fate was known and recorded, only a single one was listed as "living" (*wei wang*). Every single one of the others was marked as "dead" (*wang/si*). In Danicourt's accompanying letter, he mentioned that only 5 children of the more than 300 had by that point survived.[70] The median length of life after baptism, moreover, as tabulated from the list, was a mere five days. More than half the children died within one week, and more than three-quarters had died within one month. Only eight children lived more than three months, and none of them lived longer than six months.

The children's genders and their eventual fates are only incidental to the main purpose of the list, however, which was to record the baptism of each child, along with a proper baptismal name. But these names, written entirely in Chinese characters, are very odd and unlike ordinary Chinese names. Their mysterious meaning is deciphered with the help of a list of twenty-eight girls' and boys' French names, appended in French script at the end. All 316 children, girls and boys alike, had been baptized with European Christian names, transliterated syllable by syllable into Chinese characters.[71] "Ma-li-ya," for example, could be deciphered as Marie, "Fang-ji-jia" as Françoise, and "Bao-lu" as Paul. Each baptismal name was then ranked, according to the number of times it had been used: "Marie . . . 62, Catherine . . . 40, Françoise . . . 38, Josephine . . . 26" and so on, down to Brigitte, Gertrude and Elizabeth, with one instance each (Figure 4.9).

The baptizers wasted no energy on creativity when it came to the first names: although there was the occasional Joakim, Thérèse or Susanne, over half the girls were named Marie, Catherine, Françoise or Joséphine, and the three most popular boys' names were Paul, Alexandre and Joseph. Danicourt explained that Chinese Christians who served as baptizers frequently repeated names because they were "afraid of making a mistake in the form by giving [the children] other names that are difficult to pronounce, and to which they are not yet accustomed."[72] There may not have been a specific French godfather or godmother for each child, but it mattered not; they were still the nominal godchildren of a Francophone bevy.

Danicourt did not remark, either, on the inclusion of a Chinese family name for each child: Catherine Gu, Françoise Zhou, Paul Kong. Perhaps these foundlings were given the surnames of the Chinese families who temporarily cared for them, or perhaps they were given the surnames of the

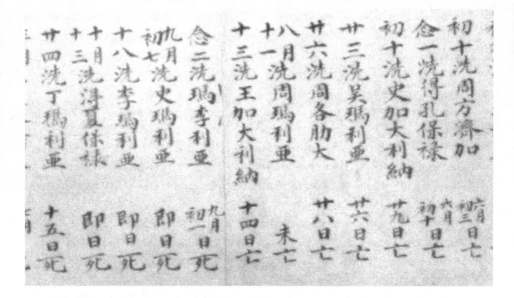

Figure 4.9. Photograph of a portion of a baptismal list from Zhejiang (1853). Each entry begins with the date of baptism, followed by the Chinese family name and a transliterated baptismal name, and ending with the date of death. The last character in each column (*wang/si*) indicates that the child has died. Only the sixth entry from the right, for "Marie Zhou," (*Zhou Ma-li-ya*), baptized on the eleventh day of the eighth month, has not yet died (*weiwang*). Other transliterated baptismal names on this portion of the list include (right to left) Françoise Zhou, Paul Kong, Catherine Shi, Marie Wu, Colette Zhou, Catherine Wang, Marie Li, Marie Shi, another Marie Li, Paul Xia and Marie Ding. Source: Author's photograph of document from the archives of the Pontificium Opus a Sancta Infantia, Rome, Folder L1.

baptizing catechists. Or yet again, perhaps each family name was merely chosen at random, like the baptismal name. Still, unlike the baptismal name, which was given to every child listed even if no other data were recorded, the Chinese family name was optional, like the dates of baptism and death. In one baptismal site with twenty-eight children, no family names were recorded, and in another site, several children in a row were given the common surname Chen.

Why is this list of names of christened Chinese children such a powerful artifact of the nineteenth-century Catholic missions in China? On the one hand, it is one of the few, if only, historical records of abandoned Chinese children by name, as individual existences, rather than as representative symbols, a collective number, or as figures in colorful anecdotes or vividly imaged scenarios. Since each child's soul mattered in this schema, each individual existence was given theological meaning and dignity, however small in measure as a brief entry on the list. But at the same time, the transliterated Francophone names are also an incredibly powerful statement of presumption. It was the French baptismal name alone that incorporated the Chinese child into the larger universe of French Catholicism, placing him or her under the protection of saints and in a relationship with a host of little French godmothers and godfathers. Acceptance into God's grace required a major change of identity.

French Catholic missionaries saw this list as a reason to rejoice, not as a reason for sadness, for the souls of every single one of the 316 children had been saved by the grace of baptism. But this list can be celebrated as an accomplishment only by one believing in the ultimate salvation of baptism. For those more concerned with the earthly lives of children, it is a heart-wrenching testament of failure. To be sure, the missionaries had not caused the deaths of any of the children—they were already at death's door—and did what they could to alleviate their physical suffering. The reality of poverty, disease and a lack of resources meant that nineteenth-century infant mortality rates were sky high, no matter who tried to save these children, Chinese or foreign. Yet the finality of row upon row of deaths is nonetheless sobering, marked by a string of the same Chinese characters indicating death, as neatly as headstones in a cemetery. Underneath each marker of death lies the faintest trace of a real infant life, however brief its existence. But if death was to be the fate of so many abandoned children in China, what would happen to the lucky few who survived, who were saved from infanticide? It was by no means a simple question with a single obvious answer. In Chapter 5, we consider the competition that arose for the care of Chinese children rescued from infanticide.

FIVE

Reframing Female Infanticide

The Emerging Nation

As the first editor of the Zikawei mission's Chinese-language newspaper, *Yiwen lu* (The Record of Beneficial News), the Chinese Jesuit priest Li Wenyu (1840–1911) wrote essays for Chinese audiences each week on various topics explaining Catholic theology and practice, as well as the distinctions between Christian thought and native Chinese heretical religions.[1] In 1886, Li reprinted a collection of his weekly essays from the newspaper, one of which centered upon the topic of female infanticide.[2] As Li had begun his studies at Zikawei as a novice in 1862, was ordained in 1872, and began working as a seminary teacher there in 1875, it is very possible that he had read or even helped with the preparation of Gabriel Palatre's massive study of Chinese infanticide, which was printed there in 1878.[3] Perhaps not surprisingly then, Li's essay shared a number of ideas in common with Palatre's work, including a Catholic disdain for native Chinese religions, as well as an impulse toward the visualization and enumeration of infant corpses. In Li's opinion, Buddhism's "ridiculous theories about reincarnation" made the problem of female infanticide worse, since a family could use it as an excuse to kill a newborn daughter, so that she might return in another life to a wealthier family. Li also envisioned the physical remains of infants as collective measure of death, lamenting that if all the bones of abandoned children were piled together, "even Mount Tai [a sacred Taoist mountain in Shandong Province] could not compare to its height and vastness. Alas!" Finally, Li provided a rough numerical calculation of the number of children killed every year, estimating that if several hundred were drowned in each of China's fifteen hundred counties, then "if we add them up all together, there are almost one million [infants] killed in a year."[4]

Yet unlike Palatre's study or the propaganda of the Sainte-Enfance, Li's essay did not demonize China as the world's worst offender when it came to infanticide. Instead, Li saw China as one country among many that shared the same problem: "The custom of drowning daughters," Li wrote, "did not begin in China. Different parts of Asia, India and other areas within the borders of the three continents of Australia, America, and Africa, all have this evil practice." Even Europe, Li pointed out, had not been immune to the practice of infanticide in its past: "In each of Europe's largest countries, in the times before Jesus, this custom also existed." Since that time, the situation had improved in Europe, to the point where "today they cannot bear to drown even illegitimate children." Li explained that "benevolent societies" in large European cities were able to accept unwanted children anonymously, through cabinets built into their walls. "Those who are afraid of shame put the child into the cabinet, and immediately leave. In this way the child's life is spared and reputations are not harmed. This act can be called a very great good deed [da shan]."[5] Li believed that the Christian faith had been critical in reforming European practices, but his explanation also reminded Chinese readers that Western nations had never been immune to the problem of infanticide.

Li's essay is but one example of the consequences of the co-mingling of Chinese and Western perspectives regarding female infanticide in the latter half of the nineteenth century. These cross-cultural interactions gradually reframed Chinese rationales for prohibiting female infanticide. The intentional killing of an unwanted daughter had been seen as a local custom and an individual sin against morality, liable to incur karmic retribution, but by the dawn of the Republican era in the early twentieth century, it had become a transgression against the nation's population, robbing it of potentially productive female citizens and threatening China's survival on the world stage. How did this shift occur? By and large, the conditions for change grew out of the fertile and contested milieu of China's late nineteenth-century treaty ports, coastal cities with special foreign enclaves where traders and missionaries first resided after the forced opening of China in the aftermath of the Opium War. But the process did not involve passive acceptance of foreign ideas on the part of Chinese living there: men like Li Wenyu, who came into direct contact with Westerners and Western texts, often brought together strands of thinking on female infanticide from both Chinese and Western sources in a variety of unexpected ways.

Some of these interactions were violent rejections of Western missionary interference. The Tianjin Massacre of 1870, for example, resulted in the deaths of twenty foreigners, one Chinese priest and an unknown number of Chinese Christian converts after rumors circulated of missionaries kidnapping and killing Chinese children for occult purposes. Other interactions, such as the cross-cultural cooperation that resulted in late nineteenth-century treaty port newspapers, demonstrated more gradual adaptations of Western secular ideas. Whether confrontational or collaborative, what all of these disparate examples shared was that they grappled with the problem of female infanticide within the context of an emerging national consciousness. If, as so many Western visitors, missionaries and Sinological experts had already asserted, female infanticide was indeed a special problem in China, then it would also require particular *Chinese* solutions. This meant not only a preference for institutional and structural responses to female infanticide enacted by Chinese rather than foreign participants but also the tailoring of foreign ideas to fit existing Chinese social contexts. This chapter will examine the successive stages of this cross-cultural reframing of the problem of female infanticide in China, as it moved from the realm of karmic morality for the individual to the purview of the state in its nascent attempts to control the national population.

ORPHANAGE COMPETITION

Before the late nineteenth century, Chinese foundling homes were the only institutions promoting social welfare for children in China, and their work could be regarded as simply a moral good, a philanthropic force for the betterment of society as a whole. This social landscape changed dramatically after the mid-nineteenth century, when foreign Catholic missionaries defined a Christian duty to save the souls of unwanted heathen children in China and exercised what they considered their God-given right to do so. The care of unwanted children could no longer be seen as just a moral issue, but became a contested political question, as foreign orphanages "competed" with Chinese orphanages for the right to save Chinese children.[6] Chinese and Westerners were not at odds in the fundamental human value of desiring to care for unwanted children; they disagreed on what appropriate solutions to that problem might be. Who should be allowed to care for these children and how should their care be managed? What institutions or organizations should be established to manage it? What were the larger consequences if a child were to be raised in a foreign missionary orphanage as a converted Christian, as opposed to a Chinese orphanage according to native Chinese customs?

One obvious reason for this overt sense of competition was the geographic proximity of Chinese foundling homes and foreign Catholic orphanages. According to her survey of Qing gazetteer records, Angela Leung has shown that the largest number of Chinese foundling homes was located in the Jiangnan region, with almost one-third of the approximately 1,000 foundling homes established during the Qing dynasty situated in the provinces of Jiangsu and Zhejiang.[7] Within Jiangsu there was a further concentration of foundling homes in the prefectures immediately north and south of the Yangtze River, with thirty-seven homes established in the Songjiang prefecture (which at the time included Shanghai), thirty-four in the Yangzhou prefecture and twenty-four in the Suzhou prefecture.[8] Meanwhile, according to Gabriel Palatre's 1878 survey of Catholic missionary orphanages in China, 101 such institutions, maintained by different orders and missionary organizations, had been established since the opening of treaty ports in 1842.[9] The Foreign Mission Society of Paris was responsible for the greatest number of Catholic orphanages in China, with thirty-four in the provinces of Sichuan, Yunnan, Guizhou, Guangdong, Guangxi and Manchuria. But the Jesuits could take pride in the fact that their thirteen orphanages were located in the oldest and most numerically significant Catholic jurisdiction in China—the Jiangnan Vicariate, home to 90,000 Christians in 1878.[10] The largest of the Jesuit orphanages was the one for boys at the Zikawei (a companion institution there for girls was run by the Sisters of the Society of the Helpers of the Holy Souls).

Although Palatre was publicly boastful of Christian charitable efforts in comparison to native Chinese ones, proclaiming that Christianity had "never been defeated in the arena of charity," privately he was not so confident.[11] In an 1874 letter to Sainte-Enfance leaders in Paris from his post in the Qingpu district of the Songjiang prefecture, Palatre lamented the "miserable state" of Catholic attempts to care for abandoned children there, given the numerical and financial superiority of Chinese orphanages. "I daresay that if the mandarins knew exactly how little competition we give them in the Songjiang region," he bemoaned, "they would smile out of pity."[12] Not only did a large native orphanage exist in the town of Songjiang, he explained, each of the seven subprefectures also had a secondary branch. If the resources of any secondary branch were insufficient to care for a child, the child could be transported to the central orphanage. All of these native branches were well funded by the wealthy communities in which they were located. Moreover, the Chinese orphanages collectively owned 3,000 to 4,000 acres of land, the rents on which were used to sustain the children. All of this reflected badly on the Catholic charitable enterprise, which was much smaller—indeed, no actual Catholic orphanages had been built in the prefecture—and funded much less generously.

To make his point even clearer, Palatre drew up a list directly comparing Chinese and Catholic activities in the prefecture. Those bringing an abandoned child to the Chinese orphanage were given a subsidy of 200 to 500 cash, but the missionaries could only offer 80 to 200 cash.[13] Wet-nurses employed outside of the Chinese orphanage were paid 800 cash per month, but the missionaries could only offer 600 cash per month. Heathen wet-nurses were also eligible for bonus stipends during regular inspections, but the missionaries offered nothing. Even Christian convert women were lured to work as wet-nurses for the heathen orphanage over the Catholic orphanage, since the pay was so much better. Each child under the care of the heathen orphanage received a trousseau of ten pieces of cloth, a swaddling blanket, a quilted jacket, two lined or unlined shirts, a quilted blanket for winter and a bamboo cradle, but children supported by the missionaries received no extra material support. Heathen children who died were buried in caskets, but the children supported by missionaries rarely were. Moreover, heathen children and their minders were subject to regular administrative and health checkups by orphanage managers and doctors, but missionaries did nothing of the kind. All in all, the heathen orphanages in Songjiang could take in approximately 1,250 to 1,700 children per year, but the missionaries had managed to take in only 182 children in 1872–73. In Palatre's opinion, the Chinese charity was "perfectly arranged." The missionaries could only dream of doing the same "to save the souls of children, that which the mandarins achieve when they save only their bodies."[14] By each and every one of Palatre's own measures—except for the saving of souls—the native Chinese orphanage system in Songjiang surpassed Catholic efforts.

Chinese provincial officials, however, were no less aware of the acute competition from foreign orphanages for the care of unwanted children. In 1873, Shen Bingcheng (1823–95), circuit intendant of the greater Suzhou area, wrote to his provincial superiors, the Jiangsu provincial governor and the governor-general of the region encompassing Jiangsu, Anhui and Jiangxi, urging them to institute infant protection societies in the areas under their control. The need for enacting this proposed expansion had less to do with humanitarian aims and more to do with meeting the perceived challenge from foreign orphanages. "In the past," wrote Shen, "[establishing ways to save infants] was one of the most important duties of philanthropic work. Today, this is even more [critical] because of the crisis with foreign affairs [*yangwu zhi ji*]." Shen explained, "Recently, foreigners have been setting up many orphanages to take in infants, such that the sons and daughters of China [*Zhonghua*] are abandoned in foreign territory [*yiyu*]. This is not the proper way of doing things."[15] Shen's concern mirrored that of an earlier 1870 memorial from Yang Futai, governor of Zhejiang Province, who wrote, "Chinese people [*huaren*] are poor and cannot raise their children. So the work is entrusted to foreigners [*yangren*] who have built homes to take them in."[16] Both memorials gained even wider audiences after they were reprinted in the *Xinbao*, a Shanghai newspaper, in 1877.[17]

The Qing court attempted to address the competition between native foundling homes and foreign missionary orphanages when it sent a proposed list of regulations regarding the conduct of foreign missionaries in China to the British, French and American foreign ministers in 1871. The first of these eight regulations dealt exclusively with foreign orphanages, outlining an ideal situation where Christian orphanages and Chinese orphanages could coexist. Foreign orphanages, asserted the foreign affairs board of the Qing court, should take in only the children of Chinese Christian converts, and Chinese local officials and gentry should take responsibility for all those children who "are not of the religion. . . . Thus China and foreign countries can each undertake these good works, and avoid points of contention."[18] The difficulty, the board continued, was entirely due to the fact that foreign orphanages did not operate like Chinese ones. Foreign orphanages did not allow birth families or relatives to continue relationships with their children, but instead severed all such ties and shrouded their activities in secrecy. This sort of inappropriate behavior, which did not value familial bonds, rendered foreign orphanages less than desirable in China:

> When we look at the example of China's orphanages, when a child is taken in, its background must be reported to local officials. After it enters the orphanage, its family is allowed to come and visit it. After it grows up, those without children are allowed to adopt it and raise it as a descendant, or its own family is allowed to come to the orphanage to reclaim it. . . . We have heard that when different countries set up orphanages in their own countries, they are managed about the same as those in China. It is only those orphanages established by foreign countries in China that do not ask about the origins of each child it takes in and that are reluctant to report to authorities. After the children arrive at the orphanage, other people are not allowed to adopt them, and their own families are not allowed reclaim them. Their own relatives are not even allowed to see them. How can this not arouse the suspicions of ordinary people?[19]

Because of these differences, the Qing foreign affairs board ultimately concluded that foreigners had no business at all raising Chinese children: "Any Chinese child [*Zhongguo youhai*], whether or not it is of the religion, should be returned to us to be raised. . . . Why should the Westerners mix themselves up in [charitable care], so that these good works give rise to a maze of doubts?"[20] For their parts, the British, American and French foreign ministers all dismissed the board's proposals, and no change in policy regarding foreign missionary conduct was ever enacted.

THE TIANJIN MASSACRE

All of this official concern with foreign competition regarding the care of unwanted Chinese children came as a direct response to the Tianjin Massacre, one of the most notorious late nineteenth-century episodes of violent conflict between native Chinese and foreign missionaries.[21] In the hot summer of 1870, rumors spread in the northern treaty port of Tianjin that Catholic nuns there were paying for kidnapped children to take into their orphanage, with the intention of gouging out their eyes and hearts to make medicines for nefarious purposes. Negotiations between local officials and the French consul failed to defuse the situation. After one heated exchange, the French consul, enraged at what he felt was lack of appropriate responsiveness on the part of Chinese officials, shot at the local magistrate of Tianjin, missed, and instead struck and killed one of the magistrate's servants. The witnessing crowd erupted, moving through the city on a rampage, killing the two French officials, ten nuns and one priest at the orphanage, and seven other foreigners they encountered along the way. Another Chinese priest and as many as thirty to forty native Chinese converts working for the missionaries were also killed, and the orphanage, cathedral and French Consulate, as well as other Protestant chapels, were destroyed. The episode soon turned into a major bone of contention in international diplomacy, bringing China and France to the brink of war. The outbreak of renewed Franco-Prussian aggressions, however, redirected French energies toward its own borders. Ultimately, eighteen Chinese were executed for the murders of the foreign nationals, twenty-five were punished through hard labor and two local officials were exiled to the northern province of Heilongjiang. Reparations of 250,000 taels were paid in compensation to the affected foreign countries, and China sent a diplomatic mission of apology to France the following year.

Most nineteenth-century Western observers at the time of the Tianjin Massacre dismissed the Chinese rumors about malevolent missionary behavior as completely outrageous. British plenipotentiary Thomas Wade asked with exasperation, "If even lettered Chinese can believe such evil of the women whose lives are devoted to the alleviation of suffering, what better opinions can they entertain of any foreigner?" For Wade and many other foreign observers, the crux of the problem lay with cultural misunderstandings on the part of the Chinese: what was required, argued Wade, was the "removal of those false impressions that everywhere possess the native mind." For his part, Wade did not see any problems with the overt religious agenda of the Sisters of Mercy, whose one goal, he wrote, was to bring up "hundreds of helpless infants . . . if they live, as Christians, and to be buried as Christians if they die."[22] Yet even in this simple assertion, Wade had unwittingly reversed the religious priorities of Catholic missionaries in China in this description: as discussed in Chapter 4, the main motivation for Catholic missionaries to gather abandoned Chinese children was first and foremost to redeem the children's immortal souls through baptism. Saving the children's mortal bodies was a secondary concern, only after the first had been secured.

Although the rumors that sparked the Tianjin incident seemed baseless to Western observers, they actually fit into a long-standing pattern in China of occult accusations made against community outsiders. As Barend ter Haar has explained, similar stories of witchcraft with different scapegoats circulated as early as the Tang dynasty, centered upon the idea of a person or demon trying to harness the life force (*qi*) contained in another individual's internal organs or, in some cases, a fetus. The life force of children was particularly desirable because they represented its purest form. By cooking, drying and pounding organs or fetuses into a powder, one could transform these rich sources of life force into pills, elixir or other medicines, so that the evildoer could supposedly attain immortality or so that the stolen life force could be attached to an inanimate object for malevolent purposes.[23] Those accused by mobs of occult activity were often outsiders or marginal figures in a community, such as the itinerant monks, peddlers and beggars described in Philip Kuhn's study of a 1768 sorcery scare, who were accused of clipping off the ends of queues to steal souls.[24] The fact that foreign missionaries required their own institutions to care for unwanted children, when Chinese institutions already did this same charity work, only raised suspicions that the missionaries harbored ulterior motives. One group of anonymous villagers outside Shanghai in 1863 voiced their doubts this way: "When we take in infants, we take in those who have just been born and feed them. In their orphanages, they buy boys and girls who are more than ten years old. You think about it: is this taking care of infants, or are they using them for some kind of witchcraft?"[25]

What is so striking in this entire episode of the Tianjin Massacre is that allegations of infanticide lay at the heart of both Chinese and Western reactions. The widespread impression of China as the land of infanticide had not only helped propel Catholic missionaries to do their utmost to save heathen children from an eternity in limbo, it also gave their baptismal work material and financial support in the form of contributions from Catholic children all over the world. But Chinese communities forced to encounter foreign missionaries and their baptismal efforts felt it necessary to account for this strange behavior by framing it in more familiar terms of kidnapping and killing children for occult practices. Regardless of the actual practice of infanticide in China, the *perception* of infanticide was an extraordinary motivating force in both directions. A newborn baby girl may have been the smallest, weakest and least significant member of nineteenth-century Chinese society, but the very idea of her innocence and helplessness was powerful enough to draw the adults surrounding her into violent confrontations, even edging nations to the brink of war.

Recognizing the nature of Chinese accusations against Catholic missionaries may help account for the physical brutality of the violence directed against the nuns in Tianjin, so shocking to contemporary Western observers of the time. One news story printed in Hong Kong spared no detail of their bodily injuries: "Their clothes are said to have been torn off them, their bodies stabbed and ripped open, their breasts cut off, and their eyes dug out."[26] An account included in another diplomatic report, supposedly related by a Chinese eyewitness to an English merchant, described the killing of the women in even more gruesome detail. The Mother Superior was dragged outside, while the other sisters were made to watch: "Her eyes were first scooped out, her breasts cut off, spears sufficient to bear the weight of the Body were run up the body from between her legs, she was then held up, & allowed to wriggle about on the spears for some time. then [sic] taken down, ripped up, her heart & liver cut out, & cut in small pieces, and distributed amongst the crowd, the body was then cut in pieces & thrown into the burning premises."[27]

Consider, once again, that the Sisters of Mercy were accused of kidnapping children in order to gouge out their eyes and hearts to make medicines. In the universe of Chinese morality books, punishments for women guilty of infanticide in the afterlife were inscribed directly on their bodies. They were tormented in the same ways that they had injured unborn children, or at the very site of sexual reproduction. Midwives had their hands and feet cut off or their tongues sliced out; mothers suffered from putrefying breasts, or severe birth pains in the womb. Although crudely rendered, the gruesome deaths of the Sisters of Mercy created real-life versions of these punishment tableaus from morality books, drawn in real blood. If a Chinese mob was truly convinced that these nuns had committed infanticide by gouging out the eyes and hearts of children, then these terrible bodily disfigurements may have seemed fitting and just. Instead of being delivered by gods and demons of the underworld, however, here the punishments were meted out by the collective judgment of an enraged mob. In other words, the same logic that had motivated the Sisters of Mercy to come to China in the first place, that of saving Chinese children from infanticide, had now perversely come back to torture them, in mutated form.

MIXING OLD AND NEW

The Tianjin Massacre represents one of the first historical moments when the problem of unwanted Chinese children was articulated as one requiring

a particular *Chinese* solution. Although it was one of the most explosive incidents of its kind, other more subtle, but no less significant, shifts in Chinese
perceptions of female infanticide also occurred during the late nineteenth
century. The same treaty ports that had served as points of entry for foreign
missionaries into the Chinese interior, leading to conflicts such as the Tianjin Massacre, also represented sites of cross-cultural collaboration and ex-
perimentation. Chinese texts produced in these hybrid spaces drew upon a
wide range of both familiar and unfamiliar ideas about female infanticide.
Nineteenth-century Western secular concepts, including ideas about scientific objectivity, anatomical concepts of human reproduction and equality
between the sexes, found a much broader audience than did Catholic theological ideas about baptism, primarily because they could be easily adapted to
fit an already existing Chinese social fabric.

One of the best places to see traces of this gradual transformation of late
nineteenth-century Chinese attitudes toward female infanticide is in the
pages of the first Chinese-language daily newspaper, the *Shenbao*. The *Shenbao* was established in Shanghai in 1872 by an English businessman, Ernest
Major. By the 1890s, it could claim the largest readership of all treaty port
newspapers, with a circulation of 15,000.[28] The existence of a separate, independent press in China was made possible in the late nineteenth century
through the extraterritorial status of the foreign concessions in treaty ports.
Prior to that moment, printed broadsheets, known as court gazettes, had
essentially served as organs of the government, reprinting imperial decrees,
edicts and memorials to the throne. Barbara Mittler has shown that early
Chinese newspapers such as the *Shenbao* won over new readers "not by insisting on being foreign and new but being old and Chinese."[29] In other
words, familiar Chinese expressive forms were gradually transformed into
constituent components more closely resembling what Western readers
would recognize as a daily newspaper, in a process that stretched well into
the twentieth century. Attitudes toward female infanticide printed in the
Shenbao mixed together old and new, Chinese and foreign interpretations.

In the first decade of the *Shenbao*'s existence, for example, the problem
of female infanticide was still articulated within a system of karmic rewards
and punishments, which had permeated the morality book genre of earlier
centuries. As in the past, the good were rewarded for their efforts in saving
unwanted daughters, and the bad were punished for committing infanticide. Mothers were still often blamed as the greatest villains, drowning their
daughters immediately after birth. Yet neither were these newspaper stories

exact replicas of past morality tales. The particular, odd details of these news stories—often related as gossip from a passing friend—now eschewed the more overtly didactic flavor of morality books in favor of the eerie, supernatural and sometimes titillating quality of the "literature of the strange."[30] Although these news stories still discussed the consequences of karmic retribution, they now focused exclusively on the people and events of this material world, remaining silent on the participation of gods and boddhisattvas, such as Guanyin, Wenchang or Yama. The difference is slight, yet discernible.

These elements are exemplified by an article on a case of female infanticide from an 1874 issue of *Shenbao*, related as a story told by a passing friend from Yunnan Province. A woman from Lou County, named Liu, gives birth to a daughter in 1870. Before a month passes, the infant goes blind, angering the mother so much that she decides to stop feeding the child, who eventually starves and dies. The following year, Liu gives birth to another daughter, whose hands are shaped "like pig's feet." Liu kills her second daughter by drowning it. Up to this point, the story echoes other morality tales, placing the blame for the decision to commit infanticide squarely on the mother. But then the *Shenbao* story takes an eerie turn, describing a supernatural episode quite unlike those found in earlier morality tales. The woman Liu gives birth a third time—this time to a "ball of flesh, as big as two fists." The flesh ball is covered with many tiny holes, which spin and swirl in nonstop motion. Bystanders want to throw it away, believing it to be a monstrous object, but before anything can be done, the spinning flesh ball leaps up and strikes the woman Liu dead. "Amidst the confusion, no one knew what happened to the ball. The next day they found it under the bed, but it had shrunk to the size of a chicken egg. Its color was very red. Some thought it a pill for a miracle cure and tried to cut it open, but it was so hard it could not be cut. When they threw it on to the ground, it made a clear, ringing sound." Eventually the hard flesh ball is buried together with the woman, and the narrator concludes that karmic retribution is to blame: "This must have been the vengeful spirits of the two daughters joined together [to make a flesh ball]. Otherwise how could it have struck the woman, causing her to shake with fear and die?"[31]

Over the course of the *Shenbao*'s development in the late nineteenth and early twentieth centuries, traditional tales of moral retribution gradually came to be categorized as "entertainments" rather than "serious" news, signaling a corresponding change in attitude that paid more attention to "objectivity and factuality" in news stories.[32] The specific details of each story began to break out of the narrow strictures of the morality book genre, as husbands, not wives alone, now took the blame for committing infanticide. Several authors also demonstrated growing impatience with the very concept of karmic retribution. Most prominently, authors described eyewitness accounts of physical brutality as examples of one-of-a-kind news stories, not generic, universal fables of didactic intent. The karmic fate of these parental perpetrators, in other words, was not as noteworthy as the acts of physical brutality of which they had been guilty. In a news story from 1876, for example, an anonymous author is surprised to hear of a case of female infanticide among "men occupying dignified, official positions in the provincial capital," since, he says, the "low custom of drowning daughters" is normally "found in impoverished and remote regions among poor women." A father in Nanjing, a military officer, stabs his newborn daughter to death with a sword in a fit of pique. His shocked wife dies of a hemorrhage; months later the man too dies from uncontrollable bleeding. Bystanders believe that the wife and daughter had "come to take his life in revenge," but the anonymous author dismisses this as "ridiculous and absurd talk."[33]

Another article from an 1878 issue of *Shenbao* takes an even more decisive step in the direction of factuality, presenting a story about infanticide narrated by an actual eyewitness. It is fixed firmly in time and space, down to the hour of the specific day and the single street of a verifiable business establishment in Ningbo: "On the eighth day of this month, between three and five o'clock in the afternoon, a traveler was seeing off his friend who was taking a boat from the northern bank of the Ningbo River. On the way back, he passed Xingsheng Street. In the empty space right across the street from the Tongshun Shipping Company, he heard that people were burning a baby girl." The unnamed traveler sees several hundred onlookers surrounding the pyre, and presses closer to catch a glimpse of what exactly was going on: "In the midst of all the smoke at first he heard the sound of crying, but as it continued, he heard only small whimpers. In a short while, the child's skin and bones had burnt to a crisp, like a meat pancake. A stone was tied to the remains, in order to throw them into the river." Asking the bystanders for more details, the traveler discovers that the girl was the daughter of a blacksmith on the street, whose wife had given birth to daughters three times in a row. The first two daughters had already died, and the family had determined that this one too should not survive. They had purposely used wood to burn her, "so that her soul would learn to be afraid and not return again as another fetus." The traveler is extremely upset and indignant at what he has seen.[34]

With each precise detail—the time of day, the name and location of the street, the name of the shipping company—the article builds up the event's factuality in the material world, so that this particular act of infanticide is presented as a unique case—a piece of recent news—instead of as universal morality tale. Moreover, in this eyewitness report, particular attention was paid to the status of the infant's body, "burnt to a crisp, like a meat pancake." Traditional tales had rarely described infant bodies in anything except generic terms, giving more attention to imbuing their voices with persuasive or pleading qualities. Finally, instead of an otherworldly karmic retribution for the parents, the story ends with an accusation for earthly officials: "Xingsheng Street can be found in the eight districts of the eastern part of Ningbo, and its local constable is named Mao Shanbao. How could he not have heard about this with his own ears or seen it with his own eyes? . . . Otherwise why wouldn't he say a word to stop this evil practice?"[35] The entire story does not hover in the distant past or in a distant village, with a beginning, middle and end already resolved; it is connected to a real time and place, and suggests an as-yet-unwritten outcome. Since the article implies that the local constable be held responsible, the possibility arises of changing the ending of the story in this world, not fixating on retribution in the next.

INTERPRETING THE FOREIGN

A shift toward factuality in reporting was not the only discernible change in the articles on female infanticide that appeared in pages of the late nineteenth-century *Shenbao*. Another impulse was to reconfigure ideas and illustrative examples drawn directly from Western sources. The author of one essay on female infanticide in another 1878 issue of *Shenbao*, for example, offered his own original explanation for how male and female fetuses came into being. It was ridiculous for the husband or parents-in-law to blame the mother for the birth of several daughters in a row, he wrote, because she exercised little control over whether the child would be a son or daughter. This was determined instead by the functions of a woman's reproductive anatomy, which expressed the forces of yin and yang in biological fashion. "After a girl becomes an adult," the *Shenbao* author explained, "under the sac enclosing her heart, there is an object like a ball, just like a chicken egg, with a cluster of grains hanging down from it, arranged by size. This determines the order of birth." This hanging cluster "splits into two parts, right and left, which determine [whether the child will be] male or female." The grains enclosed in the ball "descend from the left and the right, alternating." Because yang dominated the left side and yin dominated the right, "if [the grain] on the left side arrives first, a male is conceived, if [the grain] on the right side arrives first, a female is conceived."[36]

These detailed descriptions of female reproductive anatomy and function were not the random fancies of the anonymous *Shenbao* author, but drew upon a new medical textbook from the English doctor and medical missionary Benjamin Hobson (1816–73). Hobson spent almost twenty years in China, from 1839 to 1859, working for the London Missionary Society in Macao, Hong Kong, Canton and later Shanghai. His main contribution to the field of medicine in China, in addition to serving as a doctor, was his collaboration on a number of pioneering medical textbooks in Chinese, designed to introduce the basic concepts of Western medicine to a Chinese audience. The anonymous *Shenbao* author almost certainly drew his anatomical ideas from Hobson's 1858 Chinese textbook, *Fu ying xinshuo* (New Teachings [on the Medical Care of] Women and Infants).[37] In it, Hobson describes in detail the physical appearance of the female reproductive organs, as well as their functions during conception.

Hobson's Chinese text outlined the structures of the uterus, fallopian tubes and ovaries. One end of each fallopian tube was connected to the right and left sides of the uterus, and the other ends were "somewhat wider, spread out like silk threads, hanging down" next to the "sinewy sac" of the ovary. The eggs inside the ovary were described as "bubbles," which could be as large as a "mung bean" or as small as the "spawn of a fish." Each egg contained "essential fluid," which Hobson's text translated as "essence of *yin* [*yinjing*], also called 'essence pearls' [*jingzhu*]." A woman might have anywhere from fewer than ten to more than twenty pearls, with the average being around "fifteen to eighteen." The number of pearls determined the number of children a woman could have in her lifetime, as conception occurred when "the essence pearl bursts open," entering into the fallopian tube and "meeting with the male essence to become a germinating seed." Within his explanation of gynecological organs and functions, Hobson also noted why older women could no longer bear children: "If the essence pearls have not yet burst out in an older woman, they will slowly dry out, until the monthly flow ends, and then the essence pearls are no more."[38]

There is little question that the *Shenbao* author must have encountered Hobson's text, either directly or indirectly, given the many corresponding details and terms used in their descriptions. Like Hobson, the *Shenbao* author explained that a woman had a finite number of chances to give birth, with enough grains for "two times nine, or eighteen, children." Some women might get pregnant with no child resulting, he added, but this was due to "either weak *qixue* [female essence] or the grains having dried up." But the *Shenbao* author also went a step beyond Hobson's text, explaining that any difficulties with conceiving a son, such as giving birth to several daughters in a row, could be attributed to a blockage of *qixue* on the left, or male, side, which prevented those grains from descending. Those who had given birth only to daughters need not despair, as they "must also be able to give birth to males; they just need to nurture their *qixue* to let it circulate fully, so that [the grains] alternate their descent on the right and the left, and they will achieve their goal."[39]

The fascinating aspect of the *Shenbao* essay is not its anatomical or functional inaccuracies, or its infidelity to Hobson's text, but the way in which it implicitly points out the inadequacy of Hobson's biomedical description of human reproduction. Hobson may have been explicit in his precise anatomical descriptions of a woman's reproductive organs and their functions, but his text was entirely silent on the single topic that would have most interested expectant nineteenth-century Chinese parents. Of all of these anatomical parts and functions, which ones accounted for the differentiation of male and female fetuses? How, in other words, could one ensure the birth of a son? A biomedical understanding of the human body was not particularly helpful if it could not even answer this most basic desire. The *Shenbao* author's "translation" of Hobson's anatomical ideas thus filled in the necessary gaps, pasting nineteenth-century Western anatomical explanations into a familiar Chinese medical cosmology that responded to the immediate reproductive demands of a general Chinese audience.

In other words, in these cross-cultural encounters between late nineteenth-century Chinese writers and Western texts, influence did not imply deference. Chinese writers did not take on Western impressions or explanations regarding female infanticide whole cloth, but on the contrary tailored them to fit existing Chinese social fabrics. Nor did Western countries provide only enlightened representations of science and social change; one could also find there plenty of examples of negative models. This idea had been proposed long before by William Milne (1815–63), a British Protestant missionary who spent almost fourteen years in China and wrote a book about his experience in 1857. Milne conjectured that if a Chinese reader of English "were to peruse our daily journals for a month, and to note down the various cases that come up at the London police-courts of infant-exposure or infanticide," he would likely then "announce to his countrymen that the women of England and the fathers were a set of the most heartless wretches under the sun, for they were murdering their infants, male and female, right and left."[40]

One *Shenbao* article from 1879 did exactly what Milne had envisioned, describing a case of infanticide that had recently been discovered in England. The article began with a conscious recognition of China's reputation of infanticide among Westerners: "China has the issue of abandoning children and drowning daughters" and "all Westerners believe this to be hateful."[41] Yet the very same problem, in a slightly different guise, had also been found that year in England! The Chinese author was referring the Tranmere baby farming case in Liverpool, in which a married couple, John and Catharine Barnes, were prosecuted for neglecting to provide three infants in their care with sufficient food, endangering their lives. Baby farmers were notorious for taking in other people's children (often those of poor or unmarried mothers) for a small fee, and then keeping this profit while grievously neglecting the children in their care, often to the point of death.[42] During the Tranmere investigation, it emerged that the Barneses had been given the care of thirty to forty children over the course of many years, but none of their whereabouts could be traced, except for the three infants who had been initially rescued. These babies, according to reports in the *Liverpool Mercury*, were "all . . . in a shocking condition, caused by wilful neglect," "without proper clothing, their bodies being wrapped in bits of rag" and "exceedingly emaciated."[43] The basic facts of the Tranmere case were sketched out in the *Shenbao* article:

> For the past twelve years, in the area of "Li-wu-po," [Liverpool] Mr. "Luo-en" [Barnes] and his wife have adopted other people's illegitimate children. Every year they have adopted anywhere from nine to twelve children. The couple claimed they were firm believers in Jesus Christ. In the newspapers, they placed false advertisements, pretending that they had no children and wanting to find a son to adopt. Thus many people with an illegitimate child sent it over to them, or they gave the couple one hundred taels of silver, thinking that this was the fee for caring for their child. But all of those countless children they took in every year have disappeared without a trace

today. When asked about it, they said that the children had gotten sick and died. But how could all [the children] happen to have died in this way? It was simply that those who had given birth illegitimately cared only about their reputations, so no one filed a suit against them. Thus [the Barneses] were able to evade trouble, with no consequences. But I am afraid that the punishment from Heaven is difficult to escape.[44]

Once again, some of the particular details of the Tranmere case were emphasized to correspond with Chinese understandings. According to the *Shenbao* author, the Barneses had been able to find children to "adopt" in the first place only because they had claimed in their false advertisement that they had no children and wanted to find a son to adopt. This led other parents to pity them and hand children over to their care. Evading punishment had been easy for the Barneses, since these same birth parents were ashamed and wanted to hide their illegitimate births. Only karmic punishments, the article implied, would see justice done—no mention was made of the fact that in England, the Barneses had actually already been put on trial. What was perhaps most interesting was the implication in the Chinese article that the Barneses had wanted to adopt a son, specifically. In fact, the three surviving infants found at the Barneses' house—named Mabel, Alice and Florence—had all been girls.[45] Perhaps this incidental detail would have been most baffling of all to a nineteenth-century Chinese reader: why would anyone pay another person to starve a daughter to death over the course of many weeks or even months, when she could be dispatched at no cost immediately at birth, with a bucket of cold water?

FEMALE INFANTICIDE AS A WOMEN'S ISSUE

By the end of the nineteenth century, hybrid approaches to the problem of female infanticide, borne out of the context of treaty port encounters, gave way to more emphatic voices favoring far-reaching political and social reforms, particularly with regard to women. By and large these turn-of-the-century reform efforts related to women focused on two major issues, promoting education and ending the practice of footbinding.[46] Bringing an end to female infanticide was discussed in the pages of the *Shenbao* as a logical extension of achieving these two larger goals. The connection between women's education and footbinding had most famously been articulated in 1897, in an essay by the late Qing reformer Liang Qichao (1873–1929), who wrote that the only way to strengthen the country was to educate women, and the only way that women would be free to leave their homes for an education was to end the practice of footbinding. Copying the argument laid out in Liang Qichao's earlier essay, the author of a letter to the editor of the *Shenbao* in 1901 wrote that without education and with bound feet, women could "neither work with their brains, nor work with their bodies." If, he added, women's education was promoted and footbinding outlawed, then the 200 million women of China could be made intellectually and economically productive, and the harmful custom of female infanticide would decline naturally as a result, since parents would now recognize that their daughters were "useful" (*youyong*).[47]

Although the decision to drown a daughter at birth may have preceded all other considerations in the course of time, reformers saw the problem as the *result* of the social status of women, not one of its preconditions. As one author asserted in the *Shenbao* in 1907, "female infanticide is due to the various evil customs of footbinding, owning serving maids, abusing child brides, and heavy dowries."[48] This logic meant that addressing the problem of female infanticide emerged only as a secondary consequence of tackling other women's issues, particularly that of maximizing their economic productivity and intellectual potential. Indeed, it may have been that reformers subordinated the problem of female infanticide to focus on other women's issues because in comparison to the long-suffering lives of grown women, the suffering of an unwanted newborn girl would be mercifully brief. Ironically, this meant that although much more attention was being paid to women's issues overall in the early twentieth century, there may have been less of a focus on eradicating female infanticide as a particular social problem, at least when compared to the nineteenth century. In this sense, ending the practice of footbinding was emblematic as a new women's issue, since its visible rise to prominence at the end of the nineteenth century came at the expense of the older moral concern of prohibiting female infanticide. Unlike female infanticide, footbinding had never even been considered a negative social phenomenon for most of the preceding centuries.[49]

Although late nineteenth-century interactions with foreigners gave rise to some initial articulations of a proto-nationalist consciousness, such as the Tianjin Massacre, the major upheavals of the early twentieth century brought the question of China's fate as an emerging nation to the front and center of political discourse. The abolition of the traditional civil examination system in 1905, which had existed almost uninterrupted since the early seventh century, was followed by the even more unthinkable fall of the Qing dynasty in 1911. Its demise marked not only the end of the ruling dynasty, but the end of the entire dynastic system of succession, which had been in place for more than 2,000 years. Dynastic Qing rule was followed by the turbulent rise of factional warlord interests. The cultural and social ferment of these decades heightened after May 4, 1919, when Chinese students protested the terms of the Treaty of Versailles, which had ended World War I. Chinese young people felt betrayed by the earlier promises of Woodrow Wilson, who had advocated self-determination for colonial possessions, when German-occupied territories on the Chinese mainland were turned over to Japan, rather than reverting to Chinese control.

The woman question was a key feature in this iconoclastic May Fourth period, as reformers struggled to determine new social norms for the nation. During this moment of open intellectual and social ferment, expressions of the desire to free women from the shackles of Confucian family values grew more critical and vehement. The traditional family system was blamed for the prevalence of female infanticide. The family bonds that tied together daughters and parents, husbands and wives, and mothers and sons were no longer offered as an essential reason to love and cherish a newborn daughter, as Gui Zhongfu had advocated back in the eighteenth century. Instead, the family dynamic was precisely what had placed women in debased positions relative to men in the first place, and female infanticide was but one of many depraved customs to grow out of this unhealthy soil. This, at least, was the logic of the pseudonymous "Drunken Fool," who argued in a *Shenbao* article from 1922 that reforming the country had to begin with reforming the family. One urgently needed change was to enshrine "equality between men and women" (*nannü pingdeng*) within Chinese families:

> Men and women alike belong to the country's citizens. Both are constructed from the father's essence and the mother's blood. Originally there was no justification for bias, but for the past several thousand years in our country, men have been respected, while women have been debased, to the point where this is regarded as perfectly natural. Now even though the influence of Europe, where there is widespread support for the idea of equality between men and women, has been spreading to the East, if we take a closer look at the reality [in China], there is still a long way to go. In the interior hinterlands, the attitudes are even more closed-minded, and they all commonly drown their daughters, mistreat them, or take in child brides and the like. As for other matters, they still stick to old, indestructible ways.[50]

The notion of equality between men and women cited in the article, which had wafted in on the winds of European influence, was an entirely new rationale for not killing daughters. Nearly two centuries earlier, Gui Zhongfu had also asserted that boy and girl children were "all the same flesh and blood," but he had never insisted on gender equality. For Gui, gender difference, as expressed in distinctive male and female roles, was one of the fundamental building blocks of Confucian ideology, separating the inner (female) sphere from the outer (male) sphere. In this new twentieth-century world, the *Shenbao* author argued, the reason for refraining from infanticide moved beyond the family. Not only would male and female equality strengthen and "enrich families," it would also more significantly "benefit the nation and society," as both men and women could be considered useful citizens.[51]

Limited programmatic attempts were made by different Republican-era governments to prohibit female infanticide and implement social reforms to uplift women's status. Yan Xishan (1883–1960), the warlord who held de facto control of Shanxi Province from the end of the Qing dynasty in 1911 to the establishment of the People's Republic of China in 1949, was nicknamed the "model governor" for his attempts to enact an ambitious program of civil and social education across the province.[52] Yan's program of reform, which included prohibitions against footbinding, early marriage, opium smoking, gambling, excessive dowries and female infanticide, among other issues, looked much like Yu Zhi's earlier moral causes, with one major distinction: whereas Yu Zhi was preoccupied only with reforming local customs, Yan had a very explicit desire to align these "civilized" social customs with an emerging national consciousness. Yan articulated these aims as a self-conscious desire to "make people into good citizens" (*zuo hao guomin*), which meant that educating Shanxi's citizens about the harm of female infanticide was part of the same project as inculcating the values of patriotism and respect for authority. Proper civil behavior was no longer limited to a long list of Confucian dos and don'ts, but now included familiarity with globally relevant topics, such as race, treaties, lessons from the European war and pointers in how to treat foreigners.[53]

Other provincial governments under the control of the Nationalist Party issued similar statements against the practice of drowning daughters, again framing the problem as one related to women's social status. The Zhejiang Nationalist Party committee issued a ten-point proposal in 1927 regarding the status of women, in an attempt to ensure that "women and men have the same rights and privileges" in the law, government, economy, education and society. Women were to be ensured the right to two months of maternity leave, property inheritance, and freedom of choice in marriage and divorce, and new schools of continuing education for adult women were to be established. Practices that were seen as harming women, such as footbinding, concubinage, child brides, prostitution and other forms of trafficking, were to be prohibited. Among these numerous other goals, banning female infanticide fell to the last point on the list.[54] Other party and government entities, such as the Zhejiang Province Department of Civil Affairs, the Nationalist Party's Ministry of the Interior, the Shanghai County government and the Guangzhou municipal government, all followed suit by issuing similar decrees to protect women's rights, again including a prohibition against female infanticide as but one among many women's issues in need of reform.[55]

FEMALE INFANTICIDE AS A POPULATION ISSUE

If one major theme in the social context of Republican China was the categorization of female infanticide as one among many of the obstacles facing women, then the second marked shift was the articulation of female infanticide as part and parcel of a national population problem. This perspective was deeply influenced by the writings of Sun Yat-sen (1866–1925), revolutionary and political forefather of modern China, who set forth his basic concerns about China's population in his 1924 lectures on the *Sanmin zhuyi* (Three Principles of the People). Enamored of the combative idea of distinct human races, Sun believed that one of the most basic measures of the strength and viability of any particular nation was the continued growth of its population. Within the past century, Sun tabulated, each of the other great world powers had dramatically increased its national population. The population of the United States, for example, had shown the greatest increase, growing from 9 million to over 100 million, or 1,000 percent. But the populations of Russia, England, Japan had also all increased, anywhere from 300 to 400 percent. Even Germany's population had increased, in spite of the deprivations of the World War I, growing by 250 percent.[56]

On the other hand, continued Sun, China's population had remained stagnant for the past two centuries. It had already reached the 400 million mark in the eighteenth century, and a recent estimate by the American foreign minister William Woodville Rockhill even suggested that China's population was now no more than 300 million. Sun even projected that if current growth rates continued, in another century the United States would have a population of over 1 billion, surpassing China's current population by two and a half times. This would allow Americans to "subjugate" China and the Chinese would be "absorbed." Thus Sun warned that if China did not take care to increase its population relative to other nations, then "China will not only lose her sovereignty, but she will perish, the Chinese people will be assimilated, and the race will disappear."[57] Though perhaps difficult to imagine today, the early twentieth-century threat of America's population growth relative to China's was very real for Sun and his contemporaries.

In order for China to survive in the Darwinian contest of nations, then, it was critical that its population hold its own against competing countries. It was no longer possible, in other words, to think of the problem of infanticide in China on a local scale alone. Sun's reasoning may have been demographically spurious, but its implications were obvious: bodies were bodies, and even small infant female bodies could boost the total population, and by extension, the strength of the Chinese people. Several contemporary media reports made this logic clear in discussions of the larger social impact of female infanticide. One 1929 article in the Shanghai newspaper *Shibao* (Times) summarized Sun's reasoning, explaining his warnings about the "constriction of population" that threatened China's existence. One major reason that the "evil practice of drowning daughters should be prohibited and reformed," it concluded, was for the sake of the "nation's people [*minzu*]," since female infanticide reduced the total number of an already imperiled population.[58] The same article described the findings of the Zhejiang provincial assembly with regard to the problem, based upon the results of a census commissioned by the newly consolidated Nationalist government in Nanjing in 1928.[59] The Zhejiang census had counted 11,603,889 men and 9,028,812 women, meaning that there were 2,575,077 fewer women than men. Put another way, "men outnumbered women by 8 percent." The "evil custom of drowning daughters" was particularly to blame for this gender imbalance.[60] Another related article, printed in a 1930 issue of the *Shenbao*, tried to enumerate the extent of the province's shortage of women even more precisely, reporting on the sex ratio in each one of Zhejiang's seventy-five counties.[61]

By the 1920s, the strategy for dealing with the problem of infanticide in China was no longer a matter of convincing individuals to change their moral behavior, one family at a time, as Yu Zhi had once envisioned. Instead, concerns centered on affecting the sexual and reproductive behavior of the national population as a whole, through the scientific means of birth control. Although Sun Yat-sen had advocated population growth as a sign of national strength and health, other Republican-era reformers took the opposite position, arguing that China's excessive birth rate resulted in too many poor people lacking the basic means of subsistence, leading to female infanticide and other social ills. Chen Changheng (1888–1987) was the foremost of China's early demographic pioneers, having studied at Harvard University and earned a master's degree there in economics in 1917. He soon returned to China and set out the basic tenets of a new, scientific approach to population management in his first book, *Zhongguo renkou lun* (On China's Population), published in 1918 and reprinted numerous times in subsequent years.[62] Another reformer, Chen Dongyuan (1902–1978), wrote the first modern history of Chinese women, *Zhongguo funü shenghuo shi* (The History of Women's Lives in China) (1928), which detailed the collective trials and tribulations of Chinese women, dynasty by dynasty.[63]

Both men advocated use of birth control, but took different stances on whether to rely solely on "natural" methods, or whether other forms of contraception should be encouraged. Chen Changheng, the demographer and economist, was directly inspired by the writings of Thomas Malthus, the late eighteenth-century English curate whose *Essay on the Principle of Population* (1798) had advocated sexual abstinence and delayed marriage as moral checks on population growth. Chen's program of reform for China's population also focused on delaying marriage and childbirth. With regard to controlling birth within marriage, Chen briefly mentioned two other methods, timing sexual intercourse during the "safe period" of the latter half of a woman's menstrual cycle, or adhering to "restrained relations" on the part of the man, which meant refraining from ejaculation at the climax of sexual intercourse. Since these methods cost nothing, Chen believed they were appropriate for "rich and poor, clever and foolish alike." Birth control for Chen Changheng, in other words, ultimately translated into male self-control.[64]

In constrast, Chen Dongyuan, author of the first modern Chinese history of women, whole-heartedly advocated the use of artificial contraception. He was inspired by the lectures and writings of Margaret Sanger, the American pioneer of sex education and birth control, who had come to China in 1922 on a three-week lecture tour, speaking to audiences in both

Beijing and Shanghai. In her speech to students at Peking University, Sanger was very explicit in describing how to use different forms of contraception, including condoms, but she primarily advocated use of a diaphragm or a vaginal sponge soaked in a simple spermicidal solution of vinegar and water.[65] Unlike Chen Changheng, who was in favor of methods of birth control that relied primarily on the self-control of men, Chen Dongyuan shared Sanger's desire to place the initiative for birth control in the hands of women, suggesting that birth control methods could even possibly be a part of a new curriculum for women's education: "It seems that women with any education should all consider it a disgrace if they do not know anything about controlling birth!"[66]

What was most impressive about Sanger's speech, though, as Chen Dongyuan noted, was that she had single-handedly broken the taboo that had surrounded public discussions of sex. He vividly recalled how her message was heard, read and discussed with enthusiasm by Chinese audiences:

> The audience of the talk at the time squeezed in to listen, and after the talk was published, it made an even greater stir. There were those who felt it was very timely and prescient, and there were those who felt they were very strange words. But certainly she counts as the first person to shatter the mysterious atmosphere surrounding "sex" that has existed everywhere in Chinese society! In the past, when ever has anyone in China taken "sexual intercourse" as the topic of a public lecture in a front of a huge crowd? Apart from sowing the seeds of birth control, in this speech Sanger also initiated a proper attitude, allowing Chinese people to understand that the matter of "sex" is worth discussing, even in terms of scientific methods![67]

Science and sex, in other words, went hand in hand for Chen Dongyuan and like-minded urban elites. In this regard, Chen emphasized that "scientific methods of birth control are urgently needed in China," in order to prevent the widespread female infanticide and abortion.

This potent combination of science and sex in the form of birth control reached its most heightened expression in the idea of eugenics, which was championed by many international population control advocates of the time and was likewise discussed in China.[68] Chen Changheng, the economist and demographer, coauthored a book on Darwinism, evolution and eugenics, entitled *Jinhua lun yu shanzhong xue* (Evolution and Eugenics) (1923). His coauthor Zhou Jianren (1888–1984), a biologist and translator, explained that eugenics was the study of "how to improve the human race" by employing "methods of selecting breeds to maintain the good, in order to aid the reproduction of society's superior elements," while using "peaceful methods to eliminate the 'seedlings' of inferior elements," such as those with hereditary or other diseases, those of low intellectual abilities or criminals.[69] Such eugenic principles have been largely discredited since the end of WWII, but in the 1920s they still appealed to population control advocates as an obvious corollary to improve not only the quantity but also the quality of a given population.

Although eugenics eventually came to be known in Chinese as "the study of superior births" (youshengxue), in the early twentieth century several alternative Chinese terms still circulated.[70] In the title of their work, Chen and Zhou used a Chinese phrase, shanzhong xue, that literally meant "race improvement studies." This alternative neologism for eugenics succinctly marks the modern transformation of rhetoric surrounding the practice of female infanticide in China. The very same Chinese character, shan, which had in the previous century been included as part of terms connoting the positive improvement of public moral virtues and institutions—shanshu (morality book), shanren (benevolent person), shanju (moral play)—was now in the twentieth century being applied to the brave new context of shanzhong, or improving the biological health of the human race. As Zhou Jianren explained, his use of the term shanzhong xue was deliberate: "'Race improvement studies' [shanzhong xue] is a translation of the term 'Eugenics.' It has also been called 'racial evolution studies' [jinzhong xue], or more recently, 'superior birth studies' [yousheng xue], or 'sagacious descendent studies' [zhesi xue]. Although these other terms have classical and elegant meanings, unfortunately they cannot be understood in a single glance, so here we will just use the term 'race improvement studies.'"[71]

Underlying eugenic principles was the notion of biological determinism, emphasizing the fatalistic imprint of genetic inheritance above all else: the feeble-minded begot the feeble-minded, who would always remain feeble-minded, and the diseased begot the diseased, who would always remain diseased. The "unfit" (buliang) were forever trapped in the prisons of their own bodies. Although, as Zhou explained, many eugenicists recognized the strong influence of environmental factors in how an individual might ultimately turn out, it was still essential to have the right biological roots. "Education can only guide development of intelligence, so it is necessary to possess already the foundation for intelligence. The feeble-minded absolutely cannot be educated into the clever. Under the same type of education, there will still be the wise and the foolish. It is the same with an innately weak person; although he has ways of making a living, he can only support himself with difficulty, and cannot be transformed into a vigorous man." Thus it was necessary to breed out the unfit, reducing their impact on society.[72]

Yu Zhi would not have recognized this stance. To him, nothing was more important than moral virtue, including social standing or bookish intelligence. Yu had faith in the promise of moral education and in the capacity of all to change for the better, from the most backward and uneducated villager to the best-trained scholars with wealth to support them with appropriate guidance. An entire community needed the guidance of moral uplift, not just the lower classes, the poor or the diseased. Elite scholars fooled themselves if they believed that they were somehow absolved from moral culpability, since the existence of the problem of infanticide in any corner of society indicated that scholars, the purported leaders of society, had not done enough to prevent it or ameliorate its conditions. Even an ordinary villager could change for the better: hearing the moral exhortation at a village lecture or joining an infant protection society could inspire even the most intransigent fathers to reform, such that they would now cherish their daughters. The path of self-improvement and moral cultivation, in other words, was always open to any person who wished to try.

Whereas nineteenth-century practitioners of infanticide may have sinned against the cosmos or their own karmic fate, twentieth-century practitioners of infanticide were now guilty of thwarting the essential project of nation-building by decreasing the population. Though on the face of it such a shift might seem abrupt and bewildering, it actually evolved gradually over the course of half a century. Building upon a base of Chinese and Western cultural conceptions explored in the first four chapters of this book, this final chapter has traced the development of Chinese ideas about female infanticide in the late nineteenth and early twentieth centuries through a series of cross-cultural interactions that were alternately competitive and collaborative. Whether we consider the violence of the Tianjin Massacre in 1870, the mix of Chinese and foreign ideas in *Shenbao* articles, or the population theories of Sun Yat-sen, the critical thread connecting all of these expressions was the constant determination to find *Chinese* solutions to what eventually came to be understood as a particularly Chinese problem of female infanticide. Rather than reifying the West as the source of these outside influences, it seems more critical to consider how such ideas were adapted, interpreted and disseminated on the ground in China, in Chinese idioms, for Chinese audiences.

Certainly the attractions of moral education would never entirely be eliminated from twentieth-century Chinese society, yet the answers to some of China's most pressing problems, including female infanticide, would henceforth be articulated primarily through scientific principles. One final example might best represent this overlap of both old and new historical contexts for understanding the problem of female infanticide in China. In the tumult of Republican China, the appearance of reprints of earlier nineteenth-century editions of morality books against infanticide seemed to return to a simpler time and place, one which Yu Zhi would have recognized and embraced. The titles of these works, such as *Zhengying tongyan* (Urgent Words on Saving Infants) (1932) and *Zhengying men* (Gateway to Saving Infants) (1933), called forth the same karmic principles as their nineteenth-century predecessors. In certain cases, they were presented as exact duplicates of earlier editions, such as the *Chongbian zhengying lu* (Re-edition of the Record of Saving Infants) (1929). Like their older counterparts, these more recent editions contained tales of karmic rewards and punishments with accompanying illustrations, essays, songs and poems against the practice of female infanticide. On the surface, the publication of these morality books seemed to signal an overall sameness, a continued moral attitude toward the prevention of female infanticide from the late nineteenth century to the early twentieth century.

But although the contents of the texts were by and large verbatim copies of the nineteenth-century editions, the contexts of their production and consumption had changed dramatically. The reprinting of morality books in early twentieth-century China was part of a modern revival of Buddhist educational and philanthropic institutions, in an attempt to make the religion more relevant to the modern world.[73] These new, modern elements come to light when comparing the nineteenth and twentieth-century illustrated versions of the tale of the mother having her breasts bitten by the avenging ghosts of two daughters whom she had earlier drowned. (Figure 5.1; cf. Figure 1.4).

The twentieth-century morality book was itself the product of new, mechanized typesetting and lithographic illustration processes, instead of woodblock printing. The illustrations too had been entirely updated, revealing a modern visual vocabulary and sentiment. Horse-headed demons and avenging ghosts still danced across the page, but now the human figures were drawn in detailed late Qing-period costumes, and placed in elaborate bedroom settings complete with furniture and accessories, emphasizing the

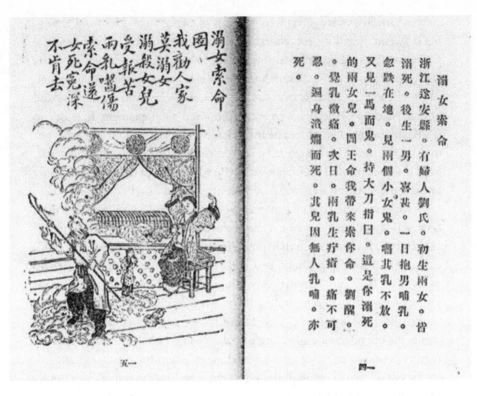

Figure 5.1. Story and illustration from a twentieth-century edition of a morality book against female infanticide. The content duplicates the nineteenth-century version, featuring a mother having her breasts bitten by the avenging ghosts of her dead daughters, as karmic punishment. However, the visual presentation of both story and illustration has changed dramatically, as a result of new, mechanized printing technologies. Compare to Figure 1.4. Source: *Chongbian zhengying lu* (1929), from the collection of the Shanghai Library.

formal perspective of the composition. In a modern society no longer configured by the "ladder of success" of the examination system, stories about preventing female infanticide and its resultant examination success now carried with them the distinct flavor of the antiquarian past, although karmic principles of reward and retribution may still have seemed relevant to some readers.

Textual distinctions between the two versions were even more telling than the updated illustrations. At the end of the twentieth-century edition, two entirely different texts were appended, which pointed to a new set of state actors. These new texts were reprints of two 1929 articles from Shanghai's *Shibao*, detailing the efforts of the Zhejiang and Shanxi provincial governments to eradicate female infanticide in each respective region.[74] Apart from reporting on census results and the crisis of an imperiled national population already described above, the two articles went on to list actions and policies each provincial government proposed to implement in order to eradicate the problem of female infanticide. Now the responsibility for humanitarian action no longer fell solely on the shoulders of an idiosyncratic, local do-gooder like Yu Zhi, but was to be addressed more systematically by local, provincial and national governments, for the benefit of all citizens.

What is striking about the nascent state efforts described in each article, however, is not only how much they echo nineteenth-century ameliorative efforts, but also how much they prefigure some of the later population policies of the People's Republic of China (PRC). Some of these initiatives would have been very familiar to Yu Zhi, including establishing more infant protection societies and foundling homes, or offering financial incentives to those who raise daughters. Others initiatives, such as enforcing punishments for offenders or registering populations and births, would implicitly require coordinated, widespread government action for regulation and enforcement. China's Nationalist government may have been unable to implement such far-reaching changes, but eventually the PRC would succeed. Although it took until the post-Mao era of the late 1970s for the PRC to adopt population control as one of the primary building blocks of the state agenda, it would more than make up for its tardiness by implementing in a few short years one of the most thoroughgoing attempts to control population growth that the modern world has ever seen.

Conclusion

In the course of her work as a journalist and radio presenter in Nanjing, Xinran Xue (1958–)finds herself in the impoverished Yimeng Mountain region of Shandong Province in 1989, invited to dinner at the home of a local village head whose daughter-in-law is about to give birth. While the group is encouraged by their host to continue eating, the sound of a woman in labor breaks in from the other room. Soon everything is silent and no baby's cries are heard, only the muttered curse of the young husband from the next room. Xinran thinks she hears something behind her and turns around to see the midwife wiping her hands on an apron and gathering her fee to leave. What happens next seems torn from the pages of a nineteenth-century morality book: "Suddenly, I thought I heard a slight movement in the slops pail behind me, and automatically glanced towards it. I felt ice in my blood. To my absolute horror, I saw a tiny foot poking out of the pail. I couldn't believe what I was seeing. Then the tiny foot twitched! It wasn't possible. The midwife must have dropped that tiny baby alive into the slop pail! I nearly threw myself at it, but the two policemen [who were accompanying Xinran] held my shoulders in a firm grip. 'Don't move, you can't save it, it's too late!'"[1]

On one level, Xinran's contemporary story stands as a chilling reminder of the stubborn persistence of the cultural preference for sons in China that remains unshaken even in the post-Mao era. Xinran's distress at her encounter with female infanticide echoes that of Su Shi, the eleventh-century Song statesman who, upon learning of the custom of drowning daughters in Hubei Province, sighed, "I felt miserable. I could not eat." Upon closer examination, however, Xinran's story offers some hint of the wildly different social, political and economic contexts affecting contemporary Chinese experiences of female infanticide. After the incident, the mother-in-law attempts to comfort Xinran by saying, " 'Doing' a baby girl is not a big thing around here. You city folk are shocked the first time you see it, right?" Xinran cannot remotely comprehend how they could drown a "living child." The peasant woman corrects her: "It's not a child. If it was, we'd be looking after it, wouldn't we? . . . It's a girl baby and we can't keep it."[2] She explains that girls are not counted in the government allocation of farmland, such that there is no way a family can afford to raise a girl, who would otherwise starve anyway. No longer is this the distant encounter of the male Chinese official, writing about actions and people he has never seen; here, the female rural subject is given a chance to talk back. When she does, it is Xinran, as the urbanite reporter, who finds that she has much to learn. Their interaction is made possible by their shared gender identity, as the mother-in-law willingly offers Xinran a glimpse into her interior world, one woman to another.

As illustrated in the preceding chapters of this book, responses to female infanticide in China have always been historically and culturally conditioned, depending on the values, experiences and perspectives of the people involved. In the nineteenth century, Chinese responses to female infanticide were framed within the context of a moral universe of karmic retribution, before the arrival of foreign missionaries turned the care of unwanted children into a contested political space, reframing the issue as a challenge for the newly emerging nation. In the past thirty years of the post-Mao reform era, Chinese experiences of female infanticide have been shaped by a vastly different set of circumstances, the most prominent of which have been rapid economic development and the implementation of state family planning policies. Following Deng Xiaoping's directive to put into practice "socialism with Chinese characteristics," free-market reforms in major coastal cities during the 1980s opened them to foreign investment, resulting in broad opportunities for wealth and prosperity. At the same time, the People's Republic of China (PRC) has made an energetic commitment to controlling population growth, most notably by implementing its One-Child policy in 1980. Having examined nineteenth-century experiences of female infanticide in China in the preceding chapters, we can now use this historical perspective to shed light on the distinctive features of this contemporary moment. Four areas in particular stand out: the economic and political factors influencing its practice, the involvement of foreign parents in adopting Chinese children, the domestic response of the PRC state in addressing sex ratio imbalances and finally, the emotional experiences of Chinese mothers who choose not to give birth to their daughters.

SEX-SELECTIVE ABORTION AND THE ONE-CHILD POLICY

In spite of the arresting impact of Xinran's story about the drowning of an unwanted newborn daughter in rural Shandong in 1989, in contemporary China postnatal infanticide has been largely superseded by sex-selective abortion.[3] Ansley Coale and Judith Banister have suggested that although female infanticide was still responsible for the high sex ratio imbalances in China recorded intermittently through the 1930s and 1940s, the practice mostly declined after the establishment of the PRC in 1949. The national sex ratio at birth (SRB) fell to its lowest levels in the two decades that immediately followed, with SRBs of 104.9 in 1953 and 103.8 in 1964.[4] Coale and Banister attribute this fall to a combination of continued high fertility and state policies promoting gender equality. Subsequently, when measured in the first census of the reform era in 1982, childhood sex ratios were still only slightly higher than normal in only a handful of provinces, a gap attributable to female infanticide or postpartum neglect.[5] After this point, however, childhood sex ratio imbalances gradually increased in coastal and central areas, followed by inland provinces, mimicking the pattern of diffusion of marketization and ultrasound technology.[6] Nationally, the SRB began to climb rapidly in the 1980s, from 107.2 in 1982 to 113.1 in 1987, to 111.3 in 1990 and to 116.8 in 1995, before leveling off somewhat in the late 1990s, from 119.9 in 2000 to 120.5 in 2005.[7] In 2010, the SRB dropped slightly to 118.06.[8]

General economic development in China over the past thirty years, in other words, has not in this instance improved chances of survival for girls, but on the contrary seems to have worsened them. Despite repeated attempts since 1986 by the PRC government to outlaw ultrasound use to reveal fetal sex, parents intent on having a son have still found ways to circumvent such prohibitions.[9] Today's Chinese parents, many of whom would otherwise never have considered killing a daughter by drowning her in a bucket of water, now have a much easier and earlier option to terminate an unwanted female fetus through sex-selective abortion.[10] This technological change represents the most significant difference between nineteenth-century and twentieth-century expressions of son preference in China. Though the two practices may yield a similar result, it is important to point out that for the majority of Chinese people today, there is a clear distinction between neonatal infanticide and postnatal abortion: according to one 1997 survey of more than 600 Chinese respondents regarding their attitudes toward abortion, 69 percent felt that abortion was not equivalent to killing an infant, and 73 percent felt that it was not equivalent to killing a human being.[11]

The other major factor during this period has been the implementation of the One-Child policy in 1980, demonstrating the tremendous capacity of the Chinese state to devise, implement and monitor population policies affecting the reproductive decisions of all of its citizens.[12] Already in the 1970s, the PRC initiated more serious and sustained efforts to control population growth, including a national campaign launched to encourage "later, longer, and fewer" births.[13] This slogan referred to later first births, longer spacing between births and fewer births overall. These early programs and subsequent economic development initiated desired fertility declines, yet they were deemed insufficient as China's population surpassed the one billion mark in 1980. The stricter regulations of the One-Child policy were set in place in 1980, limiting both urban and rural couples of the majority Han ethnicity to one child only.

In the years immediately following the establishment of the One-Child policy, coercive enforcement, coupled with an undiminished social preference for sons, particularly in rural areas, briefly led to a resurgence of actual cases of neonatal female infanticide. One report from the All-China Women's Federation Fifth National Congress in 1983, for example, drew sharp attention to this renewal of antifemale violence: "What is intolerable is the fact that some ugly phenomena that had been wiped out long ago in new China have begun to recur. Criminal acts of drowning female infants . . . have occurred frequently. In some areas these have reached serious propor-

tions."[14] Government cadres eventually recognized that the One-Child policy had to be relaxed somewhat to allow for son preference in rural areas,
and in 1983 rural parents were allowed a second child if their firstborn was
a daughter. Still, in spite of its worldwide notoriety, the PRC's One-Child
policy has not by itself caused the increase of sex ratio imbalances in contemporary China: a number of other countries without such state-mandated
family planning policies, such as India and South Korea, also evince sex
ratio imbalances.

INTERNATIONAL ADOPTIONS

Apart from this change in the technological and political conditions cir-
cumscribing sex-selective abortion today, the most dramatic shift from the
nineteenth century to the present has occurred in Chinese perceptions of
foreign involvement in the care for unwanted Chinese children. In contrast
with the position of nineteenth-century Chinese officials, such as Shen
Bingcheng, who believed that under no circumstances should a Chinese
child be left to languish in "foreign territory," openness to foreign investment
in China in the reform era has been echoed by openness to international
adoptions. Since 1991, the PRC government has allowed international adoptions of Chinese children. From that year until 2009, more than 120,000
Chinese children have been adopted internationally, with the vast majority
coming to the United States, which has received more than 74,000 Chinese
children in the intervening years.[15] As of 2008, the PRC has allowed international adoptions of Chinese children to citizens of the following seventeen
countries: United States, Canada, United Kingdom, France, Spain, Italy,
Holland, Belgium, Denmark, Norway, Sweden, Finland, Iceland, Ireland,
Australia, New Zealand and Singapore.[16] What all of these countries have in
common is a much higher and more sustained level of economic development than China.

Popular attitudes of Chinese families with regard to the adoption of
Chinese children by foreign parents have also been influenced by general
perceptions about the relative levels of economic development in the West
versus China. Contrary to their counterparts in Tianjin in the nineteenth
century, at least some contemporary Chinese families have expressed the
belief that a child raised in the more economically developed West will

have better chances in life. The journalist Xinran describes how in 1991, she once again encounters the rural Shandong couple whose first daughter was drowned at birth, when they come to Nanjing to ask for her help in finding jobs in the city. Xinran talks with the young mother at length. Since that time, the woman has given birth to two more daughters. The twist in the story, however, is this: instead of drowning the daughters at birth, her father-in-law sent the two girls south, to be taken to orphanages where they can be "adopted by foreigners." In another anecdote, a married woman who herself worked in an orphanage secretly arranges to give up her own daughter to be adopted by a foreign family, because she and her husband initially believe that "it must be much better for a child to be adopted into a middle- or upper-class family in the West than to have to put up with a life in a society as fiercely competitive as ours." Although this mother later expresses tremendous regret at her unthinkable actions, she says, "If those girls can go to Western families and live happy, healthy lives and get excellent schooling . . . that's so much better than them suffering the same sad fate that their mothers did, or even worse. They'll be valued emotionally and physically a thousand times more if they're adopted abroad."[17]

More recently, however, a renewed sense of "competition" over the care of abandoned Chinese children may be returning, echoing tensions exposed during the nineteenth century. In 2007, the China Center of Adoption Affairs, the PRC's state agency responsible for dealing with adoptions, announced more restrictive guidelines for foreigners seeking to adopt Chinese children, including a ban on previously allowed single, older or obese parents or those who fail to meet certain financial criteria. These new restrictions led some Western critics, including one American adoptive mother writing an op-ed in the *New York Times*, to suggest that the PRC merely wants to save face by minimizing an ugly social consequence of the One-Child policy—orphanages overflowing with unwanted girl children—through the control of their adoption by foreigners.[18] For its part, though, the Chinese state adoption agency has claimed that there are simply fewer girl children available for foreigners to adopt, given the gradual development of the domestic adoption system since 1992. No doubt the increase in sex-selective abortion has also lessened the number of births of unwanted girl children in intervening years. The adoption affairs agency has made an explicit goal of placing eight Chinese children domestically for every two placed through international adoption.[19]

CARE FOR GIRLS PROGRAM

Ironically, in spite of the extensive power of the PRC state to set and enforce domestic family planning policies as well as international adoption
policies, what seems most striking today is the relatively limited range of
options that the state has at its disposal to discourage couples from aborting daughters, or conversely, to encourage them to bear and raise daughters. The methods now in use are not at all far removed from nineteenth-
century attempts to prevent female infanticide as advocated by Yu Zhi,
particularly the distribution of moral tracts and the establishment of infant
protection societies. The PRC state has also largely focused on ameliorative
efforts, brought together under the name of the Care for Girls program
(*guan'ai nühai*). The primary goal of the program has been to change cultural attitudes about the value of girl offspring through a combination of
public education, economic incentives and preferential practices for families with only one or two daughters.[20] Harsher punitive measures against
those aborting female fetuses have also been introduced as part of the program's mandate, but those measures have not received as much attention
and seem difficult to enforce, given the numerous ways to circumvent sur-
veillance. The Care for Girls program began as an experimental pilot research project in one county in Anhui Province in 2000, and within three
years of implementation in this single county, the SRB dropped from 125 to
114.[21] Encouraged by the results, the National Population and Family Planning Commission began to establish the Care for Girls program in one
representative county of each of China's twenty-four provinces from 2003
to 2005.[22] Since 2006 the program has been expanded nationwide to hundreds more counties.[23]

As a public campaign with official state support, the Care for Girls program has produced copious amounts of visual and textual teaching materials to encourage families (rural ones in particular) to keep and value their
daughters.[24] These modern educational materials have similar didactic
goals as nineteenth-century morality books, yet the motivation for valuing
a girl has been entirely transformed. In place of a nineteenth-century moral
universe, drawing upon a pantheon of gods, ghosts and demons and emphasizing a woman's integral reproductive role in the family network, the
twenty-first-century state emphasizes the importance of girl children to the
proper functioning of Chinese society at large. Some slogans dispel traditional

notions about the divided family roles and responsibilities of men and women: "The times have changed; boys and girls are all the same" (*Shidai butongle, nannü dou yiyang*) or "Girls can be successful, girls can be entrepreneurial, girls can establish a household, girls can provide for the elderly" (*Nüer neng chengcai, nüer neng chuangye, nüer neng lihu, nüer neng yanglao*).[25] Others focus on the importance of sex ratio balance for the future of Chinese society at large: "Caring for girls means paying attention to the future of the nation" (*Guan'ai nühai jiu shi guanzhu minzu de weilai*) or "Together, husband and wife create a happy household; together, men and women create a harmonious society" (*Fuqi gongjian xingfu jiating, nannü gongjian hexie shehui*).[26] Indeed, the severe imbalance of sex ratios in China today does threaten future social stability, as many scholars have pointed out: large numbers of unmarried men are already shut out of the marriage market, particularly at the lower economic levels, and the shortage of women has led to an increase in the trafficking of women.[27]

Visual propaganda materials from the Care for Girls program deploy the same strategies, attempting to reeducate older generations about the importance of girls to the Chinese nation-state. One cartoon from an exhibit of campaign posters mounted in 2004, for example, shows a modern one-child family with parents, school-aged daughter and grandma, all together watching television.[28] The television screen shows what appears to be an Olympic medal ceremony, featuring two female athletes standing proudly next to each other, apparently having won both gold and silver medals for China, national flags prominently displayed behind them. The granddaughter turns to tug on the knee of her grandmother, saying, "Granny, do you still say that little girls are not as good as little boys?" The old woman is chastened and blushes with embarrassment, while the parents sit behind, secretly smiling at their daughter's precocity. In this new, modern tableau, the worth of a Chinese daughter has been entirely recalibrated. No longer is it a matter of what a daughter might mean to her own parents or family, as a dutiful and caring child, or even to her husband's family, as an essential instrument of biological reproduction to continue the family line. Instead, she contributes to society and country by bolstering national pride. Through the rigorous physical training of their bodies, these young, female athletes compete on the world's most consciously international stage and emerge victorious for China.

The question remains, however, as to whether these contemporary educational efforts and financial subsidies will be any more effective today than they were in the nineteenth century. Are appeals on behalf of the social needs of the modern state and the intrinsic worth of the girl child, in other words, any more compelling to potential parents than warnings about one's individual karmic destiny and reminders of the essential familial role of women? It is entirely possible for one to comprehend intellectually the social need for more balanced sex ratios, the negative consequences of so many missing women and the principle of gender equality yet still desire a son when it comes to one's own offspring. One recently married young rural woman reported just such a contradictory mix of personal reactions and public pressures: "If I don't get a son, I will consider that my fate is bad. After all, boys or girls are the same. I am a graduate of senior high school, but I still think boys are better. Of course, if I have a daughter, I will love her. At home, my mother and grandmother think it's bad to have a daughter. Most people think if you have no son, you will still want another. If you only have a daughter at home, you are considered incapable. That is stupid, but people in the villages think that way."[29]

WOMEN'S PERSONAL EXPERIENCES

Finally, we return to the point at which we started, by considering women's personal experiences of sex-selective abortion. Readers of this book may have difficulty imagining choosing to have an abortion for reasons of fetal sex alone, but as the example of the woman Ye revealed, these hard choices are not necessarily made without a range of conflicting human emotions, including regret, remorse, frustration, sympathy and anger. Approaching sex-selective abortion in current times with a similar sensitivity can avoid the all-too-easy judgments that come with the territory. For example, in Chu Junhong's 2001 survey of 820 married women in rural central China, 92 percent agreed that "it was not right to have female fetuses aborted" and the practice "represented unfair treatment of girls."[30] Yet of the 301 abortions reported by the women surveyed, 36 percent were acknowledged to be for reasons of sex-selection.[31] In other words, some of the same women who felt the practice was wrong still chose to have sex-selective abortions, due to pressure from their husbands or parents-in-law, pressure from rural society at large or pressure that they gave to themselves. These mothers somehow concluded, as did the woman Ye many centuries earlier, that they did not have the emotional or financial resources to care for a (usually second or third) daughter, particularly in the face of a strong competing desire for a son.

Particularly revealing in this regard was the response of one Chinese woman interviewed in 1997 who had one abortion, due to fetal abnormality, then gave birth to one daughter, then had another abortion to conform to the One-Child policy. Her physically painful abortion experiences confirmed to her that "to be a woman is really miserable."[32] Although she kept and raised her daughter, this mother expressed great sadness at her birth, since it meant "my daughter would have to suffer the various pains and bitterness I do."[33] Her words hauntingly echo the feelings of both the woman Ye and the infanticidal mother-in-law in the late imperial morality tale, who starkly announces, "All daughters would have the same bitter fate as me. It would be better to put her into a bucket of water at the start." Likewise a pregnant Chinese woman trapped in unsupportive family circumstances today may choose to abort a female fetus out of a complex combination of motives, which may appear from the outside to be selfish but might from her own perspective seem savagely selfless.

Ultimately, a more nuanced understanding of the history of female infanticide in nineteenth-century China can help dismantle some of our own taken-for-granted assumptions about the problem of female infanticide in the Chinese past, as well as the challenge of sex-selective abortion in China today. It is not uncommon, for example, to see opinions expressed like those of the journalists Nicholas Kristof and Sheryl WuDunn, who declare in *Half the Sky: Turning Oppression into Opportunity for Women Worldwide* (2009), their recent manifesto promoting women's rights around the world: "A century ago, China was arguably the worst place in the world to be born female. Foot-binding, child marriage, concubinage and female infanticide were embedded in traditional Chinese culture."[34] They acknowledge that it may have been "cultural imperialism for Westerners to criticize foot-binding and female infanticide. . . . But it was also the right thing to do. If we believe firmly in certain values, such as the equality of all human beings regardless of color or gender, then we should not be afraid to stand up for them."[35]

One purpose in delineating both Chinese and Western efforts to end female infanticide in nineteenth-century China in this book has been to avoid perpetuating this popular but inaccurate notion that Westerners alone should be credited with an impulse for instituting moral reforms. Such claims promote more than just bad history. They also continue to advance notions of civilizational hierarchies and progressive versus oppressive cultures, as well as reinforcing a presumed Eurocentric monopoly on moral righteousness. As this book has shown, Western influence did not initiate the wholesale "enlightenment" of a backward and hidebound Chinese culture in matters of human values regarding female infanticide. The impulse to do something about the problem of female infanticide had always been expressed in China; what changed in the face of nineteenth-century Western contact was the articulation of the specific reasons for ending the practice.

Nowadays, our own most meaningful gauge of the problem of unwanted daughters in China is the statistical measurement of sex ratio imbalance, emphasized by demographers, journalists and government officials alike. We are so habituated to statistical thinking as the normative manner of meaning-making in contemporary society, essential for measuring, predicting, assessing and targeting change, that we may be blind to some of its implicit limitations. Our own historical context, in other words, exerts no less firm a grip on our values, thinking and imagination than Yu Zhi's did in his own day. A modern demographic orientation clearly makes it possible to measure and track the severity of female infanticide (or, more accurately, its contemporary cousin, sex-selective abortion), yet statistics also render otherwise messy, conflicted and human situations into flat, uniform packages of data. In such a framework, populations replace individuals as the locus of concern, and the significance of a single couple or family making a unique decision about their own daughter's fate—a decision so crucial to a nineteenth-century man like Yu Zhi—is lost. Focusing on the enumeration of female victimhood through the single demographic measure of sex ratios may oversimplify our analysis of contemporary factors by leaving out the range of adults surrounding an infant girl, all of whom may have complex motives and play different parts in the decision to end a daughter's life. How to expand the space between an unwanted Chinese daughter's birth and death, in order to give her a real chance at life, remains a question to be answered as much today as in the nineteenth century.

Reference Matter

Notes

1. Su Shi, "Lun jiuninü shu" [Letter on rescuing girls from drowning], *Xuying lu* (1873), 2a.

2. See, for example, the March 6, 2010 issue of *The Economist*, the front cover of which reads "Gendercide: What Happened to 100 Million Baby Girls?" Outside of China, female infanticide in India has attracted the most scholarly and journalistic attention. See Rashmi Dube Bhatnagar, Renu Dube and Reena Dube, *Female Infanticide in India: A Feminist Cultural History* (Albany: State University of New York Press, 2005); Satadru Sen, "The Savage Family: Colonialism and Female Infanticide in Nineteenth-Century India," *Journal of Women's History* 14, no. 3 (Autumn 2002): 53–79; Lalita Panigrahi, *British Social Policy and Female Infanticide in India* (Delhi: Monoharlal, 1972).

3. "New Campaign Targets Gender Ratio Imbalance," *People's Daily Online*, August 17, 2011, http://english.peopledaily.com.cn/90882/7571975.html, accessed December 4, 2012.

4. Chu Junhong, "Prenatal Sex Determination and Sex-Selective Abortion in Rural Central China," *Population and Development Review* 27, no. 2 (June 2001): 259–81.

5. On the development and implementation of the One-Child policy, see Tyrene White, *China's Longest Campaign: Birth Planning in the People's Republic, 1949–2005* (Ithaca, NY: Cornell University Press, 2006) and Susan Greenhalgh, *Just One Child: Science and Policy in Deng's China* (Berkeley: University of California Press, 2008).

6. William Langer, "Infanticide: A Historical Survey," *History of Childhood Quarterly* 1 (1973): 353.

7. For a brief overview of infanticide around the world, see Langer, "Infanticide." On the history of infanticide in Britain, see Barbara A. Kellum, "Infanticide in England in the Later Middle Ages," *History of Childhood Quarterly* 1, no. 3 (Winter 1974): 367–88; R. Sauer, "Infanticide and Abortion in Nineteenth-Century Britain," *Population Studies* 32, no. 1 (March 1978): 81–93; George Behlmer, "Deadly Motherhood: Infanticide and Medical Opinion in Mid-Victorian England," *Journal of the History of Medicine and Allied Sciences* 34, no. 4

(October 1979): 403–27; Lionel Rose, *The Massacre of Innocents: Infanticide in Britain, 1800–1939* (London: Routledge, 1986); Laura Gowing, "Secret Births and Infanticide in Seventeenth-Century England," *Past and Present* 156, no. 1 (1997): 87–115; Ann Higginbotham, "Sin of the Age: Infanticide and Illegitimacy in Victorian London," in *Victorian Scandals: Representations of Gender and Class*, ed. Kristine Ottesen Garrigan (Athens: Ohio University Press, 1992), 257–88; Mark Jackson, *New-Born Child Murder: Women, Illegitimacy and the Courts in Eighteenth-Century England* (Manchester: Manchester University Press, 1996); Mark Jackson, ed., *Infanticide: Historical Perspectives on Child Murder and Concealment, 1550–2000* (Aldershot, England: Ashgate, 2002); Jennifer Thorn, ed., *Writing British Infanticide: Child-Murder, Gender and Print, 1722–1859* (Newark: University of Delaware Press, 2003); Josephine McDonagh, *Child Murder and British Culture, 1720–1900* (Cambridge: Cambridge University Press, 2003). On infanticide in France, see K. McQuillan, "Were Traditional Societies Really Traditional? Illegitimacy, Infanticide and Abandonment in Nineteenth Century Alsace," *Population Studies Centre Discussion Paper* 87, no. 14 (December 1987); James Donovan, "Infanticide and Juries in France, 1825–1913," *Journal of Family History* 16, no. 2 (1991): 157–76; Brigitte Bechtold, "Infanticide in 19th Century France: A Quantitative Interpretation," *Review of Radical Political Economics* 33 (2001): 165–87; Annick Tillier, *Des criminelles au village: Femmes infanticides en Bretagne (1825–1865)* (Rennes: Universitaires de Rennes, 2001). On Germany, see Otto Ulbricht, *Kindsmord und Aufklärung in Deutschland* (München: R. Oldenbourg, 1990); Jeffrey Richter, "Infanticide, Child Abandonment and Abortion in Imperial Germany," *Journal of Interdisciplinary History* 28, no. 4 (Summer 1998): 511–51. On infanticide in the United States, see Peter Hoffer and N. E. H. Hull, *Murdering Mothers: Infanticide in England and New England, 1558–1803* (New York: New York University Press, 1981); Kenneth Wheeler, "Infanticide in Nineteenth-Century Ohio," *Journal of Social History* 31, no. 2 (1997): 407–18.

8. Sarah Blaffer Hrdy, *Mother Nature: Maternal Instincts and How They Shape the Human Species* (New York: Ballantine Books, 2000); Glenn Hausfater and Sarah Blaffer Hrdy, eds., *Infanticide: Comparative and Evolutionary Perspectives* (New York: Aldine, 1984).

9. See Jackson, *Infanticide* and McDonagh, *Child Murder*.

10. Broad overviews of female infanticide in Chinese history include D. E. Mungello, *Drowning Girls in China: Female Infanticide Since 1650* (Lanham, MD: Rowman and Littlefield, 2008), 4–7; Feng Erkang, "Niying de fumu" [Infanticidal parents], in *Qu guren de tingyuan sanbu: Gudai shehui shenghuo tuji* (Beijing: Zhonghua shuju, 2005), 131–36; Bernice J. Lee, "Female Infanticide in China," *Historical Reflections / Reflexions Historiques* 8, no. 3 (Fall 1981): 163–78; Sogabe Shizuo, "Ninü kao" [Investigation of female infanticide], *Wenxing zazhi* 55, no. 10 (1962, orig. pub. in Japanese in 1941): 52–57; Nishiyama Eikyu, "Shina minken no Infanticide nitsuite" [About infanticide among Chinese people], *Toa keizai kenkyu* 13, no. 1 (1929): 36–71.

11. David Mungello begins his study with Arthur Waley's 1937 translation of the two relevant *Shijing* stanzas: "So he bears a son, / And puts him to sleep upon

a bed, / Clothes him in robes, / Gives him a jade scepter to play with. / The child's howling is very lusty; / In red greaves shall he flare, / Be lord and king of house and home. / Then he bears a daughter, / And puts her upon the ground, / Clothes her in swaddling-clothes, / Gives her a loom-whorl to play with. / For her no decorations, no emblems; / Her only care, the wine and food, / And how to give no trouble to father and mother." Mungello, *Drowning*, 4. Bernice J. Lee includes this excerpt from *Han Feizi*: "Moreover, parents' attitude to children is such that when they bear a son they congratulate each other, but when they bear a daughter they kill her. Both come from parents' love, but they congratulate each other when it is a boy and kill it if it is a girl because they are considering their later convenience and calculating their long-term interests." Lee, "Female Infanticide in China," 164.

12. T'ien Ju-k'ang, *Male Anxiety and Female Chastity: A Comparative Study of Chinese Ethical Values in Ming-Ch'ing Times* (Leiden: Brill, 1988), 25n36.

13. On dowry as an economic burden influencing the practice of female infanticide during the late imperial period, see Ann Waltner, "Infanticide and Dowry in Ming and Early Qing China," in *Chinese Views of Childhood*, ed. Anne Behnke Kinney (Honolulu: University of Hawaii, 1995), 193–217; Xiao Qian, "Qingdai Jiangxi ninü fengsu zhong de 'shejia' wenti" [Extra-dowry in the custom of infanticide in Qing dynasty Jiangxi], *Jiangnan daxue xuebao* 4, no. 4 (August 2005): 53–56.

14. On infanticide in early imperial China, see Lee Jen-der [Li Zhende], "Han Sui zhijian de shengzi buju wenti" [On the problem of giving birth to and not raising a child from the Han to the Sui dynasty], *Zhongyang yanjiuyuan lishi yüyan yanjiusuo jikan* 66, no. 3 (1995): 747–812 and Anne Behnke Kinney, "Infant Abandonment in Early China," *Early China* 18 (1993): 107–38.

15. On infanticide the Song dynasty, see Liu Jingzhen, *Bu ju zi: Songren de shengyu wenti* [To not raise a child: The problems of birth in the Song dynasty] (Banqiao, Taiwan: Daoxiang chubanshe, 1998) and Liang Qizi [Angela Leung], "Shaying, qiying, yuyingtang" [Infanticide, abandonment, orphanages], *Lishi yuekan* 3 (1988): 42–45. Liu lists forty-eight references to the practice of infanticide in Song sources citing economic or other reasons, and only four references include gender-specific reasons, such as excessive dowries. See Liu, *Bu ju zi*, 85–91.

16. On infanticide in the Ming and Qing dynasties, see Chang Jianhua, "Mingdai niying wenti chutan" [An initial inquiry into the problem of infanticide during the Ming dynasty], in *Zhongguo shehui lishi pinglun* 4 (Beijing: Shangwu yinshuguan, 2002); Chang Jianhua, "Qingdai niying wenti xintan" [A new inquiry into the problem of infanticide during the Qing dynasty], in *Hunyin jiating yu renkou xingwei*, ed. Li Zhongqing [James Lee], Guo Songyi and Ding Yizhuang (Beijing: Peking University Press, 1999), 197–219. In a nonsystematic sampling of local gazetteers from the Qing, Feng Erkang lists twenty-seven specific references to *female* infanticide in particular. Feng Erkang, "Qingdai de hunyin zhidu yu funü de shehui diwei shulun" [A discussion of marriage practices and women's social status in the Qing], *Qingshi yanjiu ji* 5 (1986): 320–21.

17. Kinney, "Abandonment," 107–8.

18. Liu, *Bu ju zi*.

19. For details on how this rate of female infanticide was calculated, see James Lee and Cameron Campbell, *Fate and Fortune in Rural China: Social Organization and Population Behavior in Liaoning 1774–1873* (Cambridge: Cambridge University Press, 1997), 65–70, in particular the notes and discussion to table 4.4. See also James Lee, Cameron Campbell and Guofu Tan, "Infanticide and Family Planning in Late Imperial China: The Price and Population History of Rural Liaoning, 1774–1873," in *Chinese History in Economic Perspective*, ed. Thomas Rawski and Lillian Li (Berkeley: University of California Press, 1992), 145–76.

20. James Lee, Wang Feng and Cameron Campbell, "Infant and Child Mortality Among the Qing Nobility: Implications for Two Types of Positive Check," *Population Studies* 48, no. 3 (November 1994): 395–411.

21. On the nature of the estimates and data, see James Lee, Cameron Campbell and Wang Feng, "Positive Check or Chinese Checks?" *Journal of Asian Studies* 61, no. 2 (May 2002): 598.

22. James Z. Lee and Wang Feng, *One Quarter of Humanity: Malthusian Mythology and Chinese Realities, 1700–2000* (Cambridge, MA: Harvard University Press, 1999).

23. Arthur Wolf, "Is There Evidence of Birth Control in Late Imperial China?" *Population and Development Review* 27, no. 1 (March 2001): 134.

24. Infanticide was prosecuted as a crime in imperial Germany (1882–1914), for example, where the conviction rate reached a high of 25.44 convictions per 100,000 births. See Richter, "Infanticide," 514, table 1. Conviction rates, of course, do not necessarily capture every instance of infanticide. Possible rates of infanticide in two counties in nineteenth-century Ohio have been estimated at 1.11 to 1.76 per 100,000 population. See Wheeler, "Infanticide," 410–11.

25. As cited in Langer, "Infanticide," 358.

26. As cited in John Boswell, *The Kindness of Strangers: The Abandonment of Children in Western Europe from Late Antiquity to the Renaissance* (Chicago: University of Chicago Press, 1998), 15–16nn27–31.

27. Langer, "Infanticide," 358–59.

28. "Abandonment is at one extreme of a continuum that ranges between termination of investment and the total commitment of a mother. . . . [It] is the default mode for a mother terminating investment. Infanticide occurs when circumstances . . . prevent a mother from abandoning it." Hrdy, *Mother Nature*, 297.

29. Langer, "Infanticide," 354.

30. On "moral revolutions," see Kwame Anthony Appiah, *The Honor Code: How Moral Revolutions Happen* (New York: W. W. Norton, 2010). Appiah argues that the moral influence of Western missionaries was crucial for the demise of footbinding in late nineteenth-century China.

31. Only one nineteenth-century Chinese source seems to have openly promoted the practice of female infanticide, as an extreme method of population control, along with celibacy and capital punishment for minor offenses. This rare

and eccentric stance appears in the diary of Wang Shiduo (1802–89), a scholar from Nanjing who kept a diary from 1855 to 1856, published posthumously in 1936. See Frank Dikötter, "The Limits of Benevolence: Wang Shiduo (1802–1889) and Population Control," *Bulletin of the School of Oriental and African Studies* 55, no. 1 (1992): 110–15.

32. Dipesh Chakrabarty, *Provincializing Europe: Postcolonial Thought and Historical Difference* (Princeton, NJ: Princeton University Press, 2000), 6.

33. Timothy Brook, Jérôme Bourgon and Gregory Blue, *Death by a Thousand Cuts* (Cambridge, MA: Harvard University Press, 2008).

34. Larissa N. Heinrich, *The Afterlife of Images: Translating the Pathological Body Between China and the West* (Durham, NC: Duke University Press, 2008).

35. Dorothy Ko, *Cinderella's Sisters: A Revisionist History of Footbinding* (Berkeley: University of California Press, 2005), 41–42 and Ko, *Every Step a Lotus: Shoes for Bound Feet* (Berkeley: University of California Press, 2001), 131–32.

36. Brook et al., *Death*, 23.

37. For a variety of examples of specific images, see Grace Lau, *Picturing the Chinese: Early Western Photographs and Postcards of China* (San Francisco: Long River Press, 2008). See also Ko, *Every Step*, 130–32; Brook et al., *Death*, 1–34, 152–202. On visual representations of native peoples in colonial contexts, see James Ryan, *Picturing Empire: Photography and the Visualization of the British Empire* (Chicago: University of Chicago Press, 1997) and Mary Louise Pratt, *Imperial Eyes: Travel Writing and Transculturation* (London: Routledge, 1992).

CHAPTER I

1. Nineteenth-century Western female missionaries did record Chinese women's accounts of infanticide, but these are rendered in English and foreground the importance of the conversion experience. For a discussion, see Chapter 3 of this book.

2. Chen Que, "Fu Jueyan gong" [On my father, the honorable Jueyan], in *Chen Que ji* (Beijing: Zhonghua shuju, 1979), 530–35. For another discussion of this passage from Chen Que, see Liang Qizi [Angela Leung], "Shaying, qiying, yuyingtang" [Infanticide, abandonment, orphanages], *Lishi yuekan* 3 (1988): 42–45.

3. On the encounter between male doctors and female patients, see Charlotte Furth, "A Doctor's Practice: Narratives of the Clinical Encounter in Late Ming Yangzhou," in *A Flourishing Yin: Gender in China's Medical History* (Berkeley: University of California Press, 1999), 224–65.

4. Biographical information on Ye and her family can be gleaned from the life of her son, Chen Que. See Wang Ruichang, *Chen Que pingzhuan* [A critical biography of Chen Que] (Nanjing: Nanjing daxue chubanshe, 2002), 11–33.

5. On a typical late imperial elite woman's life course, see Susan Mann, *Precious Records: Women in China's Long Eighteenth Century* (Stanford, CA: Stanford University Press, 1997), 45–75.

6. On Chen Que's surviving sister, see the family history (*jiapu*) as quoted in Wang, *Chen Que pingzhuan*, 25.

7. Charlotte Furth, "From Birth to Birth: The Growing Body in Chinese Medicine," in *Chinese Views of Childhood*, ed. Anne Behnke Kinney (Honolulu: University of Hawaii Press, 1995), 182.

8. Chen Que, "Fu Jueyan gong," 533.

9. On the various subjects of literate women's writing in the late imperial period, see Kang-i Sun Chang and Haun Saussy, eds., *Women Writers of Traditional China: An Anthology of Poetry and Criticism* (Stanford, CA: Stanford University Press, 1999); Ellen Widmer and Kang-i Sun Chang, eds., *Writing Women in Late Imperial China* (Stanford, CA: Stanford University Press, 1997); Mann, *Precious Records*. Although Qing women did not write poetry about infanticide, Qing men did, in their efforts to prevent it. See the poems about infanticide collected in Zhang Yingchang, ed., *Qingshi duo* [The bell of Qing poetry] (Beijing: Zhonghua shuju, 1960 [orig. 1869]).

10. On women's efforts in the nineteenth century to manage the household economy and supplement the family income, see Susan Mann, *The Talented Women of the Zhang Family* (Berkeley: University of California Press, 2007).

11. Chen Que, "Fu Jueyan gong," 531.

12. Chen Que, "Fu Jueyan gong," 531.

13. Chen Que, "Fu Jueyan gong," 531.

14. Weijing Lu, "'A Pearl in the Palm': A Forgotten Symbol of the Father-Daughter Bond," *Late Imperial China* 31, no. 1 (June 2010): 62–97.

15. Lu, "Pearl"; Hsiung Ping-chen, "Girlhood," in *A Tender Voyage: Children and Childhood in Late Imperial China* (Stanford, CA: Stanford University Press, 2005); Mann, *Talented Women*.

16. Mann, *Precious Records*, 63.

17. Gui Zhongfu is mentioned in the *Dantu xianzhi* [Dantu county gazetteer] (1803 ed.), *juan* 17, 14b. He also played a role in reestablishing a local academy.

18. *Jie ninü wen* [Essay prohibiting the drowning of girls] (1882), 3a–b. Gui's essay against infanticide appeared in numerous nineteenth-century morality books, such as *Chongding anshideng lu* [Re-edition of the Record of Light for a Darkened Room] (1831 ed., with an earlier preface dated 1816), *Anshideng zhujie* [Annotated version of Light for a Darkened Room] (1842 ed.), *Zhengying baoying lu* [Record of rewards and retributions for saving infants] (1855, 1869 eds.), *Cihang pudu ce* [The compassionate raft of salvation for all beings] (1870 ed.) and *Jie ninü tushuo* [Illustrated book of prohibiting the drowning of girls] (1873 ed.). The essay was also reprinted on its own as *Jie ninü wen* [Essay prohibiting the drowning of girls] (1876, 1882 ed.). It was also translated into English in 1848. See "Infanticide: translation of an essay warning people against the practice of drowning their female children by Kwei Chungfu of Hunan," *Chinese Repository* 17, no. 1 (January 1848): 11–16.

19. *Jie ninü wen* (1882), 3b–4a.

20. "He Longtu ninü ge" [He Longtu's song on drowning daughters], cited in "Jie ninü shuo," in *Quanren juyue* (1800), *juan* 3: 50b–51a.

21. One fascinating and exceptional nineteenth-century family, where uxorilo-cal marriage was the rule, is described in Mann, *Talented Women*.

22. Fangqin Du and Susan Mann pinpoint a change of emphasis on a woman's loyalty during the Song dynasty, from that of a woman serving her own parents to that of her serving her parents-in-law. See Du and Mann, "Competing Claims on Womanly Virtue in Late Imperial China," in *Women and Confucian Cultures in Premodern China, Korea, and Japan*, ed. Dorothy Ko, JaHyun Kim Haboush and Joan R. Piggott (Berkeley: University of California Press, 2003), 219–50.

23. On the story of Ti-Ying, see Lisa Raphals, *Sharing the Light: Representations of Women and Virtue in Early China* (Albany: State University of New York Press, 1998), 47–48 and 133–36. Han dynasty versions of the Ti-Ying story originally emphasized her literary ability, and later Ming dynasty versions focused on her filiality.

24. For a discussion of Chinese medical conceptions of gender difference, see Charlotte Furth, *A Fluorishing Yin: Gender in China's Medical History, 960–1665* (Berkeley: University of California Press, 1999), 19–58 and, by the same author, "From Birth to Birth: The Growing Body in Chinese Medicine," in *Chinese Views of Childhood*, ed. Anne Behnke Kinney (Honolulu: University of Hawaii Press, 1995), 157–91.

25. See Furth, "From Birth to Birth"; Angela Kiche Leung, "Autour de la naissance: La mere et l'enfant en Chine aux XVIe et XVIIe siècles," *Cahiers inter-nationaux de Sociologie* 56 (1984): 51–69; Li Zhende [Lee Jen-der], "Han-Tang zhijian qiuzi yifang shitan—jianlun fuke lanshang yu xingbie lunshu" [A preliminary investigation of reproductive medicine from the Han to the Tang dynasty: On the birth of gynecology and gender discourse], *Zhongyang yanjiuyuan lishi yüyan yan-jiusuo jikan* 68, no. 2 (1997): 283–367.

26. Lee, "Qiuzi yifang," 289–90.

27. Chen Ziming as cited in Leung, "Autour," 56.

28. Chu Cheng as cited in Furth, "From Birth to Birth," 164.

29. On herbal remedies, see Lee, "Qiuzi yifang," 301–9.

30. Wan Quan, *Yuying jiami*, in *Gujin tushu jicheng*, as cited in Leung, "Aut-our," 58. See also citations from early imperials texts, which also included "shoot-ing an angry pheasant" and "looking at a tiger or panther" to ensure the birth of a boy in Lee, "Qiuzi yifang," 309.

31. Yan Chunxi, *Taichan xinfa* [Teachings on giving birth] (1731) 1: 8b–9b, re-printed in *Xuxiu siku quanshu*, ed. Gu Tinglong (Shanghai: Shanghai guji chu-banshe, 1998), vol. 1008.

32. Chün-fang Yü, "A Sütra Promoting the White-Robed Guanyin as Giver of Sons," in *Religions of China in Practice*, ed. Donald S. Lopez (Princeton, NJ: Princeton University Press, 1996), 97–105.

33. Ling-in Lilian Chuu, "Cult of Guanyin Who Brings Sons," MA thesis in Asian Studies, University of British Columbia (2001).

34. Chuu, "Cult of Guanyin Who Brings Sons."

35. On the popularity, probable authorship and free distribution of *Dasheng bian*, see Yi-Li Wu, *Reproducing Women: Medicine, Metaphor, and Childbirth in*

Late Imperial China (Berkeley: University of California Press, 2010), 67–70 and 75–81; on its tone and contents, see Wu, *Reproducing*, 147–87.

36. Jizhai jushi, *Dasheng bian* [On successful childbirth] (Jingyitang canban, 1774), 1: 13b, as reprinted in *Xuxiu siku quanshu*, ed. Gu Tinglong (Shanghai: Shanghai guji chubanshe, 1998), vol. 1008, 99–115. The citations refer to the original page numbers.

37. On late imperial midwifery, see Furth, *Flourishing Yin*, 266–300 and Angela Ki Che Leung, "Women Practicing Medicine in Premodern China," in *Chinese Women in the Imperial Past: New Perspectives*, ed. Harriet T. Zurndorfer (Leiden: Brill, 1999), 105–16.

38. Jizhai jushi, *Dasheng bian*, 1: 6a.

39. On the squatting position and use of external supports, see Jen-der Lee, "Childbirth in Early Imperial China," *Nan nü* 7, no. 2 (2005): 234–41.

40. Jizhai jushi, *Dasheng bian*, 1: 8a–b and 13a–b.

41. Sun Simiao, *Beiji qianjin yaofang* as cited in Lee, "Childbirth," 254.

42. "Jiuming sushuo" [Simple words on saving lives], in *Deyi lu*, ed. Yu Zhi (Taipei: Huawen shuju, 1969 [reprint of 1869 ed.]), 172.

43. "Jiuming," 172.

44. For legal and medical aspects of infanticide in nineteenth-century Britain, see Mark Jackson, ed., *Infanticide: Historical Perspectives on Child Murder and Concealment, 1550–2000* (Aldershot, England: Ashgate, 2002). For a comprehensive cultural study of eighteenth- and nineteenth-century infanticide in Britain, see Josephine McDonagh, *Child Murder and British Culture, 1720–1900* (Cambridge: Cambridge University Press, 2003).

45. For a general overview of morality books, see Tadao Sakai, "Confucianism and Popular Educational Works," in *Self and Society in Ming Thought*, ed. Wm. Theodore de Bary (New York: Columbia University Press, 1970), 341–45 and You Zian, *Quanhua jinzhen: Qingdai shanshu yanjiu* [Golden needles of exhortation: A study of Qing dynasty morality books] (Tianjin: Tianjin renmin chubanshe, 1999).

46. On references to infanticide in the earliest Song morality books, see Catherine Bell, "'A Precious Raft to Save the World': The Interaction of Scriptural Traditions and Printing in a Chinese Morality Book," *Late Imperial China* 17, no. 1 (1996): 158–200.

47. Cynthia Brokaw, "Yuan Huang (1533–1606) and the *Ledgers of Merit and Demerit*," *Harvard Journal of Asiatic Studies* 47, no. 1 (June 1987): 137–95 and, by the same author, *The Ledgers of Merit and Demerit: Social Change and Moral Order in Late Imperial China* (Princeton, NJ: Princeton University Press, 1991).

48. Brokaw, "Yuan Huang," 192–95.

49. Examples of moral tales against infanticide appear already in the Song dynasty. See Liu Jingzhen, *Bu ju zi: Songren de shengyu wenti* [To not raise a child: The problems of birth in the Song dynasty] (Banqiao, Taiwan: Daoxiang chubanshe, 1998), 23–46.

50. The ninety-three tales against the practice of infanticide, some of which were duplicates or close variants, were found in the following six nineteenth-

century editions of morality books: *Jie ninü tushuo* [Illustrated book prohibiting the drowning of girls] (1812); *Zhengying baoying lu* (1855); *Cihang pudu ce* (1870); *Guobao tu* [Illustrated rewards and retributions] (1872); *Jie ninü tushuo* (1873); *Jiuying jiefa* [A quick way to saving infants] (1882). Each tale was counted as a separate occurrence, regardless of any repetitions or overlap.

51. On this dynamic of fathers absent at birth during the nineteenth century, see Mann, *Talented Women*.

52. On the negative impression of midwives in the Ming and Qing, see Furth, *Flourishing*, 268–72 and Leung, "Women Practicing Medicine," 105–16.

53. *Chongzuan Fujian tongzhi* [Re-edition of the Fujian province gazetteer] (1871), 55: 28a–b. For an alternative discussion and translation, see T'ien Ju-k'ang, *Male Anxiety and Female Chastity: A Comparative Study of Chinese Ethical Values in Ming–Ch'ing Times* (Leiden: Brill, 1988), 30.

54. Furth, *Flourishing*, 278.

55. On mortality rates for daughters after birth, see James Lee et al., "Infant and Child Mortality Among the Qing Nobility: Implications for Two Types of Positive Check," *Population Studies* 48, no. 3 (November 1994): 395–411. See also James Lee, Wang Feng and Cameron Campbell, *Fate and Fortune in Rural China: Social Organization and Population Behavior in Liaoning 1774–1873* (Cambridge: Cambridge University Press, 1997), 70n23.

56. *Zhengying baoying lu* (1855), 34b–35a.

57. On midwife's tongue being cut out: *Zhengying baoying lu* (1855), 9b–10a; *Guobao tu* (1872), 5a–5b; *Jie ninü tushuo* (1873), 8b–9a.

58. On Chinese Buddhist concepts of hell, see Xiao Dengfu, *Daofo shiwang diyu shuo* [On the Taoist-Buddhist Ten Kings of Hell] (Taipei: Xinwenfeng chubanshe, 1996); Stephen Teiser, *The Scripture on the Ten Kings and the Making of Purgatory in Medieval Chinese Buddhism* (Honolulu: University of Hawaii Press, 1994); Wolfram Eberhard, *Guilt and Sin in Traditional China* (Berkeley: University of California Press, 1967).

59. *Cihang pudu ce* (1870), 28b–29b.

60. *Guobao tu* (1872), 3a–3b.

61. On this custom in northern Taiwan in the late nineteenth and early twentieth centuries, see Arthur Wolf and Chieh-Shan Huang, *Marriage and Adoption in China, 1845–1945* (Stanford, CA: Stanford University Press, 1980), particularly chapters 6 and 17.

62. Guo Songyi, "Qingdai de tongyangxi hunyin" [Child bride marriages during the Qing], in *Hunyin jiating yu renkou xingwei*, ed. Li Zhongqing, Guo Songyi and Ding Yizhuang (Peking University Press, 1999), 33, Table 1.

63. Guo, "Tongyangxi," 45, Table 4b.

64. "Gengzizi yueshen yu tongjie ponüe tongxi wen" [Essay strongly forbidding the abuse of child brides by mothers-in-law, issued by the moon goddess on the date *gengzizi*], *Cihang pudu ce* (1870), 33a–b. A shorter, similar essay against child bride abuse can be found in "Quanjie buke lingnüe baoyangtongxi" [Urging against the abuse of child brides], in *Jie ninü tushuo* (1873).

65. "Gengzizi," 33b.

66. "Gengzizi," 35b.

67. "Gengzizi," 33a–34a.

68. *Zhengying baoying lu* (1855), 33a–33b.

69. This version is from *Jie ninü tushuo* (1873), 2b–3a. Alternate version: *Guobao tu* (1872), 2a–2b.

70. On Wenchang, see Terry Kleeman, *A God's Own Tale: The Book of Transformations of Wenchang, the Divine Lord of Zitong* (Albany: State University of New York Press, 1994).

71. On the karmic reward for freeing captive animals, see Joanna Handlin Smith, *The Art of Doing Good: Charity in Late Ming China* (Berkeley: University of California Press, 2009), 19–21. On the karmic reward for refusing to sleep with another man's concubine, see Benjamin Elman, *A Cultural History of Civil Examinations in Late Imperial China* (Berkeley: University of California Press, 2000), 306.

72. Brokaw, *Ledgers*, 230.

73. Yu Zhi, *Nü ershisi xiao tushuo* [Twenty-four illustrated stories of filial piety for girls] (1872), 18b–19a.

74. On the relationship between mothers and sons in late imperial China, see Hsiung, *Tender Voyage*, 130.

75. Francesca Bray, "Reproductive Hierarchies," in *Technology and Gender: Fabrics of Power in Late Imperial China* (Berkeley: University of California Press, 1997), 335–68.

76. Stories about mothers-in-law and household mistresses forcing their daughters-in-law or female servants to commit infanticide can be found in *Zhengying baoying lu* (1855), 33a–34a.

77. *Cihang pudu ce* (1870), 21b–22a. See also *Zhengying baoying lu* (1855), 24b–25a.

78. *Quanren juyue* [Rules of conduct for the perfect person] (1800), 50b.

79. Anthony Yu, "'Rest, Rest, Perturbed Spirit!' Ghosts in Traditional Chinese Prose Fiction," *Harvard Journal of Asiatic Studies* 47, no. 2 (December 1987): 397–434.

80. *Zhengying baoying lu* (1855), 7b–8a. See also *Guobao tu* (1872), 10a–10b; *Jie ninü tushuo* (1873), 5b–6a.

81. Judith Zeitlin, "Embodying the Disembodied: Representations of Ghosts and the Feminine," in *Writing Women in Late Imperial China*, ed. Ellen Widmer and Kang-i Sun Chang, 249 (Stanford, CA: Stanford University Press, 1997).

82. *Jie ninü tushuo* (1812), 15b–16a; *Zhengying baoying lu* (1855), 28b–29b; *Jiuying jiefa* (1882), 6a–6b.

83. *Jie ninü tushuo* (1873), 4b–5b and 7b–8a.

84. *Zhengying baoying lu* (1855), 10b–11a. See also *Guobao tu* (1872), 8a–8b; *Jie ninü tushuo* (1873), 6b–7a.

85. Yu, "Perturbed Spirit," 415–22.

86. *Zhengying baoying lu* (1855), 6b–7a.

87. Wronged women who committed suicide gained a similar type of power after death in late imperial fiction. See Paola Zamperini, "Untamed Hearts: Eros

and Suicide in Late Imperial Chinese Fiction," in *Passionate Women: Female Suicide in Late Imperial China*, ed. Paul S. Ropp, Paola Zamperini and Harriet T. Zurndorfer (Leiden: Brill, 2001), 77–104.

88. "Guanyin dashi zhongjie ninü ge" [Song of the boddhisattva Guanyin strictly forbidding the drowning of girls], *Cihang pudu ce* (1870), 7b–9a. See also *Zhengying baoying lu* (1855), 18a–19a.

CHAPTER 2

1. Yu Zhi's depictions of widespread human suffering in Jiangnan during the Taiping Rebellion were so riveting that fifteen years later, other authors copied some of his illustrations and used them in a booklet for their own cause, during one of the most devastating famines in northern China, from 1876 to 1879. For a direct comparison between *Jiangnan tielei tu* and the similarly titled *Henan qihuang tieleitu*, see Zhu Hu, *Difangxing liudong ji qi chaoyue: Wan Qing yizhen yu jindai Zhongguo de xin chen daixie* [Local movements and beyond: Late Qing humanitarian relief and its renewal in modern China] (Beijing: Renmin daxue chubanshe, 2006), 176–79. See also Kathryn Edgerton-Tarpley, *Tears from Iron: Cultural Responses to Famine in Nineteenth-Century China* (Berkeley: University of California Press, 2008), 132–41.

2. Yu Zhi, *Jiangnan tielei tu* [Illustrated account of Jiangnan (that would make a man of) iron cry] (1864; Taipei: Taiwan xuesheng shuju, 1969), 42. Page numbers refer to this modern edition.

3. The title of *shanren* was not unique to Yu Zhi, but it came into prominence already in the late Ming. See [Angela Leung] Liang Qizi, *Shishan yu jiaohua: Ming Qing de cishan zuzhi* [Charitable works and moral education: Benevolent institutions during the Ming and Qing dynasties] (Shijiazhuang: Hebei jiaoyu chubanshe, 2001), 83 and You Zian, *Shan yu rentong: Ming Qing yilai de cishan yu jiaohua* [In company with goodness: Charity and morality in China, 1600–1930] (Beijing: Zhonghua shuju, 2005), 90–103.

4. Yu Zhi, "Baoying hui guitiao" [Rules and regulations of the Infant Protection Society], in *Deyi lu* (Suzhou, 1869; Taipei: Huawen shuju, 1969), 113. Page numbers refer to this modern edition.

5. Yu Zhi, "Baoying hui guitiao," 114–15.

6. See the following localized studies of female infanticide using gazetteer data: Wang Qiang, "Jiangxi gudai ninü luoxi mantan" [A discussion of the backward practice of female infanticide in premodern Jiangxi], *Nanfang wenwu* 4 (2004): 114–15; Xiao Qian, "Qingdai Jiangxi ninü fengsu zhong de 'shejia' wenti" [Extra-dowry in the custom of infanticide in Qing dynasty Jiangxi], *Jiangnan daxue xuebao* 4, no. 4 (August 2005): 53–56; Xiao Qian, "Qingdai Jiangxi minjian ninü yu tongyang" [Female infanticide and child brides in Qing dynasty Jiangxi], *Wuxi qinggong daxue xuebao shehui kexue ban* 2, no. 3 (September 2001): 239–43; Xiao Qian, "Qingdai Jiangxi ninü zhuangkuang yu jinjiewen" [The condition of female infanticide and its prohibition in Qing dynasty Jiangxi], *Shilin* 1 (2001):

63–68; Xu Xiaowang, "Cong niying xisu kan Fujian lishishang de renkou ziran goucheng wenti" [On issues resulting from the natural composition of the population in Fujianese history, as influenced by the custom of infanticide], *Fujian luntan (jingji shehui ban)* 3 (2003): 52–56; Yang Jianli, "Jindai huabei diqu de ninü xisu" [The custom of female infanticide in modern northern China], *Beijing ligong daxue xue bao (shehui kexue ban)* 5, no. 4 (August 2003): 79–81.

7. Feng Erkang, "Qingdai de hunyin zhidu yu funü de shehui diwei shulun" [A discussion of marriage practices and women's social status in the Qing], *Qingshi yanjiu ji* 5 (1986): 320–21.

8. As cited in Chang Jianhua, "Mingdai niying wenti chutan" [An initial exploration of the problem of infanticide during the Ming dynasty], *Zhongguo shehui lishi pinglun* (Beijing: Shangwu yinshuguan, 2002), n4.

9. Chang, "Mingdai niying wenti."

10. Feng Erkang, "Qingdai de hunyin zhidu," 320–26.

11. Chang Jianhua, "Qingdai niying wenti xintan" [A new inquiry into the problem of infanticide during the Qing dynasty], in *Hunyin jiating yu renkou xingwei*, ed. Li Zhongqing [James Lee], Guo Songyi and Ding Yizhuang (Beijing: Peking University Press, 1999), 201.

12. Chang, "Qingdai niying wenti," 201.

13. Xiao, "Qingdai Jiangxi ninü fengsu," 54.

14. *The Great Qing Code*, trans. William C. Jones (Oxford: Clarendon Press, 1994), 304–5.

15. Françoise Lauwaert, *Le meurtre en famille: Parricide et infanticide en Chine (XVIIIe–XIXe siècle)* (Paris: Éditions Odile Jacob, 1999), 235–45.

16. *Xuying lu* (1873), 1a–b.

17. "Liangchang zushi jiuniying shuo" [Master Liangchang's words on rescuing infants from drowning], *Xuying lu* (1873), 5a–7b.

18. "Yu Xiaohui xiansheng nianpu" [Chronological biography of Mr. Yu Xiaohui], in *Beijing tushuguan cangzhenben nianpu congkan* 156, ed. Zhou Heping (1875; Beijing: Beijing tushuguan chubanshe, 1999), 297. Page numbers refer to this modern edition.

19. "Nianpu," 322.

20. Benjamin Elman, *A Cultural History of Civil Examinations in Late Imperial China* (Berkeley: University of California Press, 2000), 237.

21. "Nianpu," 322.

22. On the range of Yu's philanthropic activities, see "Nianpu," 313–16, 319, 321.

23. Joanna Handlin Smith, *The Art of Doing Good: Charity in Late Ming China* (Berkeley: University of California Press, 2009), 10.

24. Zhu Xi, "Lesser Learning," in *Learning to Be a Sage: Selections from the Conversations of Master Chu, Arranged Topically*, trans. Daniel K. Gardner (Berkeley: University of California Press, 1990), 93.

25. As cited by Catherine Bell, "Stories from an Illustrated Explanation of the Tract of the Most Exalted on Action and Response," in *Religions of China in Practice*, ed. Donald S. Lopez (Princeton, NJ: Princeton University Press, 1996), 439.

26. *Zhengying baoying lu* [Record of rewards and retributions for saving infants] (1855 ed.), 22a.

27. Identical versions of the same tale appear in *Zhengying baoying lu* (1855), 23a–23b and *Cihang pudu ce* (1870), 23b–24a.

28. Justus Doolittle, *Social Life of the Chinese* (New York: Harper and Bros., 1865), vol. 1, 164.

29. *Zhengying baoying lu* (1855), 22b.

30. Smith, *Art of Doing Good*, 11.

31. Yu Zhi, "Zixu" [Author's preface], *Shujitang jinyue* (1880 ed.), *juan* 1, 3a.

32. Yu Zhi, "Zixu," *juan* 1, 3a.

33. Yu Zhi, "Zixu," *juan* 1, 3a.

34. Yu Zhi, *Jiangnan tielei tu*, 86.

35. Stephen H. West and Wilt L. Idema, "The Status of Wang Shifu's *Story of the Western Wing* in Chinese Literature," in *The Story of the Western Wing*, ed. and trans. West and Idema (Berkeley: University of California Press, 1995), 3–18.

36. James Legge translation, chapter 3 of "Mencius," *Chinese Classics*, vol. 2 (orig. trans. 1895), http://sacred-texts.com/cfu/menc/menc03.htm.

37. Yu Zhi, "Liyan" [introductory remarks], *Shujitang jinyue* (1880 ed.), *juan* 1, 26a.

38. Yu Zhi, "Liyan," *juan* 1, 26a.

39. Yu Zhi, "Yuguai tu," in *Shujitang jinyue, juan* 4, 1a–22b.

40. Yu Zhi, "Yuguai tu," 5a.

41. Yu Zhi, "Yuguai tu," 4a.

42. Yu Zhi, "Yuguai tu," 6a.

43. Liao Ben, "Shenmiao xitai" [Temple stages], *Zhongguo xiju tushi* (Zhengzhou: Daxiang chubanshe, 2000), 84.

44. Tanaka Issei, "The Social and Historical Context of Ming-Ch'ing Local Drama," in *Popular Culture in Late Imperial China*, ed. David Johnson, Andrew J. Nathan and Evelyn S. Rawski (Berkeley: University of California Press, 1985), 143–60. See also Huan Tu, "Xiangcunju tan" [Speaking of village operas], *Xiju yuekan* 1, no. 1 (1928), as cited in Joshua Goldstein, *Drama Kings: Players and Publics in the Re-Creation of Peking Opera, 1870–1937* (Berkeley: University of California Press, 2007), 47.

45. Andrea Goldman, "Opera in the City: Theatrical Performance and Urbanite Aesthetics in Beijing, 1770–1900" (Ph.D. dissertation, University of California, Berkeley, 2005), 214.

46. Lu Jiye, "'Zhushazhi' de zuozhe Yu Zhi: Yige tongsu wenxue zuozhe de shengping shilüe" [Yu Zhi, the author of the *Red Birthmark*: A biographical sketch of an author of popular literature], in *Zhongguo jindai wenxue lunwenji (1919–1949)*, ed. Liang Shu'an (Beijing: Zhongguo shehuikexue chuanshe, 1988), 422.

47. "Nianpu," 327.

48. Yan Chen, "Yu Liancun guangwen" [Yu Liancun, educator], *Mohuayinguan ganjiu huairen ji* (n.d.), Qingdai zhuanji congkan 29 (Taipei: Minwen shuju, 1985), 409.

49. Qi Rushan as quoted in Zhang Mingqi, "Woguo qianyishiji de dazhong xiju zuojia jian shijianzhe" [An author and producer of mass dramas from China's previous century], in *Zhongguo jindai wenxue lunwenji (1919–1949)*, ed. Liang Shu'an (1940; Beijing: Zhongguo shehuikexue chubanshe, 1988), 440–41.

50. Lu Jiye, " 'Zhushazhi,' " 421.

51. William Theodore de Bary, "The Community Compact," in *Asian Values and Human Rights: A Confucian Communitarian Perspective* (Cambridge, MA: Harvard University Press, 1998), 58–89.

52. Criticism of the village lecture system, from the *Chinese Repository*, as cited in Victor Mair, "Language and Ideology in the Written Popularizations of the *Sacred Edict*," in *Popular Culture in Late Imperial China*, ed. David Johnson, Andrew J. Nathan and Evelyn S. Rawski (Berkeley: University of California Press, 1985), 353.

53. Yu Zhi, *Jiangnan tielei tu*, 84.

54. Yu Zhi, "Baoying hui jishi" [Chronicle of the Infant Protection Society], *Deyi lu* (Taipei: Huawen shuju, 1969, orig. 1869), 131.

55. Yu Zhi, "Baoying hui jishi," 131.

56. Yu Zhi, "Baoying hui jishi," 131.

57. Yu Zhi, "Baoying hui jishi," 131–32.

58. Yu Zhi, "Baoying hui jishi," 131–32.

59. Yu Zhi, "Xuetang jiangyu ba" [Postscript to *School Lectures*], *Zun xiaoxue zhai wenji* (1883 ed.), *wen ji* 4, 11b.

60. One of Yu Zhi's pithy poems for children laid forth all of these behaviors. See "Xu shentong shi" (Poem of the Child Prodigy Continued), *Xiaoxue yishu zhangcheng* (1892 ed.).

61. Charles Muller, trans., chapter 8, "The Doctrine of the Mean" (1991), www .hm.tyg.jp/~acmuller/contao/docofmean.htm.

62. *Nianpu*, 333.

63. Mary Backus Rankin, *Elite Activism and Political Transformation in China, Zhejiang Province, 1865–1911* (Stanford, CA: Stanford University Press, 1986); William Rowe, *Hankow: Conflict and Community in a Chinese City, 1796–1895* (Stanford, CA: Stanford University Press, 1989), especially chapter 3, "Popular Welfare," 91–134.

64. Yu Zhi, "Yuying tang zhangcheng," *Deyi lu, juan* 3, 1a–3a.

65. Yu Zhi, "Yuying tang zhangcheng," *Deyi lu, juan* 3, 3a–7a.

66. Yu Zhi, "Yuying tang zhangcheng," *Deyi lu, juan* 3, 5a–5b.

67. Fuma Susumu, "Qingmo de baoying hui" [Infant protection societies at the end of the Qing], in *Zhongguo shanhui shantangshi yanjiu*, trans. Wu Yue, Yang Wenxin and Zhang Xuefeng (Beijing: Shangwu yinshuguan, 2005), 275–76.

68. Angela Kiche Leung, "L'accueil des enfants abandonnés dans la Chine du bas-Yangzi aux XVIIe et XVIIIe siècles," *Études Chinoises* 4, no. 1 (Spring 1985): 32.

69. Rachel Ginnis Fuchs, *Abandoned Children: Foundlings and Child Welfare in Nineteenth-Century France* (Albany: State University of New York Press, 1984), 142.

70. Yu Zhi, "Baoying hui guitiao" [Rules and regulations of the Infant Protection Society], *Deyi lu*.

71. On earlier prototypes of the infant protection society, see Susumu, "Qingmo de baoying hui," 279–80.

72. Yu Zhi, "Baoying hui jishi," 129.

73. Liang, *Shishan*, 254.

74. Yu Zhi, "Baoying hui guitiao," 107.

75. Yu Zhi, "Baoying hui guitiao," 112.

76. Liang, *Shishan*, 252.

77. Yu Zhi, "Baoying hui guitiao," 105.

78. Peng Yunzhang as cited in Fuma, "Qingmo," 281.

79. Yu Zhi, "Baoying hui jishi," 129.

80. Fuma, "Qingmo," 291.

81. Fuma, "Qingmo," 289–90.

82. Fuma, "Qingmo," 289–90.

83. Fuma, "Qingmo," 282.

84. Fuma, "Qingmo," 282.

85. A circuit intendant was an interregional, intermediary official, serving as a midlevel bureaucrat between a provincial governor and local county magistrates. For more detail, see R. Kent Guy, *Qing Governors and Their Provinces: The Evolution of Territorial Administration in China, 1644–1796* (Seattle, WA: University of Washington Press, 2010).

86. On Shen Bingcheng's efforts to promote infant protection societies, see *Jiangsu susongtaidao banli baoying binggao tiaogui* [Report and regulations on dealing with infant protection from the circuit intendant of Su-Song-Tai, Jiangsu], (N.p., n.d.).

87. Yu Zhi, "Baoying hui jishi," 129–30.

88. Yu Zhi, "Baoying hui jishi," 129–30.

89. "Nianpu," 337.

90. In 1835, Yu was named a supplementary student (*fusheng*); in 1858, he was promoted to the rank of assistant instructor (*xundao*); in 1863, he was given an honorary blue feather (*lanling*) and his deceased parents were honored; in 1866, he was named as a principal (*jianyuan*) of a foreign language school in Shanghai; and in 1867, his status was raised to the fifth rank (*wupindingdai*), and his deceased grandparents were honored. See *Nianpu*, 313, 326, 329, 330, 331.

91. "Nianpu," 330 and 337. For more on the Language Institute in Shanghai, see Xiong Yuezhi, *Xixue dongjian yu wanqing shehui* [The dissemination of Western learning and late Qing society] (Shanghai: Shanghai renmin chubanshe, 1994), 334–49.

92. On the consequences of differing translations of treaty documents, see Lydia Liu, *The Clash of Empires: The Invention of China in Modern World Making* (Cambridge, MA: Harvard University Press, 2004).

93. On Yu's insistence on Lesser Learning as a principle, see "Nianpu," 331. For the curricular standards in 1870, see "Jicheng zhuoni guang fangyan guan kecheng

shitiao" [A draft petition under consideration on ten points of the curriculum of the *Guang fangyan guan*], in *Guang fangyan guan quan'an* (Shanghai: Shanghai guji chubanshe, 1989).

CHAPTER 3

1. A. C. Moule, "Herbert Allen Giles," *Journal of the Royal Asiatic Society of Great Britain and Ireland* 3 (July 1935): 577.

2. Herbert A. Giles, "Autobibliographical, Etc." (ca. 1925), MS Add. 8964/1, p. 41, Cambridge University Library.

3. Herbert A. Giles, "Infanticide in China," *Adversaria Sinica* (Shanghai: Kelly and Walsh, 1914), vol. 1, 410.

4. "The Prevalence of Infanticide in China," *Journal of the North China Branch of the Royal Asiatic Society* [hereafter, *JNCBRAS*] 20 (1885): 25.

5. For more on infanticide in Britain, see Josephine McDonagh, *Child Murder and British Culture, 1720–1900* (Cambridge: Cambridge University Press, 2003); Mark Jackson, ed., *Infanticide: Historical Perspectives on Child Murder and Concealment, 1550–2000* (Aldershot, England: Ashgate, 2002); Lionel Rose, *The Massacre of the Innocents: Infanticide in Great Britain, 1800–1939* (London: Routledge, 1986). On infanticide in France, see Rachel Ginnis Fuchs, *Abandoned Children: Foundlings and Child Welfare in Nineteenth-Century France* (Albany: State University of New York Press, 1984) and *Poor and Pregnant in Paris: Strategies for Survival in the Nineteenth Century* (New Brunswick, NJ: Rutgers University Press, 1992); R. Burr Litchfield and David Gordon, "Closing the 'Tour': A Close Look at the Marriage Market, Unwed Mothers and Abandoned Children in Mid-Nineteenth Century Amiens," *Journal of Social History* 13 (Spring 1980): 458–73. On infanticide in America, see Peter Hoffer and N. E. H. Hull, *Murdering Mothers: Infanticide in England and New England, 1558–1803* (New York: New York University Press, 1981); Sherri Broder, "Child Care or Child Neglect?: Baby-Farming in Late-Nineteenth-Century Philadelphia," *Gender and Society* 2, no. 2 (June 1988): 128–48; Paul Gilje, "Infant Abandonment in Early Nineteenth-Century New York City: Three Cases," *Signs* 8, no. 3 (Spring 1983): 580–90.

6. McDonagh, *Child Murder*, 123.

7. Margaret L. Arnot, "Infant Death, Child Care and the State: The Baby-Farming Scandal and the First Infant Life Protection Legislation of 1872," *Continuity and Change* 9 (1994): 271–311.

8. Margaretha Weppner, *The North Star and the Southern Cross* (London: Sampson Low, Marston, Low and Searle, 1875), vol. 1, 261.

9. Jennifer Holmgren, "Myth, Fantasy or Scholarship: Images of the Status of Women in Traditional China," *Australian Journal of Chinese Affairs* 155, no. 6 (July 1981), 162.

10. Cf. David Mungello, *Drowning Girls in China: Female Infanticide Since 1650* (Lanham, MD: Rowman and Littlefield, 2008). See note 81 below.

11. Cf. Mungello, *Drowning Girls*, particularly chapter 4, 63–65. Mungello attributes this apparent debate to the "lack of knowledge of the facts" on the part of Protestant "infanticide deniers," as opposed to Catholic missionaries, who were "more knowledgeable" about the subject, given their management of orphanages in China.

12. Otto van der Sprenkel, as cited in Colin Mackerras, *Western Images of China* (Hong Kong: Oxford University Press, 1989), 30n5.

13. Isabelle and Jean-Louis Vissière, eds., *Lettres édifiantes et curieuses de Chine: 1702–1776* (Paris: Garnier-Flammarion, 1979), 28–29.

14. "Preface," *Journal of the Shanghai Literary and Scientific Society* 1 (June 1858): i.

15. On the history of Royal Asiatic Society branches in Asia, see Harold Otness, "Nurturing the Roots for Oriental Studies: The Development of the Libraries of the Royal Asiatic Society Branches and Affiliates in Asia in the Nineteenth Century," *International Association of Orientalist Librarians Bulletin* 43 (1998): 9–17.

16. "List of Members," *JNCBRAS* 20 (1885): 106–14.

17. In 1886 the NCBRAS sought to remedy the lack of Catholic missionary participation by electing the Jesuit Father Angelo Zottoli as Honorary Member; see "Proceedings," *JNCBRAS* 20, no. 5 and 6 (1885): 292.

18. On nineteenth-century scholarly societies, see the Scholarly Societies Project website, www.scholarly-societies.org, sponsored by the University of Waterloo Library.

19. "List of Members," *JNCBRAS*, 106–14.

20. "Prevalence of Infanticide," *JNCBRAS*, 36.

21. "Prevalence of Infanticide," *JNCBRAS*, 38–39.

22. "Prevalence of Infanticide," *JNCBRAS*, 49.

23. Samuel Wells Williams, *The Middle Kingdom: A Survey of the Geography, Government, Literature, Social Life, Arts, and History of the Chinese Empire and Its Inhabitants* (Rev. ed.) (New York: C. Scribner's Sons, 1882), vol. 2, 239–43.

24. François Xavier d'Entrecolles, letter to Madame ***, October 19, 1720, in *Lettres édifiantes et curieuses, écrites des Missions Étrangeres: Mémoires de la Chine, &c.* (Paris, 1781), vol. 19, 102.

25. Letter from du Baudory as cited in Gaubil to Mgr. de Normond, November 4, 1722, *Lettres édifiantes et curieuses, écrites des Missions Étrangeres: Mémoires de la Chine, &c.* (Paris, 1781), vol. 19, 253.

26. Olof Torén, "O. Toreens Reise nach Suratte," in Pehr Osbeck et al., *Reise nach Ostindien und China* (Rostock, 1765), 235–36.

27. For a translation of Zhu Xi's *Family Rituals*, see Patricia Buckley Ebrey, trans., *Chu Hsi's Family Rituals: A Twelfth-Century Chinese Manual for the Performance of Cappings, Weddings, Funerals and Ancestral Rites* (Princeton, NJ: Princeton University Press, 1991). On the use of Zhu Xi's text in early modern Chinese funerary rituals, see Nicolas Standaert, *The Interweaving of Rituals: Funerals in the*

Cultural Exchange Between China and Europe (Seattle: University of Washington Press, 2008).

28. Zhu Xi, *Family Rituals*, 96.

29. J. J. M. de Groot, *The Religious System of China: Its Ancient Forms, Evolution, History and Present Aspect, Manners, Customs and Social Institutions Connected Therewith*, vol. 3, part 1, "Disposal of the Dead" (Leiden: Brill, 1897), 1387.

30. de Groot, *Religious System*, 1075.

31. Huang Liuhong, "Yuyang ying'er," *Fuhui quanshu* (17th c.), *juan* 31, 18b–19c.

32. D'Entrecolles to Madame ***, October 19, 1720, 108.

33. Susan Naquin, *Peking: Temples and City Life, 1400–1900* (Berkeley: University of California Press, 2000), 646–47.

34. Joseph-Marie Amiot, letter to M***, September 28, 1777, in *Mémoires concernant l'histoire, les sciences, les arts, les moeurs, les usages, &c. des Chinois, par les missionnaires de Pe-kin* (Paris, 1780), vol. 6, 323.

35. On charitable burial societies, see Liang Qizi (Angela Leung), *Shishan yu jiaohua: Ming Qing de cishan zhuzhi* [Charitable works and moral education: Benevolent institutions during the Ming and Qing dynasties] (Shijiazhuang, Hebei: Hebei jiaoyu chubanshe, 2001), 278–306.

36. "Xinfeng yiguta" [Xinfeng's bone collection tower], *Nanhu wanbao* [Nanhu Evening News], November 16, 2008, http://nhwb.cnjxol.com/html/2008-11/16/content_189275.htm, accessed November 29, 2010.

37. de Groot, *Religious System*, vol. 3, 1387–89.

38. W. Somerset Maugham, "The Sights of the Town," in *On a Chinese Screen* (New York: George H. Doran, 1922), 167–68.

39. George Wingrove Cooke, *China: Being "The Times" Special Correspondence from China in the Years 1857–58* (London: Routledge and Co., 1859), 98–99.

40. Cooke, *China*, 100.

41. Henry Auchincloss, "Shanghai: Its Streets, Shops and People," *The Continental Monthly* 6 (July–December 1864), 648.

42. Mary Isabella Bryson, *Child Life in Chinese Homes* (London: Religious Tract Society, 1885), 17.

43. C. F. Gordon Cumming, *Wanderings in China* (Edinburgh: William Blackwood, 1886), vol. 2, 61–62.

44. Maugham, "Sights of the Town," 168.

45. John Scarth, *Twelve Years in China: The People, the Rebels, and the Mandarins, by a British Resident* (Edinburgh: Thomas Constable, 1860), 103.

46. Auchincloss, "Shanghai: Its Streets, Shops, and People," 648.

47. For illustrations and photographs of baby towers, see Scarth, *Twelve Years in China*, 102; Mrs. J. F. Bishop, *Chinese Pictures: Notes on Photographs Made in China* (New York: Charles L. Bowman, 1900?), 60–61; E. A. Ross, *The Changing Chinese: The Conflict of Oriental and Western Cultures in China* (New York: The Century Co., 1911), 208. See also photographs contained in the archival collections

Ralph G. Gold, Yale Divinity Library Special Collections, (1911–13), baby tower at Fuzhou, and Sidney Gamble, Duke University Archives (1917–19), baby tower at Guan Xian in Sichuan.

48. On the Chefoo baby tower, see Carl Crow, *The Travelers' Handbook for China* (San Francisco: San Francisco News Co., 1913), 166. On the Shanghai baby tower, see William Frederick Mayers, Nicholas B. Dennys and Charles King, *The Treaty Ports of China and Japan: A Complete Guide to the Open Ports of Those Countries, Together with Peking, Yedo, Hongkong and Macao, Forming a Guide Book and Vade Mecum for Travellers, Merchants and Residents in General, with 29 Maps and Plans* (London, Trübner, 1867), 406.

49. Mary Ninde Gamewell, *New Life Currents in China* (New York: Methodist Book Concern, 1919), 178.

50. Theodore M. Porter, *Trust in Numbers: The Pursuit of Objectivity in Science and Public Life* (Princeton, NJ: Princeton University Press, 1995), ix.

51. "Prevalence of Infanticide," *JNCBRAS*, 35.

52. John Barrow, *Travels in China*, 2nd ed. (London, 1806), 172–76.

53. Barrow, *Travels*, 169–70.

54. Barrow, *Travels*, 176.

55. On the development of statistics in the nineteenth century, see Theodore Porter, *The Rise of Statistical Thinking, 1820–1900* (Princeton, NJ: Princeton University Press, 1986).

56. William Petty, *Political Arithmetick* (orig. London, 1690), http://socserv2.mcmaster.ca/~econ/ugcm/3113/petty/poliarith.html, accessed January 16, 2006.

57. David Abeel, "Notices of Infanticide Collected from the People of Fukien," *Chinese Repository* 12, no. 10 (October 1843): 542.

58. Abeel, "Infanticide," 542.

59. Abeel, "Infanticide," 546–48.

60. Adele M. Fielde, *Pagoda Shadows: Studies from Life in China* (London, 1887), 25–26.

61. Fielde, *Pagoda Shadows*, 20.

62. Fielde, *Pagoda Shadows*, 173–74.

63. Fielde, *Pagoda Shadows*, 136.

64. Fielde, *Pagoda Shadows*, 26.

65. Gabriel Palatre, *L'infanticide et l'oeuvre de la Sainte-Enfance en Chine* (Shanghai: Mission Catholique, l'Orphelinat de Tou-sè-wè, 1878), xiii.

66. Palatre, *L'infanticide*, 112.

67. Aloysius Pfister, "Avertissement," in Palatre, *L'infanticide*, i.

68. Palatre, *L'infanticide*, xi.

69. Joseph de la Servière, *Histoire de la mission du Kiang-nan* (Shanghai, 1914), vol. 2, 278.

70. Palatre, *L'infanticide*, 57.

71. Palatre, *L'infanticide*, 65.

72. Palatre, *L'infanticide*, 113.

73. Palatre, *L'infanticide*, 183.

74. It is unclear whose translation mistake this may have been. Palatre credits the French translations of the Chinese texts in his book to another Jesuit missionary, Father Durandière. See Palatre, *L'infanticide*, xiii.

75. Palatre unknowingly cited the following four titles and editions by Yu Zhi: [Deyi lu] *Té-i-lou*, "Recueil de choses utiles" [Collection of useful things] (1869); [Xuetang jiangyu] *Hio-tang-kiang-iu*, "Discours moraux destinés aux Ecoliers" [Moral speeches intended for schoolboys] (1860); [Xuetang riji] *Hio-tang-je-ki*, "Recueil d'histoires quotidiennes à l'usage des Ecoles" [Collection of daily stories for use by schools] (1860, 1868, 1872 eds.); [Jiangnan tieleitu xinbian] *Kiang-nan-tié-lei-tou-sin-pien*, "Nouvelle description malheurs du Kiang-nan" [New description of the misfortunes of Jiangnan] (n.d.).

76. Palatre, *L'infanticide*, 59n1.

77. "Prevalence of Infanticide," *JNCBRAS*, 26.

78. Léon Lallemand, *Histoire des infants abandonnés et délaissés* (Paris, 1885), 604–22.

79. Éduoard Chappet, *Société de Géographie de Lyon, Séance mensuelle du 8 janvier 1885, L'infanticide et l'oeuvre de la Sainte-Enfance en Chine par le Père Palatre* (Lyon, 1885).

80. J.-J. Matignon, "Infanticide et avortement," *Superstition, Crime et Misère en Chine* (Lyon: Storck and Co., 1902), 157–84.

81. Herbert A. Giles, "Infanticide in China," *Adversaria Sinica* (Shanghai: Kelly and Walsh, 1914), vol. 1, 421.

82. The replication of the Chinese contents of Palatre's work continues today. Palatre's chapter divisions, much of his textual evidence, and twenty of his illustrations have been entirely reproduced in David Mungello's recent study of female infanticide in China, *Drowning Girls in China*, in particular chapters 2 and 3. Mungello offers no analytical commentary on his extensive recycling of Palatre's work, drawing upon it directly as Chinese evidence regarding infanticide.

83. Adolphe Vasseur, *Un orphelinat chinois de la Sainte-Enfance à l'exposition internationale d'imagerie de Rouen et l'infanticide en Chine prouvé à M. Tchen-Ki-Tong par ses compatriotes* (Paris, n.d.), 2.

84. Charles de Harlez, "L'infanticide en Chine," *Le Muséon: Revue Internationale* 4, no. 2–4 (1885): 205–10, 269–80, 424–36.

85. Charles de Harlez, "Infanticide in China According to Chinese Documents," *Dublin Review* 111 (July 1892): 117–43.

CHAPTER 4

1. *Iu-Chien-Tchou-Iom. Trois entretiens illustrés sur la Chine donnés à Québec, Avril 1872 par le R. P. Vasseur, S. J., Missionnaire Apostolique en Chine, Directeur de l'Oeuvre Chinoise de St. Luc pour la Propagation de la Foi* (n.p., n.d.), 9–25.

2. *Iu-Chien-Tchou-Iom*, 12–25.

3. *Iu-Chien-Tchou-Iom*, 10.

4. Henrietta Harrison has discussed the Sainte-Enfance as an early prototype of the contemporary "transnational aid organization." See Harrison, "'A Penny for the Little Chinese': The French Holy Childhood Association in China, 1843–1951," *American Historical Review* 113, no. 1 (February 2008): 72–92.

5. Thomas Laqueur, "Bodies, Details, and the Humanitarian Narrrative," in *The New Cultural History*, ed. Lynn Hunt (Berkeley: University of California Press, 1989), 176–78.

6. Luc Boltanski, *Distant Suffering: Morality, Media and Politics*, trans. Graham Burchell (Cambridge: Cambridge University Press, 1999).

7. "Decree for the Armenians, issued at the Council of Florence in 1439," Medieval Sourcebook: The Seven Sacraments: Catholic Doctrinal Documents, www.fordham.edu/halsall/source/ 1438sacraments.asp#armen, accessed September 2, 2011.

8. St. Augustine, "On the Merit and the Forgiveness of Sins, and the Baptism of Infants" (Book 3), www.newadvent.org/fathers/15013.htm, accessed September 2, 2011.

9. St. Thomas Aquinas, *Summa Theologica*, Supplement to the Third Part, Question 70, Article 1 and 2, www.newadvent.org/summa/5070.htm, accessed September 2, 2011.

10. Both Breton cases are discussed in Annick Tillier, *Des criminelles au village: Femmes infanticide en Bretagne, 1825–1865* (Rennes: Presses universitaires de Rennes, 2001), 195–96.

11. St. Thomas Aquinas, *Summa Theologica*, Part III, Question 68, Article 10, www.newadvent.org/summa/4068.htm#article9, accessed September 2, 2011.

12. Jules Corblet, *Histoire dogmatique, liturgique et archéologique du sacrement de baptême* (Paris: Société Générale de Librairie Catholique, 1881), vol. 1, 395.

13. François Xavier d'Entrecolles to Madame ***, October 19, 1720, in *Lettres édifiantes et curieuses, écrites des Missions Étrangeres: Mémoires de la Chine, &c.* (Paris, 1781), vol. 19, 100–101.

14. Du Baudory as cited in Antoine Gaubil to Mgr. de Nemond, November 4, 1722, in *Lettres édifiantes et curieuses, écrites des Missions Étrangeres: Mémoires de la Chine, &c.* (Paris, 1781), vol. 19, 250.

15. Du Baudory as cited in Antoine Gaubil, 251–52.

16. Corblet, *Baptême* 1, 394.

17. Bureaux du Conseil Central de l'oeuvre de la Sainte-Enfance, *Manuel de l'oeuvre de la Sainte-Enfance* (Paris, 1872), 27.

18. Sainte-Enfance, *Manuel*, 16–17.

19. Father Delvaux, as quoted by Alain Sauret, "China's Role in the Foundation and Development of the Pontifical Society of the Holy Childhood," in *Historiography of the Chinese Catholic Church: Nineteenth and Twentieth Centuries*, ed. Jeroom Heyndrickx (Leuven: Ferdinand Verbiest Foundation, 1994), 248.

20. Sainte-Enfance, *Manuel*, 16–17.

21. Sainte-Enfance, *Manuel*, 32.

22. Sainte-Enfance, *Manuel*, 53–54.

23. Sainte-Enfance, *Manuel*, 36. For more on the activity of the Propagation de la Foi, see J. P. Daughton, *An Empire Divided: Religion, Republicanism, and the Making of French Colonialism, 1880–1914* (Oxford: Oxford University Press, 2006).

24. Sainte-Enfance, *Manuel*, 63–64.

25. Corblet, *Baptême* 2, 171–310.

26. Sainte-Enfance, *Manuel*, 64.

27. Sainte-Enfance, *Manuel*, 65.

28. On the phenomenon of Marian apparitions as revealed to children, see Sandra Zimdars-Swartz, *Encountering Mary: From La Salette to Medjugorje* (Princeton, NJ: Princeton University Press, 1991).

29. "Compte général des Recettes et Dépenses, du 18 avril 1845 au 20 mai 1846," *Annales de l'Oeuvre de la Sainte-Enfance* 1, no. 2 (1845–46): 152–59.

30. Daughton, *An Empire Divided*, 38.

31. "Exercice 1874–1875, Compte général de l'année," *Annales de l'Oeuvre de la Sainte-Enfance* 26, no. 164 (1874–75): 146–55.

32. "Exercice 1899–1900, Compte général de l'année," *Annales de l'Oeuvre de la Sainte-Enfance* 51, no. 314 (1899–1900): 152–79.

33. Louis Hermand, *Les Étapes de la Mission du Kiang-nan, 1842–1922* (Zi-ka-wei, Shanghai: Imprimerie de la Mission Zi-Ka-Wei, 1926), 28.

34. Hermand, *Étapes*, 22.

35. Hermand, *Étapes*.

36. Sainte-Enfance, *Manuel*, 59.

37. Sainte-Enfance, *Manuel*, 59.

38. M. le Curé de Notre-Dame de Châteauroux, "Petit catechisme de l'Oeuvre de la Sainte-Enfance," *Annales* 12, no. 76 (1860): 352.

39. M. le Curé, "Petit catechisme," 352–53.

40. Sainte-Enfance, *Manuel*, 21.

41. M. le Curé, "Petit catechisme," 354–55.

42. Harrison, "'A Penny for the Little Chinese,'" 85.

43. Harrison, "'A Penny for the Little Chinese,'" 86.

44. As quoted in Sauret, "Holy Childhood," 259.

45. Harrison, "'A Penny for the Little Chinese,'" 80.

46. Tcheng-Ki-Tong (Chen Jitong), *Les Chinois peints par eux-mêmes* (Paris: Calmann Lévy, 1884), 175–76.

47. M. le Curé, "Petit catechisme."

48. M. le Curé, "Petit catechisme."

49. M. le Curé, "Petit catechisme."

50. Sainte-Enfance, *Manuel*, 58.

51. The articles ran from late November to late December 1875. As a result of these accusations, the director of the Sainte-Enfance filed a defamation case against Sarcey and the editor of the newspaper, Edmond About. Eventually the two were fined 700 francs and required to pay damages of 1,000 francs. See Edmond About, "Condamnés," *Le XIXe Siècle*, December 25, 1875.

52. Sarcey, "Les petits chinois," *Le XIXe Siècle*, November 30, 1875.

53. Sarcey, "Les petits chinois," *Le XIXe Siècle*, December 8, 1875.

54. Sarcey, "Les petits chinois," *Le XIXe Siècle*, November 30, 1875.

55. Sarcey, "Les petits chinois," *Le XIXe Siècle*, December 8–9, 1875.

56. See, for example, the 1881 play about an African slave child, "Suema, petite esclave africaine," *Annales* 32, no. 199 (1881): 82 ff.

57. "Les Jeunes Herboriseurs, ou les petits bergers de Savoie," *Annales* 12, no. 77 (1860): 420–25.

58. "Les Jeunes Herboriseurs," 426–31.

59. "Rosalie et Berthe, ou les filles d'un pêcheur Normand," *Annales* 13, no. 78 (1861): 59–71.

60. "Sin-a-li, ou l'orphelin de Zi-ka-wei," *Annales* 14, no. 88 (1862): 361–83; "Maria Siao, ou l'aveugle de Kiou-kiang," *Annales* 22, no. 136 (1870): 330–60; Le Directeur diocésain de l'Oeuvre de la Sainte-Enfance à Moutiers-Tarentaise, "Sio-Tsia, ou l'orpheline de Pen-choui," *Annales* 28, no. 178 (1877): 330–52.

61. For "useless," "piece of furniture," "vile crocodile" and "ignoble hippopotamus," see "Sio-tsia." For "disgusting little monster," see "Maria Siao." For "viper" and "lazy," see "Sin-a-li."

62. Harrison, "'A Penny for the Little Chinese,'" 72 and 88.

63. "Sin-a-li," 361–64.

64. "Sin-a-li," 373–76.

65. "Sin-a-li," 376–79.

66. "Sin-a-li," 379–83.

67. Danicourt refers to the list (mistakenly giving the total as 317 children) in a letter to the Sainte-Enfance dated November 28, 1853, mentioned in *Annales* 7, no. 47 (1855): 440.

68. [Zhejiang baptismal list], Folder L1, Pontificium Opus a Sancta Infantia archives, Rome.

69. François-Xavier Danicourt to M. le vice-président de l'Oeuvre de la Sainte-Enfance, letter dated April 4, 1851, in *Annales* 4, no. 24 (1852): 66–72.

70. Danicourt's letter in *Annales* 7, no. 47 (1855): 440.

71. The Chinese transliterations of European Christian names were standardized at some earlier point of missionary contact, probably from their Italian or Portuguese versions. Henrietta Harrsion, personal communication, May 27, 2013.

72. Danicourt to M. le vice-président, letter dated April 4, 1851.

CHAPTER 5

1. On the publication of the *Yiwen lu*, see Auguste Colombel, *Histoire de la Mission du Kiang-nan, Troisième partie, II L'Episcopat de Mgr. Languillat (1865–1878)* (Shanghai, 1895–1905), 246 and also *Troisième partie, III—L'Episcopat de Mgr. Garnier (1879–1898)*, 418.

2. Li Di [Li Wenyu], "Ninü lun" [On drowning daughters], *Li Ku* (1886).

3. Li Wenyu came from a family that had been Catholic for some eight generations, when one of his early ancestors had converted. See *Li Ku*, 1b. For more on the life of Li Wenyu, see Joachim Kurtz, "Messenger of the Sacred Heart: Li Wenyu (1840–1911) and the Jesuit Periodical Press in Late Qing Shanghai," in *From Woodblocks to the Internet: Chinese Publishing and Print Culture in Transition, Circa 1800 to 2008*, ed. Cynthia Brokaw and Christopher Reed (Leiden: Brill, 2010), 81–110.

4. Li Di, "Ninü lun" [On drowning daughters], *Li Ku, juan* 9, 9b–10a.

5. Li Di, "Ninü lun," *Li Ku, juan* 9, 8b.

6. Competition between native Chinese and foreign missionary charitable efforts has been described for famine relief as well. See Andrea Janku, "Sowing Happiness: Spiritual Competition in Famine Relief Activities in Late Nineteenth-Century China," *Minsu quyi* 143 (March 2004): 89–118.

7. There were 182 foundling homes established during the Qing dynasty in Jiangsu and another 131 in Zhejiang. See the appendix in Liang Qizi [Angela Leung], *Shishan yu jiaohua: Ming Qing de cishan zhuzhi* [Charitable works and moral education: Benevolent institutions during the Ming and Qing dynasties] (Shijiazhuang, Hebei: Hebei jiaoyu chubanshe, 2001), 327–67. See also Angela Leung, "L'accueil des enfants abandonnés dans la Chine du bas-Yangzi aux XVIIe et XVIIIe siècles," *Études Chinoises* 4, no. 1 (Spring 1985): 15–54; Fuma Susumu, "Qingdai qianqi de yuying shiye" [Early Qing foundling home enterprises], in *Zhongguo shanhui shantangshi yanjiu* (Beijing: Shangwu yinshuguan, 2005).

8. Liang, *Shishan*, 327–67.

9. Gabriel Palatre, *L'infanticide et l'oeuvre de la Sainte-Enfance en Chine* (Shanghai: Mission Catholique, l'Orphelinat de Tou-sè-wè, 1878), 165–70.

10. Louis Hermand, *Les Étapes de la Mission du Kiang-nan, 1842–1922* (Zi-ka-wei, Shanghai: Imprimerie de la Mission Zi-Ka-Wei, 1926), 24.

11. Palatre, *L'infanticide*.

12. Letter from Gabriel Palatre to R. P. Foucault, March 2, 1874. Pontificium Opus a Sancta Infantia (POSI) archives, Series C, File 368.

13. "Copper cash" coins (made of a copper and zinc alloy) were the basis for small, daily transactions in imperial China. In theory, a string of 1000 cash was equivalent to one silver tael, but in practice, the exchange value of cash to tael was not standardized across the empire. Writing in the last years of the nineteenth century, Joseph Edkins, a British Protestant missionary, estimated that a Chinese workman required 200 cash per day to live, whereas two centuries earlier, he would have required only 100 cash for daily necessities. See Joseph Edkins, *Chinese Currency* (Shanghai: Presbyterian Mission Press, 1901), 117.

14. Palatre to Foucault, POSI archives, Series C, File 368.

15. Shen Bingcheng, "Qingtongshi geshu juban baoyinghui bing" [Letter requesting the circulation of instructions to affiliated areas to establish infant protection societies] (12th year of Tongzhi, 1st month, 3rd day [January 31, 1873]), *Jiangsu susongtaidao banli baoying binggao tiaogui* [Report and regulations on dealing with infant protection from the circuit intendant of Su-Song-Tai, Jiangsu], (N.p., n.d.).

16. Yang Futai, "Zhejiang xunfubuyuan Yang tongshi gezhouxian juban bao-ying yuanzha" [Original letter from the Zhejiang governor and vice-president of the board, Yang, informing each district and county to establish infant protection societies] (9th year of Tongzhi, 8th month [September 1870]), *Jiangsu susongtaidao banli baoying binggao tiaogui*.

17. *Xinbao*, March 9–20, 1877. The *Xinbao* reprint included Shen Bingcheng's version of rules and regulations for infant protection societies, which was based on Yu Zhi's original template. It also included a complete English translation of the memorials and regulations, suggesting that Chinese philanthropic concern for unwanted children was of interest to foreign audiences as well.

18. "Zongli yamen zhi geguo gongshi shu" [Letter from the Zongli Yamen to the envoys of various countries], in *Fangyangjiao shuwenjietie xuan*, ed. Wang Minglun (Jinan: Qilu shushe, 1984), 381.

19. "Zongli yamen," 381. For more on this dynamic, see Henrietta Harrison, "'A Penny for the Little Chinese': The French Holy Child Association in China, 1843–1951," *American Historical Review* 113, no. 1 (February 2008): 72–92.

20. "Zongli yamen," 382.

21. Antiforeign activity in China increased dramatically after the treaty marking the conclusion of the Second Opium War in 1860 allowed missionaries to roam freely in the Chinese interior. See Paul A. Cohen, *China and Christianity: The Missionary Movement and the Growth of Chinese Antiforeignism, 1860–1870* (Cambridge, MA: Harvard University Press, 1963). Cohen discusses the Tianjin Massacre in particular in chapter 9. See also John King Fairbank, "Patterns Behind the Tientsin Massacre," *Harvard Journal of Asiatic Studies* 20, no. 3–4 (1957): 480–511.

22. Wade to Prince of Kung, July 9, 1870, Enclosure 1 in Despatch no. 36, in *Papers Relating to the Massacre of Europeans at Tien-tsin on the 21st June, 1870*, China series, no. 1 (London: Great Britain Foreign Office, 1871), 82.

23. Barend J. ter Haar, *Telling Stories: Witchcraft and Scapegoating in Chinese History* (Leiden: Brill, 2006), 92–94.

24. Philip Kuhn, *Soulstealers: The Chinese Sorcery Scare of 1768* (Cambridge, MA: Harvard University Press, 1990).

25. "Mifang wenda" [Questions and answers from a secret visit], *Fanyangjiao shuwenjietie xuan*, ed. Wang Minglun (Jinan: Qilu shushe, 1984), 117.

26. "Tientsin Massacre Confirmed," *China Mail Extra*, July 10, 1870.

27. Enclosure in Foreign Office file 17/608, Public Records Office (London).

28. Leo Ou-fan Lee and Andrew J. Nathan, "The Beginnings of Mass Culture: Journalism and Fiction in the Late Ch'ing and Beyond," in *Popular Culture in Late Imperial China*, ed. David Johnson, Andrew J. Nathan and Evelyn S. Rawski (Berkeley: University of California Press, 1985), 362.

29. Barbara Mittler, *A Newspaper for China? Power, Identity and Change in Shanghai's News Media, 1872–1912* (Cambridge, MA: Harvard University Press), 53.

30. On this genre of works in late imperial Chinese literary history, see Judith Zeitlin, *Historian of the Strange: Pu Songling and the Chinese Classical Tale* (Stanford, CA: Stanford University Press, 1993).

31. "Ninü ebao" [Drowning daughter leads to karmic retribution], *Shenbao*, May 14, 1874.

32. Mittler, *Newspaper*, 94–97.

33. "Shanü sangqi" [Killing a daughter means losing a wife], *Shenbao*, April 7, 1876.

34. "Yinghai cansi" [Baby dies tragically], *Shenbao*, May 18, 1878.

35. "Yinghai cansi," *Shenbao*.

36. "Lun ninü lousu" [On the ignorant custom of drowning daughters], *Shenbao*, December 11, 1878.

37. Benjamin Hobson, *Fuying xinshuo* [New teachings (on the medical care of) women and infants] (Shanghai: Renji yiguan, 1858), reprinted in vol. 380, *Gugong zhenben congkan* (Haikou: Hainan chubanshe, 2000).

38. Hobson, *Fuying xinshuo*, 2a (original pagination).

39. "Lun ninü lousu," *Shenbao*.

40. William C. Milne, *Life in China* (London: Routledge, 1857), 42.

41. "Jiehai mouli" [Using children to gain a profit], *Shenbao*, December 12, 1879.

42. On baby farming in nineteenth-century England, see Margaret L. Arnot, "Infant Death, Child Care and the State: The Baby-Farming Scandal and the First Infant Life Protection Legislation of 1872," *Continuity and Change* 9 (1994): 271–311.

43. "Alleged Baby Farming in Tranmere," *Liverpool Mercury*, September 5, 1879. The Tranmere case was covered over the course of several issues through the month of September.

44. "Jiehai mouli," *Shenbao*.

45. "Alleged Baby Farming in Tranmere," *Liverpool Mercury*, September 5, 1879.

46. On women's education in the early twentieth century, see Paul Bailey, *Gender and Education in China: Gender Discourses and Women's Schooling in the Early Twentieth Century* (London: Routledge, 2007). On footbinding, see Dorothy Ko, *Cinderella's Sisters: A Revisionist History of Footbinding* (Berkeley: University of California Press, 2005).

47. "Qing jin nüzi chanzu peicheng youyong zhi cai qi laigao zhaodeng" [A letter to the editor on forbidding women's footbinding in order to develop useful talent], *Shenbao*, November 5, 1901.

48. "Jiangxi sidao yanjin ninü shiwen" [A Jiangxi official's instructions on strictly forbidding drowning daughters], *Shenbao*, January 22, 1907.

49. Ko, *Cinderella's Sisters*.

50. "Gailang jiating zhi zuiyao banfa" [The most critical ways to reform the family system], *Shenbao*, September 10, 1922.

51. "Gailang jiating," *Shenbao*.

52. On Yan's reform efforts, see Donald Gillin, *Warlord: Yen Hsi-shan in Shansi Province, 1911–1949* (Princeton, NJ: Princeton University Press, 1967).

53. "Shanxi tongxin: Mofangsheng jiaomin zhengce" [Correspondence from Shanxi: The policies of the model province on educating the people], *Shenbao*,

March 11, 1922. The *Shenbao* repeatedly praised Yan Xishan's reform efforts. See also the March 24, 1922 and October 22, 1922 issues.

54. "Zhejiang zuijin zhenggang" [Zhejiang's recent political program], *Shenbao*, March 28, 1927.

55. For prohibitions against female infanticide from the following government agencies, see the following issues of the *Shenbao*: Zhejiang provincial government's department of civil affairs, "Hangzhou kuaixin" [Hangzhou express correspondence], July 15, 1927; Jiangsu provincial government's department of civil affairs, "Susheng shiqinian du shizeng dagang" [Jiangsu 1928 administrative summary], June 15, 1928; national government's ministry of the interior, "Neibu tongling baohu nüquan" [Ministry of Interior orders the protection of women's rights], June 16, 1928; Shanghai country government, "Neizhengbu baozhang nüquan zhi tongling" [The order of the Ministry of the Interior guaranteeing women's rights], June 26, 1928; Guangzhou municipal government, "Yuesheng jinwen" [Recent news from Guangdong], July 15, 1928.

56. Sun Yat-sen, *San min chu i* [The Three Principles of the People], ed. L. T. Chen, trans. Frank W. Price (Shanghai: China Committee, Institute of Pacific Relations, 1927), 12–25.

57. Sun, *San min chu i*, 22–26.

58. "Zhesheng yanjin ninü louxi" [Zhejiang Province strictly forbids the backward habit of drowning girls], *Shibao*, February 18, 1929.

59. The results of the 1928 census were deemed unreliable by later social scientists. See Jiang Tao, *Zhongguo jindai renkou shi* [A history of China's modern population] (Hangzhou: Zhejiang renmin chubanshe, 1993), 100–107. For more on the rise of the social survey in twentieth-century China, see Tong Lam, *A Passion for Facts: Social Surveys and the Construction of the Chinese Nation-State, 1900–1949* (Berkeley: University of California Press, 2011).

60. "Zhesheng yanjin ninü louxi," *Shibao*.

61. "Zhejiangsheng queshao nüzi, yue erbaiwushiwan ren" [Zhejiang Province has a shortage of women, approximately 2.5 million people], *Shenbao*, May 12, 1930.

62. Chen Changheng, *Zhongguo renkou lun*, 8th ed. [On China's population] (Shanghai: Shangwu yinshuguan, 1928).

63. Chen Dongyuan, *Zhongguo funü shenghuo shi* [The History of Women's Lives in China] (Shanghai: Shanghai wenshu chubanshe, 1990 [1928]).

64. Chen Changheng, *Zhongguo renkou lun*, 21–24.

65. Shan-ge-er furen [Margaret Sanger], "Shengyu zhicai de shenme yu zenyang" [The what and how of birth control], *Funü zazhi* [The Ladies' Journal], (June 1, 1922), 130–32.

66. Chen Dongyuan, *Zhongguo funü shenghuo shi*, 417.

67. Chen Dongyuan, *Zhongguo funü shenghuo shi*, 414.

68. For more on eugenics in early twentieth-century China, see Frank Dikötter, *Imperfect Conceptions: Medical Knowledge, Birth Defects and Eugenics in China* (New York: Columbia University Press, 1998) and Yuehtsen Juliette Chung, *Struggle for*

National Survival: Eugenics in Sino-Japanese Contexts, 1896–1945 (New York: Routledge, 2002).

69. Zhou Jianren, "Shanzhongxue de lilun yu shishi" [The theory and implementation of eugenics], in *Jinhualun yu shanzhongxue* [Evolution and eugenics] (Shanghai: Shanghai shangwu yinshuguan, 1923), 63.

70. Chung, *Struggle*, 14.

71. Zhou Jianren, "Shanzhongxue yu qi jianlizhe" [Eugenics and its founders], in *Jinhualun yu shanzhongxue*, 49.

72. Zhou Jianren, "Shanzhongxue de lilun yu shishi," 72–73.

73. See Holmes Welch, *The Buddhist Revival in China* (Cambridge, MA: Harvard University Press, 1968).

74. "Zhejiang minzhengting jin'ge ninü banfa an" [Proposed methods for prohibiting female infanticide from the Zhejiang people's assembly] and "Shanxi shengzhengfu gechu ninü banfa an" [Proposed methods for abolishing female infanticide from the Shanxi provincial government], *Chongbian zhengying lu* [Reedition of the Record of Saving Infants] (1929), 69–74.

CONCLUSION

1. Xinran, *Message from an Unknown Chinese Mother: Stories of Loss and Love*, trans. Nicky Harman (London: Chatto and Windus, 2010), 34–37.

2. Xinran, *Message*, 34–37.

3. Judith Banister, "Shortage of Girls in China Today," *Journal of Population Research* 21, no. 1 (2004): 19–45.

4. Ansley Coale and Judith Banister, "Five Decades of Missing Females in China," *Demography* 31, no. 3 (August 1994): 459–79.

5. Banister, "Shortage of Girls," 19–45.

6. Banister, "Shortage of Girls," 19–45.

7. Li Shuzhuo, "Imbalanced Sex Ratio at Birth and Comprehensive Intervention in China," paper for the 4th Asia Pacific Conference on Reproductive and Sexual Heath and Rights, Hyderabad, India, 2007. Figure 2, SRB in China, overall tendency and regional differences, 1982–2005. www.unpfa.org/gender/docs/studies/china.pdf, accessed November 25, 2011.

8. "New Campaign Targets Gender Ratio Imbalance," *People's Daily Online*, August 17, 2011, http://english.peopledaily.com.cn/90882/7571975.html, accessed December 4, 2012.

9. Li, "Imbalanced Sex Ratio at Birth," appendix, Table 1.

10. Monica Das Gupta first identified this pattern of increased sex discrimination at higher levels of economic development in northern regions of India, including Haryana and Punjab. See an overview of her findings in Tina Rosenberg, "The Daughter Deficit," *New York Times Magazine*, August 19, 2009. See also Chu Junhong, "Sex Determination and Sex-Selective Abortion in Rural Central China," *Population and Development Review* 27, no. 2 (June 2001): 249–81.

11. Jing-Bao Nie, *Behind the Silence: Chinese Voices on Abortion* (Lanham, MD: Rowman and Littlefield, 2005), 110.

12. On the relative influence of sex-selective abortion and the One-Child policy on sex ratio imbalances in China, see Wei Xing Zhu, Li Lu and Therese Hesketh, "China's Excess Males, Sex Selective Abortion, and One Child Policy: Analysis of Data from 2005 National Intercensus Survey," *British Medical Journal* (April 9, 2009) 338: b1211 doi: 10/1136/bmj.b1211.

13. On the history of population control policies in the PRC, see Susan Greenhalgh and Edwin Winckler, *Governing China's Population: From Leninist to Neoliberal Biopolitics* (Stanford, CA: Stanford University Press, 2005); Tyrene White, *China's Longest Campaign: Birth Planning in the People's Republic, 1949–2005* (Ithaca, NY: Cornell University Press, 2006); Susan Greenhalgh, *Just One Child: Science and Policy in Deng's China* (Berkeley: University of California Press, 2008).

14. As cited in Elisabeth Croll, *Endangered Daughters: Discrimination and Development in Asia* (London: Routledge, 2000), 167.

15. Peter Selman, "Transnational Adoption of Children from Asia in the Twenty-First Century," unpublished paper, as cited in Leslie Wang, "Children on the Margins: The Global Politics of Orphanage Care in Contemporary China," unpublished Ph.D. dissertation in sociology, University of California, Berkeley (2010), 80.

16. "Basic Procedures for Foreigners to Adopt from China," August 27, 2008, China Center of Adoption Affairs, www.china-ccaa.org/site%5Cinfocontent %5CSWSY_20080827102804406_en.htm, accessed November 25, 2011.

17. Xinran, *Message*, 38–43 and 143–49.

18. Beth Nonte Russell, "The Mystery of the Chinese Baby Shortage," *New York Times*, January 23, 2007, www.nytimes.com/2007/01/23/opinion/23russell.html ?pagewanted=all, accessed November 25, 2011.

19. Joshua Zhong, "China Domestic Adoption," *Chinese Children Adoption International Circle Newsletter*, www.chinesechildren.org/Newsletter%5CWindow% 20to%20China/WTC_03_2002.pdf, accessed December 14, 2012.

20. Li "Imbalanced Sex Ratio," 9.

21. Li, "Imbalanced Sex Ratio," 9.

22. Li, "Imbalanced Sex Ratio," 9–10.

23. Li, "Imbalanced Sex Ratio," 10.

24. Quanguo guan'ai nühai xingdong lingdao xiaozu bangongshi [Office of the national leadership group of the Care for Girls campaign] ed., *Guan'ai nühai xingdong: Gongzuo zhinan* [Handbook of the Care for Girls campaign] (Beijing: Zhongguo renkou chubanshe, 2006); *Guan'ai nühai: Quanguo manhuazhan zuopinji* [Care for Girls: National cartoon exhibition catalog] (Beijing: Zhongguo renkou chubanshe, 2004).

25. *Guan'ai nühai xingdong: Gongzuo zhinan*, 37–38.

26. *Guan'ai nühai xingdong: Gongzuo zhinan*, 37–38.

27. Valerie M. Hudson and Andrea M. Den Boer, *Bare Branches: The Security Implications of Asia's Surplus Male Population* (Cambridge, MA: MIT Press, 2004).

28. Wang Yinhua, "Nainai likui bu zisheng" [Granny is convinced and speechless], in *Guan'ai nühai: Quanguo manhuazhan zuopinji*, 15.

29. As cited by Elisabeth Croll, *Endangered Daughters*, 81–82.

30. Chu, "Sex-Selective Abortion," 274–75.

31. Chu, "Sex-Selective Abortion," 274–75.

32. Nie, *Behind the Silence*, 141.

33. Nie, *Behind the Silence*, 141.

34. Nicholas D. Kristof and Sheryl WuDunn, *Half the Sky: Turning Oppression into Opportunity for Women Worldwide* (New York: Alfred A. Knopf, 2009), 206–7.

35. Kristof and WuDunn, *Half the Sky*, 206–7.

Selected Bibliography

Abeel, David. "Notices of Infanticide Collected from the People of Fukien." *Chinese Repository* 12, no. 10 (October 1843): 540–42.

"Alleged Baby Farming in Tranmere." *Liverpool Mercury*, September 5, 1879.

Amiot, Joseph-Marie. Letter to M***, September 28, 1777. In Vol. 6, *Mémoires concernant l'histoire, les sciences, les arts, les moeurs, les usages, &c. des Chinois, par les missionnaires de Pe-kin*, 275–346. Paris, 1780.

Annales de l'Oeuvre de la Sainte-Enfance. Paris: Oeuvre Pontificale de la Sainte-Enfance, 1846–1900.

Anshideng zhujie [Annotated version of Light for a Darkened Room]. 1842 ed.

Appiah, Kwame Anthony. *The Honor Code: How Moral Revolutions Happen*. New York: W. W. Norton, 2010.

Arnot, Margaret L. "Infant Death, Child Care and the State: The Baby-Farming Scandal and the First Infant Life Protection Legislation of 1872." *Continuity and Change* 9 (1994): 271–311.

Auchincloss, Henry B. "Shanghai: Its Streets, Shops, and People." *The Continental Monthly* 6 (July–December 1864): 633–50.

Bailey, Paul. *Gender and Education in China: Gender Discourses and Women's Schooling in the Early Twentieth Century*. London: Routledge, 2007.

Banister, Judith. "Shortage of Girls in China Today." *Journal of Population Research* 21, no. 1 (2004): 20–45.

Barrow, John. *Travels in China*. 2nd ed. London, 1806.

Bechtold, Brigitte. "Infanticide in 19th Century France: A Quantitative Interpretation." *Review of Radical Political Economics* 33 (2001): 165–87.

Behlmer, George. "Deadly Motherhood: Infanticide and Medical Opinion in Mid-Victorian England." *Journal of the History of Medicine and Allied Sciences* 34, no. 4 (October 1979): 403–27.

Bell, Catherine. " 'A Precious Raft to Save the World': The Interaction of Scriptural Traditions and Printing in a Chinese Morality Book." *Late Imperial China* 17, no. 1 (1996): 158–200.

Bell, Catherine. "Stories from an Illustrated Explanation of the *Tract of the Most Exalted on Action and Response*." In *Religions of China in Practice*, edited by Donald S. Lopez, 437–45. Princeton, NJ: Princeton University Press, 1996.

Bhatnagar, Rashmi Dube, Renu Dube and Reena Dube. *Female Infanticide in India: A Feminist Cultural History.* Albany: State University of New York Press, 2005.

Bishop, Mrs. J. F. *Chinese Pictures: Notes on Photographs Made in China.* New York: Charles L. Bowman, [1900?].

Boltanski, Luc. *Distant Suffering: Morality, Media and Politics.* Translated by Graham Burchell. Cambridge: Cambridge University Press, 1999.

Boswell, John. *The Kindness of Strangers: The Abandonment of Children in Western Europe from Late Antiquity to the Renaissance.* Chicago: University of Chicago Press, 1998.

Bray, Francesca. *Technology and Gender: Fabrics of Power in Late Imperial China.* Berkeley: University of California Press, 1997.

Broder, Sherri. "Child Care or Child Neglect?: Baby-Farming in Late-Nineteenth-Century Philadelphia." *Gender and Society* 2, no. 2 (June 1988): 128–48.

Brokaw, Cynthia. "Yuan Huang (1533–1606) and the *Ledgers of Merit and Demerit.*" *Harvard Journal of Asiatic Studies* 47, no. 1 (June 1987): 137–95.

Brokaw, Cynthia J. *The Ledgers of Merit and Demerit: Social Change and Moral Order in Late Imperial China.* Princeton, NJ: Princeton University Press, 1991.

Brook, Timothy, Jérôme Bourgon and Gregory Blue. *Death by a Thousand Cuts.* Cambridge, MA: Harvard University Press, 2008.

Bryson, Mary Isabella. *Child Life in Chinese Homes.* London: Religious Tract Society, 1885.

Bureaux du Conseil Central de l'Oeuvre de la Sainte-Enfance. *Manuel de l'Oeuvre de la Sainte-Enfance.* Paris, 1872. Collection of the Bibliotheca Zi-Ka-Wei, Shanghai.

Chakrabarty, Dipesh. *Provincializing Europe: Postcolonial Thought and Historical Difference.* Princeton, NJ: Princeton University Press, 2000.

Chang Jianhua. "Mingdai niying wenti chutan" [An initial exploration of the problem of infanticide during the Ming dynasty]. In Vol. 4, *Zhongguo shehui lishi pinglun* [Chinese social history review]. Beijing: Shangwu yinshuguan, 2002.

Chang Jianhua. "Qingdai niying wenti xintan" [A new inquiry into the problem of infanticide during the Qing dynasty]. In *Hunyin jiating yu renkou xingwei* [Marriage, family and population behavior], edited by Li Zhongqing [James Lee], Guo Songyi and Ding Yizhuang, 197–219. Beijing: Peking University Press, 1999.

Chang, Kang-i Sun, and Haun Saussy, eds. *Women Writers of Traditional China: An Anthology of Poetry and Criticism.* Stanford, CA: Stanford University Press, 1999.

Chappet, Éduoard. *Société de Géographie de Lyon, Séance mensuelle du 8 janvier 1885, L'infanticide et l'Oeuvre de la Sainte-Enfance en Chine par le Père Palatre.* Lyon, 1885.

Chen Changheng. *Zhongguo renkou lun* [On China's population]. 8th ed. Shanghai: Shangwu yinshuguan, 1928 (orig. 1918).

Chen Dongyuan, *Zhongguo funü shenghuo shi* [The History of Women's Lives in China]. 1928. Reprint, Shanghai: Shanghai wenshu chubanshe, 1990.

Chen Que. "Fu Jueyan gong" [On my father, the honorable Jueyan]. In *Chen Que ji* [Collected writings of Chen Que], 530–35. Beijing: Zhonghua shuju, 1979.

China Center of Adoption Affairs. "Basic Procedures for Foreigners to Adopt from China, August 27, 2008." www.china-ccaa.org/site%5Cinfocontent %5CSWSY_20080827102804406_en.ht. Accessed November 25, 2011.

Chongbian zhengying lu [Re-edition of the Record of Saving Infants]. Shanghai: Shanghai foxue shuju, 1929. Collection of the Shanghai Library, Shanghai.

Chongding anshideng lu [Re-edition of the Record of a Light for a Darkened Room]. 1831 ed.

Chongzuan Fujian tongzhi [Re-edition of the Fujian province gazetteer]. 1871 ed.

Chu Junhong. "Prenatal Sex Determination and Sex-Selective Abortion in Rural Central China." *Population and Development Review* 27, no. 2 (June 2001): 259–81.

Chung, Yuehtsen Juliette. *Struggle for National Survival: Eugenics in Sino-Japanese Contexts, 1896–1945.* New York: Routledge, 2002.

Chuu, Ling-in Lilian. "The Cult of Guanyin Who Brings Sons." MA thesis, University of British Columbia, 2001.

Cihang pudu ce [The compassionate raft of salvation for all beings]. Nanjing, 1870 ed. Collection of the Bibliotheca Zi-Ka-Wei, Shanghai.

Coale, Ansley, and Judith Banister. "Five Decades of Missing Females in China." *Demography* 31, no. 3 (August 1994): 459–79.

Cohen, Paul A. *China and Christianity: The Missionary Movement and the Growth of Chinese Antiforeignism, 1860–1870.* Cambridge, MA: Harvard University Press, 1963.

Colombel, Auguste. *Histoire de la Mission du Kiang-nan, Troisième partie, II L'Episcopat de Mgr. Languillat (1865–1878)* and *III L'Episcopat de Mgr. Garnier (1879–1898).* Shanghai: N.p., 1895–1905.

"Compte général des Recettes et Dépenses, du 18 avril 1845 au 20 mai 1846." *Annales de l'Oeuvre de la Sainte-Enfance* 1, no. 2 (1845–46): 152–59.

Cooke, George Wingrove. *China: Being "The Times" Special Correspondence from China in the Years 1857–58.* London: Routledge and Co., 1859.

Corblet, Jules. Vol. 1, *Histoire dogmatique, liturgique et archéologique du sacrement de baptême.* Paris: Société Générale de Librairie Catholique, 1881.

Croll, Elisabeth. *Endangered Daughters: Discrimination and Development in Asia.* London: Routledge, 2000.

Crow, Carl. *The Travelers' Handbook for China.* San Francisco: San Francisco News Co., 1913.

Cumming, C. F. Gordon. Vol. 2, *Wanderings in China.* Edinburgh: William Blackwood, 1886.

Danicourt, François-Xavier. Letter to M. le vice-président de l'Oeuvre de la Sainte-Enfance, April 4, 1851. *Annales de l'Oeuvre de la Sainte-Enfance* 4, no. 24 (1852): 66–72.

Danicourt, François-Xavier. Letter to the Sainte-Enfance, November 28, 1853. *Annales de l'Oeuvre de la Sainte-Enfance* 7, no. 47 (1855): 440.

Dantu xianzhi [Dantu county gazetteer]. 1803 ed.

Daughton, J. P. *An Empire Divided: Religion, Republicanism, and the Making of French Colonialism, 1880–1914*. Oxford: Oxford University Press, 2006.

de Bary, William Theodore. *Asian Values and Human Rights: A Confucian Communitarian Perspective*. Cambridge, MA: Harvard University Press, 1998.

"Decree for the Armenians, issued at the Council of Florence in 1439." Medieval Sourcebook: The Seven Sacraments: Catholic Doctrinal Documents. www .fordham.edu/halsall/source/1438sacraments.asp#armen. Accessed September 2, 2011.

d'Entrecolles, François Xavier. Letter to Madame ***, October 19, 1720. In Vol. 19, *Lettres édifiantes et curieuses, écrites des Missions Étrangeres: Mémoires de la Chine, &c.*, 98–164. Paris, 1781.

de Groot, J. J. M. Vol. 3, Book 1, "Disposal of the Dead," *The Religious System of China: Its Ancient Forms, Evolution, History and Present Aspect, Manners, Customs and Social Institutions Connected Therewith*. Leiden: Brill, 1897.

de Harlez, Charles. "Infanticide in China According to Chinese Documents." *Dublin Review* 111 (July 1892): 117–43.

de Harlez, Charles. "L'infanticide en Chine." *Le Muséon: Revue Internationale* 4, no. 2–4 (1885): 205–10, 269–80, 424–36.

de la Servière, Joseph. Vol. 2, *Histoire de la mission du Kiang-nan: Mgr. Borgniet (1856–1862), Mgr. Languillat (1864–1878)*. Shanghai: Imprimerie de T'ou-sé-wé, 1914.

Dikötter, Frank. *Imperfect Conceptions: Medical Knowledge, Birth Defects and Eugenics in China*. New York: Columbia University Press, 1998.

Dikötter, Frank. "The Limits of Benevolence: Wang Shiduo (1802–1889) and Population Control." *Bulletin of the School of Oriental and African Studies* 55, no. 1 (1992): 100–119.

Le Directeur diocésain de l'Oeuvre de la Sainte-Enfance à Moutiers-Tarentaise. "Sio-Tsia, ou l'orpheline de Pen-choui." *Annales de l'Oeuvre de la Sainte-Enfance* 28, no. 178 (1877): 330–52.

Donovan, James. "Infanticide and Juries in France, 1825–1913." *Journal of Family History* 16, no. 2 (1991): 157–76.

Doolittle, Justus. *Social Life of the Chinese*. 2 vols. New York: Harper and Bros., 1865.

Du, Fangqin and Susan Mann. "Competing Claims on Womanly Virtue in Late Imperial China." In *Women and Confucian Cultures in Premodern China, Korea and Japan*, edited by Dorothy Ko, JaHyun Kim Haboush and Joan R. Piggott, 219–50. Berkeley: University of California Press, 2003.

Eberhard, Wolfram. *Guilt and Sin in Traditional China*. Berkeley: University of California Press, 1967.

Ebrey, Patricia Buckley, trans. *Chu Hsi's Family Rituals: A Twelfth-Century Chinese Manual for the Performance of Cappings, Weddings, Funerals and Ancestral Rites*. Princeton, NJ: Princeton University Press, 1991.

Edgerton-Tarpley, Kathryn. *Tears from Iron: Cultural Responses to Famine in Nineteenth-Century China*. Berkeley: University of California Press, 2008.

Edkins, Joseph. *Chinese Currency*. Shanghai: Presbyterian Mission Press, 1901.

Elman, Benjamin. *A Cultural History of Civil Examinations in Late Imperial China*. Berkeley: University of California Press, 2000.

"Exercice 1874–1875, Compte général de l'année." *Annales de l'Oeuvre de la Sainte-Enfance* 26, no. 164 (1874–75): 146–55.

"Exercice 1899–1900, Compte général de l'année." *Annales de l'Oeuvre de la Sainte-Enfance* 51, no. 314 (1899–1900): 152–79.

Fairbank, John King. "Patterns Behind the Tientsin Massacre." *Harvard Journal of Asiatic Studies* 20, no. 3–4 (1957): 480–511.

Feng Erkang. "Niying de fumu" [Infanticidal parents]. In *Qu guren de tingyuan sanbu* [Strolling in the courtyards of the ancients]. Beijing: Zhonghua shuju, 2005.

Feng Erkang. "Qingdai de hunyin zhidu yu funü de shehui diwei shulun" [A discussion of marriage practices and women's social status in the Qing]. *Qingshi yanjiu ji* [Qing historical research] 5 (1986): 305–43.

Fielde, Adele. *Pagoda Shadows: Studies from Life in China*. London: T. Ogilve Smith, 1887.

Fuchs, Rachel. *Poor and Pregnant in Paris: Strategies for Survival in the Nineteenth Century*. New Brunswick, NJ: Rutgers University Press, 1992.

Fuchs, Rachel Ginnis. *Abandoned Children: Foundlings and Child Welfare in Nineteenth-Century France*. Albany: State University of New York Press, 1984.

Fuma Susumu. *Zhongguo shanhui shantangshi yanjiu* [A history of China's philanthropic societies and institutions]. Translated by Wu Yue, Yang Wenxin and Zhang Xuefeng. Beijing: Shangwu yinshuguan, 2005.

Furth, Charlotte. "Concepts of Pregnancy, Childbirth and Infancy in Ch'ing Dynasty China." *Journal of Asian Studies* 46, no. 1 (February 1987): 7–35.

Furth, Charlotte. *A Flourishing Yin: Gender in China's Medical History, 960–1665*. Berkeley: University of California Press, 1999.

Furth, Charlotte. "From Birth to Birth: The Growing Body in Chinese Medicine." In *Chinese Views of Childhood*, edited by Anne Behnke Kinney, 157–92. Honolulu: University of Hawaii Press, 1995.

"Gailang jiating zhi zuiyao banfa" [The most critical ways to reform the family system]. *Shenbao*, September 10, 1922.

Gamewell, Mary Ninde. *New Life Currents in China*. New York: Methodist Book Concern, 1919.

Gardner, Daniel K., ed. and trans. *Learning to Be a Sage: Selections from the [Zhuxi yulei] Conversations of Master Chu, Arranged Topically*. Berkeley: University of California Press, 1990.

Gaubil, Antoine. Letter to Mgr. de Nemond, November 4, 1722. In Vol. 19, *Lettres édifiantes et curieuses, écrites des Missions Étrangeres: Mémoires de la Chine, &c.*, 246–56. Paris, 1781.

"Gendercide: What Happened to 100 Million Baby Girls?" Special issue, *The Economist*, March 6, 2010.

"Gengzizi yueshen yu tongjie ponüe tongxi wen" [Essay strongly forbidding the abuse of child brides by mothers-in-law, issued by the moon goddess on the date *gengzizi*]. In *Cihang pudu ce* [The compassionate raft of salvation for all beings]. Nanjing: 1870 ed. Collection of the Bibliotheca Zi-Ka-Wei, Shanghai.

Giles, Herbert A. "Autobibliographical, Etc." [ca. 1925]. MS Add. 8964/1. Collection of the Cambridge University Library.

Giles, Herbert A. "Infanticide in China." *Adversaria Sinica*. Vol. 1. Shanghai: Kelly and Walsh, 1914.

Gilje, Paul. "Infant Abandonment in Early Nineteenth-Century New York City: Three Cases." *Signs* 8, no. 3 (Spring 1983): 580–90.

Gillin, Donald. *Warlord: Yen Hsi-shan in Shansi Province, 1911–1949*. Princeton, NJ: Princeton University Press, 1967.

Goldman, Andrea. "Opera in the City: Theatrical Performance and Urbanite Aesthetics in Beijing, 1770–1900." Ph.D. dissertation, University of California, Berkeley, 2005.

Goldstein, Joshua. *Drama Kings: Players and Publics in the Re-Creation of Peking Opera, 1870–1937*. Berkeley: University of California Press, 2007.

Gowing, Laura. "Secret Births and Infanticide in Seventeenth-Century England." *Past and Present* 156, no. 1 (1997): 87–115.

The Great Qing Code. Translated by William C. Jones. Oxford: Clarendon Press, 1994.

Greenhalgh, Susan. *Just One Child: Science and Policy in Deng's China*. Berkeley: University of California Press, 2008.

Greenhalgh, Susan, and Edwin Winckler. *Governing China's Population: From Leninist to Neoliberal Biopolitics*. Stanford, CA: Stanford University Press, 2005.

Guan'ai nühai: Quanguo manhuazhan zuopinji [Care for Girls: National cartoon exhibition catalog]. Beijing: Zhongguo renkou chubanshe, 2004.

"Guanyin dashi zhongjie ninü ge" [Song of the boddhisattva Guanyin strictly forbidding the drowning of girls]. In *Cihang pudu ce* [The compassionate raft of salvation for all beings]. 1870 ed. Collection of the Bibliotheca Zi-Ka-Wei, Shanghai.

Guobao tu [Illustrated rewards and retributions]. 1872 ed. Collection of the National Library of China, Beijing.

Guo Songyi. "Qingdai de tongyangxi hunyin" [Child bride marriages during the Qing]. In *Hunyin jiating yu renkou xingwei* [Marriage, family and population behavior], edited by Li Zhongqing [James Lee], Guo Songyi and Ding Yizhuang, 33–59. Beijing: Peking University Press, 1999.

Guy, R. Kent. *Qing Governors and Their Provinces: The Evolution of Territorial Administration in China, 1644–1796*. Seattle, WA: University of Washington Press, 2010.

"Hangzhou kuaixin" [Hangzhou express correspondence]. *Shenbao*, July 15, 1927.

Harrison, Henrietta. "'A Penny for the Little Chinese': The French Holy Child-hood Association in China, 1843–1951." *American Historical Review* 113, no. 1 (February 2008): 72–92.

Hausfater, Glenn, and Sarah Blaffer Hrdy, eds. *Infanticide: Comparative and Evolutionary Perspectives*. New York: Aldine, 1984.

Heinrich, Larissa N. *The Afterlife of Images: Translating the Pathological Body Between China and the West*. Durham, NC: Duke University Press, 2008.

Hermand, Louis. *Les Étapes de la Mission du Kiang-nan, 1842–1922*. Zi-ka-wei, Shanghai: Imprimerie de la Mission Zi-Ka-Wei, 1926.

Higginbotham, Ann. "Sin of the Age: Infanticide and Illegitimacy in Victorian London." In *Victorian Scandals: Representations of Gender and Class*, edited by Kristine Ottesen Garrigan, 257–88. Athens: Ohio University Press, 1992.

Hobson, Benjamin. *Fuying xinshuo* [New teachings (on the medical care of) women and infants], 1858. Reprinted in Vol. 380, *Gugong zhenben congkan* [National Palace Museum rare editions collection]. Haikou: Hainan chubanshe, 2000.

Hoffer, Peter and N. E. H. Hull. *Murdering Mothers: Infanticide in England and New England, 1558–1803*. New York: New York University Press, 1981.

Holmgren, Jennifer. "Myth, Fantasy or Scholarship: Images of the Status of Women in Traditional China." *Australian Journal of Chinese Affairs* 155, no. 6 (July 1981): 147–70.

Hrdy, Sarah Blaffer. *Mother Nature: Maternal Instincts and How They Shape the Human Species*. New York: Ballantine Books, 2000.

Hsiung Ping-chen. *A Tender Voyage: Children and Childhood in Late Imperial China*. Stanford, CA: Stanford University Press, 2005.

Huang Liuhong, "Yuyang ying'er" [Raising infants]. In *Fuhui quanshu juan* [Complete book concerning happiness and benevolence], 31:15b–19b (17th c.).

Hudson, Valerie M., and Andrea M. Den Boer. *Bare Branches: The Security Implications of Asia's Surplus Male Population*. Cambridge, MA: MIT Press, 2004.

"Infanticide: translation of an essay warning people against the practice of drowning their female children by Kwei Chungfu of Hunan." *Chinese Repository* 17, no. 1 (January 1848): 11–16.

Issei, Tanaka. "The Social and Historical Context of Ming-Ch'ing Local Drama." In *Popular Culture in Late Imperial China*, edited by David Johnson, Andrew J. Nathan and Evelyn S. Rawski, 143–60. Berkeley: University of California Press, 1985.

Iu-Chien-Tchou-Iom. Trois entretiens illustrés sur la Chine donnés à Québec, Avril 1872 par le R. P. Vasseur, S. J., Missionnaire Apostolique en Chine, Directeur de l'Oeuvre Chinoise de St. Luc pour la Propagation de la Foi. N.p., n.d. Collection of the Bibliotheca Zi-Ka-Wei, Shanghai.

Jackson, Mark. *New-Born Child Murder: Women, Illegitimacy and the Courts in Eighteenth Century England.*, Manchester, England: Manchester University Press, 1996.

Jackson, Mark, ed. *Infanticide: Historical Perspectives on Child Murder and Concealment, 1550–2000.* Aldershot, England: Ashgate, 2002.

Janku, Andrea. "Sowing Happiness: Spiritual Competition in Famine Relief Activities in Late Nineteenth-Century China." *Minsu quyi* 143 (March 2004): 89–118.

"Les Jeunes Herboriseurs, ou les petits bergers de Savoie." *Annales de l'Oeuvre de la Sainte-Enfance* 12, no. 77 (1860): 420–31.

Jiangsu susongtaidao banli baoying binggao tiaogui [Report and regulations on dealing with infant protection from the circuit intendant of Su-Song-Tai, Jiangsu]. N.p., n.d. Collection of the Shanghai Library, Shanghai.

Jiang Tao. *Zhongguo jindai renkou shi* [A history of China's modern population]. Hangzhou: Zhejiang renmin chubanshe, 1993.

"Jiangxi sidao yanjin ninü shiwen" [A Jiangxi official's instructions on strictly forbidding drowning daughters]. *Shenbao,* January 22, 1907.

"Jicheng zhuoni guang fangyan guan kecheng shitiao" [A draft petition under consideration on ten points of the curriculum of the *Guang fangyan guan*]. In *Guang fangyan guan quan'an* [Complete archives of the Institute for the Propagation of Area Languages]. Shanghai: Shanghai guji chubanshe, 1989.

"Jiehai mouli" [Using children to gain a profit]. *Shenbao,* December 12, 1879.

"Jie ninü shuo" [Essay prohibiting the drowning of girls]. In *Quanren juyue juan* [Rules of conduct for the perfect person], 3:49a–51b. 1800 ed. Collection of the Bibliothèque nationale de France, Paris.

Jie ninü tushuo [Illustrated book prohibiting the drowning of girls]. Guangzhou, 1812 ed. Collection of the School of Oriental and African Studies Library, London.

Jie ninü tushuo [Illustrated book prohibiting the drowning of girls]. Huzhou, Zhejiang, 1873 ed. Collection of the Bibliotheca Zi-Ka-Wei, Shanghai.

Jie ninü wen [Essay prohibiting the drowning of girls]. Shishan, 1876 ed. Collection of the Bibliotheca Zi-Ka-Wei, Shanghai.

Jie ninü wen / Jiuying jiefa [Essay prohibiting the drowning of girls / A quick way to saving infants]. Henan, 1882 ed. Collection of the Harvard-Yenching Library, Boston.

"Jiuming sushuo" [Simple words on saving lives]. In *Deyi lu* [Record of attaining (goodness)], edited by Yu Zhi. 1869 ed. Reprint, Taipei: Huawen shuju, 1969.

Jiuying xinzhang [New regulations for rescuing infants]. Wuchang, 1873 ed. Collection of the Bibliotheca Zi-Ka-Wei, Shanghai.

Jizhai jushi. *Dasheng bian* [On successful childbirth]. 1774. Reprinted in Vol. 1008, *Xuxiu siku quanshu* [Revised edition of the Complete Library of the Four Treasuries], edited by Gu Tinglong, 99–115. Shanghai: Shanghai guji chubanshe, 1998.

Kellum, Barbara A. "Infanticide in England in the Later Middle Ages." *History of Childhood Quarterly* 1, no. 3 (Winter 1974): 367–88.

Kinney, Anne Behnke. "Infant Abandonment in Early China." *Early China* 18 (1993): 107–38.

Kleeman, Terry. *A God's Own Tale: The Book of Transformations of Wenchang, the Divine Lord of Zitong*. Albany: State University of New York Press, 1994.

Ko, Dorothy. *Cinderella's Sisters: A Revisionist History of Footbinding*. Berkeley: University of California Press, 2005.

Ko, Dorothy. *Every Step a Lotus: Shoes for Bound Feet*. Berkeley: University of California Press, 2001.

Kristof, Nicholas D., and Sheryl WuDunn. *Half the Sky: Turning Oppression into Opportunity for Women Worldwide*. New York: Alfred A. Knopf, 2009.

Kuhn, Philip. *Soulstealers: The Chinese Sorcery Scare of 1768*. Cambridge, MA: Harvard University Press, 1990.

Kurtz, Joachim. "Messenger of the Sacred Heart: Li Wenyu (1840–1911) and the Jesuit Periodical Press in Late Qing Shanghai." In *From Woodblocks to the Internet: Chinese Publishing and Print Culture in Transition, Circa 1800 to 2008*, edited by Cynthia Brokaw and Christopher Reed, 81–110. Leiden: Brill, 2010.

Lallemand, Léon. *Histoire des enfants abandonnés et délaissés*. Paris, 1885.

Lam, Tong. *A Passion for Facts: Social Surveys and the Construction of the Chinese Nation-State, 1900–1949*. Berkeley: University of California Press, 2011.

Langer, William. "Infanticide: A Historical Survey." *History of Childhood Quarterly* 1 (1973): 353–66.

Laqueur, Thomas. "Bodies, Details, and the Humanitarian Narrative." In *The New Cultural History*, edited by Lynn Hunt, 176–202. Berkeley: University of California Press, 1989.

Lau, Grace. *Picturing the Chinese: Early Western Photographs and Postcards of China*. San Francisco: Long River Press, 2008.

Lauwaert, Françoise. *Le meurtre en famille: Parricide et infanticide en Chine (XVIIIe–XIXe siècle)*. Paris: Éditions Odile Jacob, 1999.

Lee, Bernice J. "Female Infanticide in China." *Historical Reflections / Reflexions Historiques* 8, no. 3 (Fall 1981): 163–78.

Lee, James, and Cameron Campbell. *Fate and Fortune in Rural China: Social Organization and Population Behavior in Liaoning 1774–1873*. Cambridge: Cambridge University Press, 1997.

Lee, James, Cameron Campbell and Guofu Tan. "Infanticide and Family Planning in Late Imperial China: The Price and Population History of Rural Liaoning, 1774–1873." In *Chinese History in Economic Perspective*, edited by Thomas Rawski and Lillian Li, 145–76. Berkeley: University of California Press, 1992.

Lee, James, Cameron Campbell and Wang Feng. "Positive Check or Chinese Checks?" *Journal of Asian Studies* 61, no. 2 (May 2002): 591–607.

Lee, James, and Wang Feng. *One Quarter of Humanity: Malthusian Mythology and Chinese Realities, 1700–2000*. Cambridge, MA: Harvard University Press, 1999.

Lee, James, Wang Feng and Cameron Campbell. "Infant and Child Mortality Among the Qing Nobility: Implications for Two Types of Positive Check." *Population Studies* 48, no. 3 (November 1994): 395–411.

Lee, Jen-der. "Childbirth in Early Imperial China." *Nan nü* 7, no. 2 (2005): 234–41.

[Lee Jen-der] Li Zhende. "Han Sui zhijian de shengzi buju wenti" [On the problem of giving birth to and not raising a child from the Han to the Sui dynasty]. *Zhongyang yanjiuyuan lishi yüyan yanjiusuo jikan* [Bulletin of the Institute of History and Philology, Academia Sinica] 66, no. 3 (1995): 747–812.

[Lee Jen-der] Li Zhende. "Han-Tang zhijian qiuzi yifang shitan—jianlun fuke lanshang yu xingbie lunshu" [A preliminary investigation of reproductive medicine from the Han to the Tang dynasty: On the birth of gynecology and gender discourse]. *Zhongyang yanjiuyuan lishi yüyan yanjiusuo jikan* [Bulletin of the Institute of History and Philology, Academia Sinica] 68, no. 2 (1997): 283–367.

Lee, Leo Ou-fan, and Andrew J. Nathan. "The Beginnings of Mass Culture: Journalism and Fiction in the Late Ch'ing and Beyond." In *Popular Culture in Late Imperial China*, edited by David Johnson, Andrew J. Nathan and Evelyn S. Rawski, 360–95. Berkeley: University of California Press, 1985.

Leung, Angela Ki Che. "L'accueil des enfants abandonnés dans la Chine du bas-Yangzi aux XVIIe et XVIIIe siècles." *Études Chinoises* 4, no. 1 (Spring 1985): 15–54.

Leung, Angela Ki Che. "Autour de la naissance: La mere et l'enfant en Chine aux XVIe et XVIIe siècles." *Cahiers internationaux de Sociologie* 56 (1984): 51–69.

Leung, Angela Ki Che. "Relief Institutions for Children in Nineteenth Century China." In *Chinese Views of Childhood*, edited by Anne Behnke Kinney, 251–78. Honolulu: University of Hawaii Press, 1995.

Leung, Angela Ki Che. "Women Practicing Medicine in Premodern China." In *Chinese Women in the Imperial Past: New Perspectives*, edited by Harriet T. Zurndorfer, 101–34. Leiden: Brill, 1999.

[Leung, Angela] Liang Qizi. "Shaying, qiying, yuyingtang" [Infanticide, abandonment, orphanages]. *Lishi yuekan* 3 (1988): 42–45.

[Leung, Angela] Liang Qizi. *Shishan yu jiaohua: Ming Qing de cishan zhuzhi* [Charitable works and moral education: Benevolent institutions during the Ming and Qing dynasties]. Shijiazhuang, Hebei: Hebei jiaoyu chubanshe, 2001.

"Liangchang zushi jiuniying shuo" [Master Liangchang's words on rescuing infants from drowning]. In *Xu ying lu* [Record of child welfare]. 1873 ed. Collection of the Bibliotheca Zi-Ka-Wei, Shanghai.

Liao Ben. *Zhongguo xiju tushi* [Illustrated history of Chinese opera]. Zhengzhou: Daxiang chubanshe, 2000.

Li Di [Li Wenyu]. *Li Ku* [Grotto of doctrines]. 1886. Collection of the Archives de la Province de France de la Compagnie de Jésus, Paris.

Li Shuzhuo. "Imbalanced Sex Ratio at Birth and Comprehensive Intervention in China." Paper presented at the 4th Asia Pacific Conference on Reproductive and Sexual Heath and Rights, Hyderabad, India, 2007. www.unpfa.org/gender /docs/studies/china.pdf. Accessed November 25, 2011.

"List of Members." *Journal of the North China Branch of the Royal Asiatic Society* 20 (1885): 106–14.

Litchfield, R. Burr and David Gordon. "Closing the 'Tour': A Close Look at the Marriage Market, Unwed Mothers and Abandoned Children in Mid-Nineteenth Century Amiens." *Journal of Social History* 13 (Spring 1980): 458–73.

Liu Jingzhen. *Bu ju zi: Songren de shengyu wenti* [To not raise a child: The problems of birth in the Song dynasty]. Banqiao, Taiwan: Daoxiang chubanshe, 1998.

Liu, Lydia. *The Clash of Empires: The Invention of China in Modern World Making*. Cambridge, MA: Harvard University Press, 2004.

Lu Jiye. "'Zhushazhi' de zuozhe Yu Zhi: Yige tongsu wenxue zuozhe de shengping shilüe" [Yu Zhi, the author of the *Red Birthmark*: A biographical sketch of an author of popular literature]. 1935. Reprinted in *Zhongguo jindai wenxue lunwenji (1919–1949)* [Collected essays on modern Chinese literature, 1919–1949], edited by Liang Shu'an, 403–23. Beijing: Zhongguo shehuikexue chubanshe, 1988.

Lu, Weijing. "'A Pearl in the Palm': A Forgotten Symbol of the Father-Daughter Bond." *Late Imperial China* 31, no. 1 (2010): 62–97.

"Lun ninü lousu" [On the ignorant custom of drowning daughters]. *Shenbao*, December 11, 1878.

Mackerras, Colin. *Western Images of China*. Hong Kong: Oxford University Press, 1989.

Mair, Victor. "Language and Ideology in the Written Popularizations of the *Sacred Edict*." In *Popular Culture in Late Imperial China*, edited by David Johnson, Andrew J. Nathan and Evelyn S. Rawski, 325–59. Berkeley: University of California Press, 1985.

Mann, Susan. *Precious Records: Women in China's Long Eighteenth Century*. Stanford, CA: Stanford University, 1997.

Mann, Susan. *The Talented Women of the Zhang Family*. Berkeley: University of California Press, 2007.

"Maria Siao, ou l'aveugle de Kiou-kiang." *Annales de l'Oeuvre de la Sainte-Enfance* 22, no. 136 (1870): 330–60.

Matignon, J.-J. *Superstition, Crime et Misère en Chine*. Lyon: Storck and Co., 1902.

Maugham, W. Somerset. "The Sights of the Town." In *On a Chinese Screen*, 166–70. New York: George H. Doran, 1922.

Mayers, William Frederick, Nicholas B. Dennys and Charles King. *The Treaty Ports of China and Japan: A Complete Guide to the Open Ports of Those Countries, Together with Peking, Yedo, Hongkong and Macao, Forming a Guide Book and Vade Mecum for Travellers, Merchants and Residents in General, with 29 Maps and Plans*. London: Trübner, 1867.

McDonagh, Josephine. *Child Murder and British Culture, 1720–1900*. Cambridge: Cambridge University Press, 2003.

McQuillan, Kevin. "Were Traditional Societies Really Traditional? Illegitimacy, Infanticide and Abandonment in Nineteenth Century Alsace." *Population Studies Centre Discussion Paper* 87, no. 14 (December 1987).

"Mifang wenda" [Questions and answers from a secret visit]. In *Fanyangjiao shuwenjietie xuan* [Selected writings against foreign teachings], edited by Wang Minglun, 117–18. Jinan: Qilu shushe, 1984.

Milne, William C. *Life in China*. London: Routledge, 1857.

Mittler, Barbara. *A Newspaper for China? Power, Identity and Change in Shanghai's News Media, 1872–1912*. Cambridge, MA: Harvard University Press, 2004.

M. le Curé de Notre-Dame de Châteauroux. "Petit catechisme de l'Oeuvre de la Sainte-Enfance." *Annales de l'Oeuvre de la Sainte-Enfance* 12, no. 76 (1860): 352–58.

Moule, A. C. "Herbert Allen Giles." *Journal of the Royal Asiatic Society of Great Britain and Ireland* 3 (July 1935): 577–79.

Mungello, David E. *Drowning Girls in China: Female Infanticide Since 1650*. Lanham, MD: Rowman and Littlefield, 2008.

Naquin, Susan. *Peking: Temples and City Life, 1400–1900*. Berkeley: University of California Press, 2000.

"Neibu tongling baohu nüquan" [Ministry of Interior orders the protection of women's rights]. *Shenbao*, June 16, 1928.

"Neizhengbu baozhang nüquan zhi tongling" [The order of the Ministry of the Interior guaranteeing women's rights]. *Shenbao*, June 26, 1928.

"New Campaign Targets Gender Ratio Imbalance." *People's Daily Online*, August 17, 2011. http://english.peopledaily.com.cn/90882/7571975.html. Accessed on December 4, 2012.

Nie, Jing-Bao. *Behind the Silence: Chinese Voices on Abortion*. Lanham, MD: Rowman and Littlefield, 2005.

"Ninü ebao" [Drowning daughter leads to karmic retribution]. *Shenbao*, May 14, 1874.

Nishiyama Eikyu. "Shina minken no Infanticide nitsuite" [About infanticide among Chinese people]. *Toa keizai kenkyu* 13, no. 1 (1929): 36–71.

Otness, Harold. "Nurturing the Roots for Oriental Studies: The Development of the Libraries of the Royal Asiatic Society Branches and Affiliates in Asia in the Nineteenth Century." *International Association of Orientalist Librarians Bulletin* 43 (1998): 9–17.

Palatre, Gabriel. *L'infanticide et l'Oeuvre de la Sainte-Enfance en Chine*. Shanghai: Mission Catholique, l'Orphelinat de Tou-sè-wè, 1878.

Palatre, Gabriel. Letter to R. P. Foucault, March 2, 1874. Series C, File 368. Pontificium Opus a Sancta Infantia (POSI) archives, Rome.

Panigrahi, Lalita. *British Social Policy and Female Infanticide in India*. Delhi: Monoharlal, 1972.

Papers Relating to the Massacre of Europeans at Tien-tsin on the 21st June, 1870. China series, no. 1. London: Great Britain Foreign Office, 1871.

Petty, William. *Political Arithmetick*. Orig. London, 1690. http://socserv2 .mcmaster.ca/~econ/ugcm/3113/petty/poliarith.html. Accessed January 16, 2006.

Porter, Theodore. *The Rise of Statistical Thinking, 1820–1900*. Princeton, NJ: Princeton University Press, 1986.

Porter, Theodore M. *Trust in Numbers: The Pursuit of Objectivity in Science and Public Life*. Princeton, NJ: Princeton University Press, 1995.

Pratt, Mary Louise. *Imperial Eyes: Travel Writing and Transculturation*. London: Routledge, 1992.

"Preface." *Journal of the Shanghai Literary and Scientific Society* 1 (June 1858): i–ii.

"The Prevalence of Infanticide in China." *Journal of the North China Branch of the Royal Asiatic Society* 20 (1885): 25–50.

"Proceedings." *Journal of the North China Branch of the Royal Asiatic Society* 20, no. 5 and 6 (1885): 292–94.

"Qing jin nüzi chanzu peicheng youyong zhi cai qi laigao zhaodeng" [A letter to the editor on forbidding women's footbinding in order to develop useful talent]. *Shenbao*, November 5, 1901.

Quanguo guan'ai nühai xingdong lingdao xiaozu bangongshi [Office of the national leadership group of the Care for Girls campaign], ed. *Guan'ai nühai xingdong: Gongzuo zhinan* [Handbook of the Care for Girls campaign]. Beijing: Zhongguo renkou chubanshe, 2006.

"Quanjie buke lingnüe baoyangtongxi" [Urging against the abuse of child brides]. In *Jie ninü tushuo* [Illustrated book prohibiting the drowning of girls]. 1873 ed. Collection of the Bibliotheca Zi-Ka-Wei, Shanghai.

Rankin, Mary Backus. *Elite Activism and Political Transformation in China: Zhejiang Province, 1865–1911*. Stanford, CA: Stanford University Press, 1986.

Raphals, Lisa. *Sharing the Light: Representations of Women and Virtue in Early China*. Albany: State University of New York Press, 1998.

Richter, Jeffrey. "Infanticide, Child Abandonment and Abortion in Imperial Germany." *Journal of Interdisciplinary History* 28, no. 4 (Summer 1998): 511–51.

"Rosalie et Berthe, ou les filles d'un pêcheur Normand." *Annales de l'Oeuvre de la Sainte-Enfance* 13, no. 78 (1861): 59–71.

Rose, Lionel. *The Massacre of the Innocents: Infanticide in Britain, 1800–1939*. London: Routledge, 1986.

Rosenberg, Tina. "The Daughter Deficit." *New York Times Magazine*, August 19, 2009.

Ross, E. A. *The Changing Chinese: The Conflict of Oriental and Western Cultures in China*. New York, NY: The Century Co., 1911.

Rowe, William. *Hankow: Conflict and Community in a Chinese City, 1796–1895*. Stanford, CA: Stanford University Press, 1989.

Russell, Beth Nonte. "The Mystery of the Chinese Baby Shortage." *New York Times*, January 23, 2007. www.nytimes.com/2007/01/23/opinion/23russell.html?pagewanted=all. Accessed November 25, 2011.

Ryan, James. *Picturing Empire: Photography and the Visualization of the British Empire*. Chicago: University of Chicago Press, 1997.

Sakai, Tadao. "Confucianism and Popular Educational Works." In *Self and Society in Ming Thought*, edited by Wm. Theodore de Bary, 331–66. New York: Columbia University Press, 1970.

Sarcey, Francisque. [Various articles.] *Le XIXe Siècle*, December 1875.

Sauer, R. "Infanticide and Abortion in Nineteenth-Century Britain." *Population Studies* 32, no. 1 (March 1978): 81–93.

Sauret, Alain. "China's Role in the Foundation and Development of the Pontifical Society of the Holy Childhood." In *Historiography of the Chinese Catholic Church: Nineteenth and Twentieth Centuries*, edited by Jeroom Heyndrickx, 247–72. Leuven: Ferdinand Verbiest Foundation, 1994.

Scarth, John. *Twelve Years in China: The People, the Rebels, and the Mandarins, by a British Resident*. Edinburgh: Thomas Constable, 1860.

Sen, Satadru. "The Savage Family: Colonialism and Female Infanticide in Nineteenth-Century India." *Journal of Women's History* 14, no. 3 (2002): 53–79.

Shan-ge-er furen [Margaret Sanger]. "Shengyu zhicai de shenme yu zenyang" [The what and how of birth control]. *Funü zazhi* [The Ladies' Journal] (June 1, 1922).

"Shanü sangqi" [Killing a daughter means losing a wife]. *Shenbao*, April 7, 1876.

"Shanxi shengzhengfu gechu ninü banfa an" [Proposed methods for abolishing female infanticide from the Shanxi provincial government]. In *Chongbian zhengying lu* [Re-edition of the Record of Saving Infants], 73–74. 1929 ed. Collection of the Shanghai Library.

"Shanxi tongxin: Mofangsheng jiaomin zhengce" [Correspondence from Shanxi: The policies of the model province on educating the people]. *Shenbao*, March 11, 1922.

Shen Bingcheng. "Qingtongshi geshu juban baoyinghui bing" [Letter requesting the circulation of instructions to affiliated areas to establish infant protection societies]. Shen Bingchen to provincial superiors, January 31, 1873. In *Jiangsu susongtaidao banli baoying binggao tiaogui* [Report and regulations on dealing with infant protection from the circuit intendant of Su-Song-Tai, Jiangsu]. N.p., n.d. Collection of the Shanghai Library, Shanghai.

"Sin-a-li, ou l'orphelin de Zi-ka-wei." *Annales de l'Oeuvre de la Sainte-Enfance* 14, no. 88 (1862): 361–83.

Smith, Joanna Handlin. *The Art of Doing Good: Charity in Late Ming China*. Berkeley: University of California Press, 2009.

Sogabe Shizuo. "Ninü kao" [Investigation of female infanticide]. 1941. Reprinted and translated in *Wenxing zazhi* 55, no. 10 (1962): 52–57.

Standaert, Nicolas. *The Interweaving of Rituals: Funerals in the Cultural Exchange Between China and Europe*. Seattle: University of Washington Press, 2008.

St. Augustine. "On the Merit and the Forgiveness of Sins, and the Baptism of Infants" (Book 3). www.newadvent.org/fathers/15013.htm. Accessed September 2, 2011.

St. Thomas Aquinas. *Summa Theologica*, Part III, Question 68, Article 10. www.newadvent.org/summa/4068.htm#article9. Accessed September 2, 2011.

St. Thomas Aquinas. *Summa Theologica*, Supplement to the Third Part, Question 70, Article 1 and 2. www.newadvent.org/summa/5070.htm. Accessed September 2, 2011.

Sun Yat-sen. *San Min Chu I: The Three Principles of the People*. Edited by L. T. Chen. Translated by Frank W. Price. Shanghai: China Committee, Institute of Pacific Relations, 1927.

"Susheng shiqinian du shizeng dagang" [Jiangsu 1928 administrative summary]. *Shenbao*, June 15, 1928.

Su Shi. "Lun jiuninü shu" [Letter on rescuing girls from drowning]. In *Xuying lu* [Record of child welfare]. 1873 ed. Collection of the Bibliotheca Zi-Ka-Wei, Shanghai.

Tcheng-Ki-Tong [Chen Jitong]. *Les Chinois peints par eux-mêmes*. Paris: Calmann Lévy, 1884.

Teiser, Stephen. *The Scripture on the Ten Kings and the Making of Purgatory in Medieval Chinese Buddhism*. Honolulu: University of Hawaii Press, 1994.

ter Haar, Barend J. *Telling Stories: Witchcraft and Scapegoating in Chinese History*. Leiden: Brill, 2006.

Thorn, Jennifer, ed. *Writing British Infanticide: Child-Murder, Gender and Print, 1722–1859*. Newark: University of Delaware Press, 2003.

T'ien Ju-k'ang. *Male Anxiety and Female Chastity: A Comparative Study of Chinese Ethical Values in Ming–Ch'ing Times*. Leiden: Brill, 1988.

"Tientsin Massacre Confirmed." *China Mail Extra*, July 10, 1870.

Tillier, Annick. *Des criminelles au village: Femmes infanticides en Bretagne (1825–1865)*. Rennes: Presses Universitaires de Rennes, 2001.

Torén, Olof. "O. Toreens Reise nach Suratte." In *Reise nach Ostindien und China*, edited by Pehr Osbeck. Rostock, 1765.

Ulbricht, Otto. *Kindsmord und Aufklärung in Deutschland*. München: R. Oldenbourg, 1990.

United Kingdom. Public Record Office. Foreign Office. File 17/608, enclosure. London.

Vasseur, Adolphe. *Un orphelinat chinois de la Sainte-Enfance à l'exposition internationale d'imagerie de Rouen et l'infanticide en Chine prouvé à M. Tchen-Ki-Tong par ses compatriotes*. Paris, n.d. Collection of the Bibliothèque nationale de France, Paris.

Vissière, Isabelle, and Jean-Louis, eds. *Lettres édifiantes et curieuses de Chine: 1702–1776*. Paris: Garnier-Flammarion, 1979.

Waltner, Ann. "Infanticide and Dowry in Ming and Early Qing China." In *Chinese Views of Childhood*, edited by Anne Behnke Kinney, 193–217. Honolulu: University of Hawaii Press, 1995.

Wang, Leslie. "Children on the Margins: The Global Politics of Orphanage Care in Contemporary China." Ph.D. dissertation, University of California, Berkeley, 2010.

Wang Qiang. "Jiangxi gudai ninü louxi mantan" [A discussion of the backward practice of female infanticide in premodern Jiangxi]. *Nanfang wenwu* [Cultural Relics from Southern China] 4 (2004): 114–15.

Wang Ruichang. *Chen Que pingzhuan* [Critical biography of Chen Que]. Nanjing: Nanjing daxue chubanshe, 2002.

Wei Xing Zhu, Li Lu and Therese Hesketh. "China's Excess Males, Sex Selective Abortion, and One Child Policy: Analysis of Data from 2005 National Intercensus Survey." *British Medical Journal* (April 9, 2009) 338: b1211 doi: 10/1136/bmj.b1211.

Welch, Holmes. *The Buddhist Revival in China*. Cambridge, MA: Harvard University Press, 1968.

Weppner, Margaretha. Vol. 1, *The North Star and the Southern Cross*. London: Sampson Low, Marston, Low and Searle, 1875.

West, Stephen H. and Wilt L. Idema. "The Status of Wang Shifu's *Story of the Western Wing* in Chinese Literature." In *The Story of the Western Wing*, ed. and trans. Stephen H. West and Wilt L. Idema, 3–18. Berkeley: University of California Press, 1995.

Wheeler, Kenneth. "Infanticide in Nineteenth-Century Ohio." *Journal of Social History* 31, no. 2 (1997): 407–18.

White, Tyrene. *China's Longest Campaign: Birth Planning in the People's Republic, 1949–2005*. Ithaca, NY: Cornell University Press, 2006.

Widmer, Ellen, and Kang-i Sun Chang, eds. *Writing Women in Late Imperial China*. Stanford, CA: Stanford University Press, 1997.

Williams, Samuel Wells. Vol. 2, *The Middle Kingdom: A Survey of the Geography, Government, Education, Social Life, Arts and History of the Chinese Empire and Its Inhabitants* (Rev. ed.). New York: C. Scribner's Sons, 1882.

Wolf, Arthur. "Is There Evidence of Birth Control in Late Imperial China?" *Population and Development Review* 27, no. 1 (March 2001): 133–54.

Wolf, Arthur, and Chieh-Shan Huang. *Marriage and Adoption in China, 1845–1945*. Stanford, CA: Stanford University Press, 1980.

Wu, Yi-Li. *Reproducing Women: Medicine, Metaphor and Childbirth in Late Imperial China*. Berkeley: University of California Press, 2010.

Xiao Dengfu. *Daofo shiwang diyu shuo* [On the Taoist-Buddhist Ten Kings of Hell]. Taipei: Xinwenfeng chubanshe, 1996.

Xiao Qian. "Qingdai Jiangxi minjian ninü yu tongyang" [Female infanticide and child brides in Qing dynasty Jiangxi]. *Wuxi qinggong daxue xuebao shehui kexue ban* [Wuxi University of Light Industry Journal, sociology edition] 2, no. 3 (September 2001): 239–43.

Xiao Qian. "Qingdai Jiangxi ninü fengsu zhong de 'shejia' wenti" [Extra-dowry in the custom of infanticide in Qing dynasty Jiangxi]. *Jiangnan daxue xuebao* [Jiangnan University Journal] 4, no. 4 (August 2005): 53–56.

Xiao Qian. "Qingdai Jiangxi ninü zhuangkuang yu jinjiewen" [The condition of female infanticide and its prohibition in Qing dynasty Jiangxi]. *Shilin* 1 (2001): 63–68.

Xinbao, March 9–20, 1877.

"Xinfeng yiguta" [Xinfeng's bone collection tower]. *Nanhu wanbao* [Nanhu Evening News], November 16, 2008. http://nhwb.cnjxol.com/html/2008-11/16/content_189275.htm. Accessed November 29, 2010.

Xinran. *Message from an Unknown Chinese Mother: Stories of Loss and Love.* Translated by Nicky Harman. London: Chatto and Windus, 2010.

Xiong Yuezhi. *Xixue dongjian yu wanqing shehui* [The dissemination of Western learning and late Qing society]. Shanghai: Shanghai renmin chubanshe, 1994.

Xu Xiaowang. "Cong niying xisu kan Fujian lishishang de renkou ziran goucheng wenti" [On issues resulting from the natural composition of the population in Fujianese history, as influenced by the custom of infanticide]. *Fujian luntan (jingji shehui ban)* [Fujian tribune, economics and society edition] 3 (2003): 52–56.

Xuying lu [Record of child welfare]. Sanguanzhen, Jiangsu, 1873 ed. Collection of the Bibliotheca Zi-Ka-Wei, Shanghai.

Yan Chen. "Yu Liancun guangwen" [Yu Liancun, educator]. In *Mohuayinguan ganjiu huairen ji* [Remembrance of past things and people from the Ink-song Study] Reprinted in *Qingdai zhuanji congkan* [Collection of Qing biographies] 29. Taipei: Minwen shuju, 1985.

Yan Chunxi. *Taichan xinfa* [Teachings on giving birth]. 1731. Reprinted in Vol. 1008, *Xuxiu siku quanshu* [Revised edition of the Complete Library of the Four Treasuries], edited by Gu Tinglong. Shanghai: Shanghai guji chubanshe, 1998.

Yang Futai. "Zhejiang xunfubuyuan Yang tongshi gezhouxian juban baoying yuanzha" [Original letter from the Zhejiang governor and vice-president of the board, Yang, informing each district and county to establish infant protection societies]. Yang Futai to local officials, September 1870. In *Jiangsu susongtaidao banli baoying binggao tiaogui* [Report and regulations on dealing with infant protection from the circuit intendant of Su-Song-Tai, Jiangsu]. N.p., n.d. Collection of the Shanghai Library, Shanghai.

Yang Jianli. "Jindai huabei diqu de ninü xisu" [The custom of female infanticide in modern northern China]. *Beijing ligong daxue xuebao (shehui kexue ban)* [Beijing Institute of Technology Journal, sociology edition] 5, no. 4 (August 2003): 79–81.

"Yinghai cansi" [Baby dies tragically]. *Shenbao*, May 18, 1878.

You Zian. *Quanhua jinzhen: Qingdai shanshu yanjiu* [Golden needles of exhortation: A study of Qing dynasty morality books]. Tianjin: Tianjin renmin chubanshe, 1999.

You Zian. *Shan yu rentong: Ming Qing yilai de cishan yu jiaohua* [In company with goodness: Charity and morality in China, 1600–1930]. Beijing: Zhonghua shuju, 2005.

Yu, Anthony. "'Rest, Rest, Perturbed Spirit!' Ghosts in Traditional Chinese Prose Fiction." *Harvard Journal of Asiatic Studies* 47, no. 2 (December 1987): 397–434.

Yü, Chün-fang. "A Sutra Promoting the White-Robed Guanyin as Giver of Sons." In *Religions of China in Practice*, edited by Donald S. Lopez, 97–105. Princeton, NJ: Princeton University Press, 1996.

[Yu Zhi] Jiyun shanren. *Jiangnan tielei tu* [Illustrated account of Jiangnan (that would make a man of) iron cry]. 1864 ed. Reprint, Taipei: Taiwan xuesheng shuju, 1969.

[Yu Zhi] Jiyun shanren. *Xuetang riji gushi tushuo* [Daily reader of illustrated stories for schools]. 1874 ed. Collection of the National Library of China, Beijing.

[Yu Zhi] Ronghu jiyun shanren. *Nü ershisi xiao tushuo* [Twenty-four illustrated stories of filial piety for girls]. 1872 ed. Collection of the Harvard-Yenching Library, Boston.

[Yu Zhi]. *Shujitang jinyue* [Music of the day near to a (moral state) hall]. Suzhou: 1880 ed. Collection of the C. V. Starr East Asian Library, University of California, Berkeley.

[Yu Zhi] Wu yun, ed. *Deyi lu* [Record of attaining (goodness)]. 1869 ed. Reprint, Taipei: Huawen shuju, 1969.

[Yu Zhi]. *Zun xiaoxue zhai wenji* [Collected works of the Respecting Lesser Learning Studio]. 1883 ed. Collection of the Peking University Library, Beijing.

"Yuesheng jinwen" [Recent news from Guangdong]. *Shenbao*, July 15, 1928.

"Yuxiaohui xiansheng nianpu" [Mr. Yuxiaohui's chronological biography]. 1875 ed. Reprinted in Vol. 156, *Beijing tushuguan cangzhenben nianpu congkan* [Beijing Library rare editions of chronological biographies collection], edited by Zhou Heping, 305–38. Beijing: Beijing tushuguan chubanshe, 1999.

Zamperini, Paola. "Untamed Hearts: Eros and Suicide in Late Imperial Chinese Fiction." In *Passionate Women: Female Suicide in Late Imperial China*, edited by Paul S. Ropp, Paola Zamperini and Harriet T. Zurndorfer, 77–104. Leiden: Brill, 2001.

Zeitlin, Judith. "Embodying the Disembodied: Representations of Ghosts and the Feminine." In *Writing Women in Late Imperial China*, edited by Ellen Widmer and Kang-i Sun Chang, 242–63. Stanford, CA: Stanford University Press, 1997.

Zeitlin, Judith. *Historian of the Strange: Pu Songling and the Chinese Classical Tale*. Stanford, CA: Stanford University Press, 1993.

Zhang Mingqi. "Woguo qianyishiji de dazhong xiju zuojia jian shijianzhe" [An author and producer of mass dramas from China's previous century]. 1940. Reprinted in *Zhongguo jindai wenxue lunwenji (1919–1949)* [Collected essays on modern Chinese literature], edited by Liang Shu'an, 431–41. Beijing: Zhongguo shehuikexue chubanshe, 1988.

Zhang Yingchang, ed. *Qingshi duo* [The bell of Qing poetry]. 1869 ed. Reprint, Beijing: Zhonghua shuju, 1960.

[Zhejiang baptismal list, 1852]. Folder L1. Pontificium Opus a Sancta Infatia archives, Rome.

"Zhejiang minzhengting jin'ge ninü banfa an" [Proposed methods for prohibiting female infanticide from the Zhejiang people's assembly]. In *Chongbian zhengying lu* [Re-edition of the Record of Saving Infants], 69–72. 1929 ed. Collection of the Shanghai Library.

"Zhejiangsheng queshao nüzi, yue erbaiwushiwan ren" [Zhejiang Province has a shortage of women, approximately 2.5 million people]. *Shenbao*, May 12, 1930.

"Zhejiang zuijin zhenggang" [Zhejiang's recent political program]. *Shenbao*, March 28, 1927.

Zhengying baoying lu [Record of rewards and retributions for saving infants]. Guangzhou, 1855 ed. Collection of the Wellcome Library, London.

Zhengying baoying lu [Record of rewards and retributions for saving infants]. Shanghai, 1869 ed. Collection of the Bibliotheca Zi-Ka-Wei, Shanghai.

Zhengying men [Gateway to saving infants]. Shanghai, 1933 ed. Collection of the Shanghai Library, Shanghai.

Zhengying tongyan [Urgent words on saving infants]. Shanghai, 1932 ed. Collection of the National Library of China, Beijing.

Zhengying tushuo jizheng [Illustrated edition of testimony on saving infants]. 1892 ed. Collection of the Shanghai Library, Shanghai.

"Zhesheng yanjin ninü louxi" [Zhejiang Province strictly forbids the backward habit of drowning girls]. *Shibao*. February 18, 1929.

Zhong, Joshua. "China Domestic Adoption." *Chinese Children Adoption International Circle Newsletter*. www.chinesechildren.org/Newsletter%5CWindow%20to%20China/WTC_03_2002.pdf. Accessed December 14, 2012.

Zhou Jianren. "Shanzhongxue de lilun yu shishi" [The theory and implementation of eugenics]. In *Jinhualun yu shanzhongxue* [Evolution and eugenics], edited by Chen Changheng and Zhou Jianren. Shanghai: Shanghai shangwu yinshuguan, 1923.

Zhou Jianren. "Shanzhongxue yu qi jianlizhe" [Eugenics and its founders]. In *Jinhualun yu shanzhongxue* [Evolution and eugenics], edited by Chen Changheng and Zhou Jianren. Shanghai: Shanghai shangwu yinshuguan, 1923.

Zhu Hu. *Difangxing liudong ji qi chaoyue: Wan Qing yizhen yu jindai Zhongguo de xin chen daixie* [Local movements and beyond: Late Qing humanitarian relief and its renewal in modern China]. Beijing: Renmin daxue chubanshe, 2006.

Zimdars-Swartz, Sandra. *Encountering Mary: From La Salette to Medjugorje*. Princeton, NJ: Princeton University Press, 1991.

"Zongli yamen zhi geguo gongshi shu" [Letter from the Zongli Yamen to the envoys of various countries]. In *Fanyangjiao shuwenjietie xuan* [Selected writings against foreign teachings], edited by Wang Minglun, 379–87. Jinan: Qilu shushe, 1984.

Chinese Character List

保祿　*Bao-lu* [Paul]
保嬰會　*baoying hui*
不舉子　*bu ju zi*
不養子　*bu yang zi*
不良　*buliang*

陳長蘅　*Chen Changheng*
陳東原　*Chen Dongyuan*
陳確　*Chen Que*
陳穎伯　*Chen Yingbo*
重編拯嬰錄　*Chongbian zhengying lu*
慈航普渡冊　*Cihang pudu ce*

大善　*da shan*
達生編　*Dasheng bian*
大學　*daxue*
得一善　*de yi shan*
得一錄　*Deyi lu*

惡習　*exi*

方濟加　*Fang-ji-jia* [Françoise]
風　*feng*
福惠全書　*Fuhui quanshu*
夫妻共建幸福家庭，男女共建和諧社會
　Fuqi gongjian xingfu jiating, nannü gongjian hexie shehui
婦嬰新說　*Fu ying xinshuo*

顧三寶　*Gu Sanbao*
關愛女孩　*guan'ai nühai*
關愛女孩就是關注民族的未來　*Guan'ai nühai jiu shi guanzhu minzu de weilai*
廣方言館　*Guang fangyan guan*

貴中孚　*Gui Zhongfu*
果報圖　*Guobao tu*

孩兒歸所　*hai'er guisuo*
華人　*huaren*
黃六鴻　*Huang Liuhong*
晦齋　*Huizhai*

戒溺女圖說　*Jie ninü tushuo*
戒溺女文　*Jie ninü wen*
江南鐵淚圖　*Jiangnan tielei tu*
積骨塔　*jigu ta*
精珠　*jingzhu*
進化論與善種學　*Jinhua lun yu shanzhong xue*
進種學　*jinzhong xue*
救嬰捷法　*Jiuying jiefa*
寄雲山人　*Jiyun shanren*

李問漁　*Li Wenyu*
蓮村　*Liancun*
梁溪　*Liangxi*
梁溪晦齋氏輯於寄雲山房　*Liangxi huizhaishi jiyu jiyun shanfang*
立物坡　*Li-wu-po* [Liverpool]
陋俗　*lousu*
羅恩　*Luo-en* [Barnes]

瑪利亞　*Ma-li-ya* [Maria/Marie]
民俗　*minsu*
民族　*minzu*

男女平等　*nannü pingdeng*
溺女　*ni nü*
女二十四孝圖說　*Nü ershisi xiao tushuo*

女兒能成才， 女兒能創業， 女兒能立戶，
　女兒能養老　*Nü'er neng chengcai,
　nü'er neng chuangye, nü'er neng
　lihu, nü'er neng yanglao*

氣　*qi*
棄嬰　*qi ying*
氣血　*qixue*
勸善　*quan shan*
勸善臺　*quan shan tai*

日記故事續記　*Riji gushi xuji*

三從　*sancong*
三民主義　*Sanmin zhuyi*
殺子　*sha zi*
善劇　*shanju*
善人　*shanren*
善書　*shanshu*
善種學　*shanzhong xue*
沈秉成　*Shen Bingcheng*
申報　*Shenbao*
時報　*Shibao*
時代不同了， 男女都一樣　*Shidai
　butongle, nannü dou yiyang*
庶幾堂今樂　*Shujitang jinyue*
死　*si*
松江　*Songjiang*
送子觀音　*Songzi Guanyin*
俗　*su*
俗多溺女　*su duo ninü*
蘇軾　*Su Shi*

太上感應篇　*Taishang ganying pian*
童養媳　*tongyangxi*

亡　*wang*
未亡　*weiwang*
文昌　*Wenchang*

習　*xi*
鄉約　*xiangyue*
小學　*xiaoxue*

薛欣然　*Xue Xinran*
學堂講語　*Xuetang jiangyu*
學堂日記故事圖說　*Xuetang riji gushi
　tushuo*

閻錫山　*Yan Xishan*
楊秀貞　*Yang Xiuzhen*
洋人　*yangren*
洋務之機　*yangwu zhi ji*
葉　*Ye*
陰精　*yinjing*
益聞錄　*Yiwen lu*
異域　*yiyu*
優生學　*yousheng xue*
有用　*youyong*
余善人　*Yu Shanren*
愈顯主榮　*yu xian zhu rong*
　[Iu-chien-tchou-iom]
余治　*Yu Zhi*
冤魂　*yuanhun*
育怪圖　*Yuguai tu*
育嬰堂　*yuying tang*

拯嬰報應錄　*Zhengying baoying lu*
拯嬰門　*Zhengying men*
拯嬰痛言　*Zhengying tongyan*
哲嗣學　*zhesi xue*
志宏　*Zhihong*
中國婦女生活史　*Zhongguo funü
　shenghuo shi*
中國人口論　*Zhongguo renkou lun*
中國幼孩　*zhongguo youhai*
中華　*zhonghua*
重男輕女　*zhongnan qingnü*
朱三郎　*Zhu Sanlang*
朱熹　*Zhu Xi*
徐家匯　*Zikawei*
尊小學齋　*Zun xiaoxue zhai*
尊小學齋文集　*Zun xiaoxue zhai wenji*
作好國民　*zuo hao guomin*

Index

Page numbers in italic indicate tables and figures.